THE CRIMINAL TRIAL IN LATER MEDIEVAL ENGLAND

THE CRIMINAL TRIAL IN LATER MEDIEVAL ENGLAND

FELONY BEFORE THE COURTS FROM EDWARD I TO THE SIXTEENTH CENTURY

J.G. BELLAMY

UNIVERSITY OF TORONTO PRESS
TORONTO BUFFALO

First published in 1998 by
Sutton Publishing Limited · Phoenix Mill
Thrupp · Stroud · Gloucestershire · GL5 2BU
Published in North America in 1998
by University of Toronto Press Incorporated
Toronto Buffalo

Canadian Cataloguing in Publication Data

Bellamy, John G., 1930–
  The English criminal trial in the middle centuries: felony before the courts from Edward I to the mid-sixteenth century

ISBN 0-8020-4295-3

1. Trials – England – History. 2. Criminal Courts – England – History. I. Title

KD370.B45 1998   345.42'07'0902   C97-932234–0

Typeset in 10/12pt Baskerville.
Typesetting and origination by
Sutton Publishing Limited.
Printed in Great Britain by
MPG Books, Bodmin, Cornwall.

CONTENTS

ACKNOWLEDGEMENTS   7

INTRODUCTION   8

1.   ACCUSATION: BY JURY AND BY APPEAL   19

2.   MAJOR CRIMES
     MURDER AND MANSLAUGHTER   57
     LARCENY, ROBBERY AND BURGLARY   69

3.   TRIAL AND THE VERDICT REVOLUTION   93

4.   AFTERMATH   134

APPENDIX 1: RAPE   162

APPENDIX 2: LESS FREQUENT FELONIES   187

GLOSSARY   195

NOTES ON COMMENTATORS   197

NOTES ON SOURCES   199

INDEX   201

For G.B. and A.G.B.

in memoriam

Acknowledgements

I wish to express my appreciation of grant support of my research for this book by the Social Sciences and Humanities Research Council of Canada. I should also like to place on record my indebtedness to my wife Annette, for her tolerance of a husband frequently engrossed with the distant English past during the last thirty or so years, and her unfailing encouragement and salutary advice.

John Bellamy
Ottawa
December 1996

INTRODUCTION

Felony, as Maitland pointed out, was a category of crime which could be prosecuted by appeal, and could result in forfeiture of life or member where the lands of the person convicted went to his lord or the king, and his chattels went solely to the latter.[1] In degree of heinousness, we may add, felony occupied the middle ground, lying between the ultimate crime of treason and the minor offence of trespass, which emerged as an indictable misdeed in the later thirteenth century. While virtually all of the capital crimes committed in late medieval England were felonies there existed no definitive list of these offences nor any clear and public statement which specified what each amounted to. Several types of felony we can trace back to Anglo-Saxon times, while others had their origins in acts of parliament from the reign of Edward I onwards, the fifteenth and sixteenth centuries being increasingly fruitful. Some of the felonies in the 'common law' category (i.e. non-statutory ones) and even some born of statute yield only reluctantly to precise definition, but to accomplish this is a most necessary task (one for the most part neglected by historians) if we are to understand the nature of serious crime in the middle centuries.

Like indictable trespasses felonies could be tried before a variety of courts. For the historian, however, there has survived no great wealth of material which describes the actual process of the criminal trial – rather the reverse. Apart from a short thirteenth-century tract designed apparently to elucidate procedure by appeal, some extended but partisan remarks on the trial process by John Fortescue in the later fifteenth century and Thomas More in the earlier sixteenth, and the more exhaustive work by Thomas Smith a few decades later, there is little that can be called direct and informed contemporary comment.[2] Of lesser value but still useful is a compendium of legal and procedural points pertaining to criminal trials that dates from late in the reign of Edward I.[3] Too early to help us substantially with the period under review yet providing some details of value is the treatise by Bracton and that known as *Britton*.[4] The remainder of any reconstruction of the criminal trial in the later medieval and early Tudor periods has to be assembled from scattered comments and facts to be discovered in the *Year Books*, the rolls of chancery, the correspondence of the king's ministers, state papers, Tudor law reports, readings at the Inns of Court, and the records of the courts. Of the last the records of the king's bench, the justices of the peace and the justices of oyer and terminer provide information of value, but the records of the justices of gaol delivery (later referred to as justices of assize) more so, because it was at gaol delivery that the majority of arraigned felons appear to have had their cases determined. The records of gaol deliveries survive from about 1300 to 1410 in fair measure and relatively long runs for individual counties enable us to make useful comparisons. The records of peace commissions (which contain indictments but no appeals and only rarely verdicts) are few and do not allow longitudinal study. Their survival appears to have been directly connected with the activities of the king's bench, either because as an itinerant court of the first instance it determined the cases of those accused before particular peace commissions, or because certain of those arraigned had been successful in getting their cases moved before it.[5] It has been suggested that the justices of the peace determined felonies in their sessions periodically in the early fifteenth century.[6] This may have been so, but the degree to which they lightened the burden of the justices of gaol delivery in this respect and the conviction rate at peace sessions is still unknown.

Any account of the criminal trial in the middle centuries (c. 1300–1600) needs to give some consideration to the English system of justice as a whole, particularly the chief dispensers of that justice, if the mechanics of accusation and trial are to be made clearer. The attitudes to criminal justice of the monarch, his advisers, his parliament, and his judges were obviously of paramount importance to its efficiency. The English rulers of this period, despite flattering talk at times by chroniclers that they aspired to be latter day Solomons, seem to have viewed criminal justice in a very mundane way. Criminal justice, as they saw it, existed primarily to help them preserve their thrones and all else, even financial profit, was subsidiary. The greatest crime, treason, was to be rooted out by every means at their disposal, the suspects convicted without fail, and then punished in a manner whose brutality was quite out of keeping with other English punishments.[7] The other serious offences under the criminal law, the felonies, were viewed very much more dispassionately, unless, that is, they involved a dangerous feud which might disturb the upper classes or substantial financial loss to the king or the royal family.[8] The interest or disinterest of particular kings in criminal justice appears to have had little effect on the rate of conviction for felony in general. Henry V, it is usually stated, was a powerful king greatly concerned with public order yet the gaol delivery conviction rate for felony in his reign was perhaps the lowest in our whole period. When, on the other hand, Henry VI, the feeblest of kings, had been on the throne about twenty years the rate seems to have reached an unprecedented high level.[9]

Whenever, in the period under review, there was some modification of the criminal justice system the impulse usually came from parliament rather than the king or his advisers. Furthermore it was likely to originate in the lower house rather than the upper. Parliamentary records of the fourteenth and fifteenth centuries contain a good number of petitions for improvement. A persistent theme was the need for the keepers or justices of the peace to have the power to try felonies without supervision, that is without professional judges or lawyers sitting with them. The compromises and experiments engendered by parliamentary pressure in this regard, which have been carefully delineated by historians, were the closest the legal category of felony ever came to being a national issue.[10] However, quite as important for the history of felony and even for the history of English criminal law administration in the round are the clues they provide about the relationship between these 'amateur' justices and the professional judges of the king's bench, the court of common pleas, and the exchequer.

The professional judges rarely numbered more than a dozen at any time. England, for its population and wealth, was thus woefully deficient in expert skills on the bench. Unless the king decided otherwise, which was rare, these judges, although appointed to hold office at the royal will, could count on remaining in their position until total incapacity or death overtook them. They received a reasonable salary with a very substantial supplement for maintenance, and additional payment when encumbered with special judicial duties (for example commissions of oyer and terminer).[11] Income which came from sources other than the king, we can be sure, was much greater, for it has been noted that in the poll tax of 1379 the assessment of a chief justice was greater than that of an earl. The unofficial income came from the fees which the judges received as retainers of the nobility (a practice parliament tried hard to stop), from serving as feoffees to uses, and most lucratively from gifts and payments from suitors and would-be suitors in their courts. The suspicion arises that the very office of professional judge was purchasable: as late as 1592 Roger Manwood, a justice of common pleas, offered Lord Burghley 500 marks for the vacant chief justiceship of the king's bench. In the fourteenth century the children or grandchildren of no fewer than eight professional judges reached the ranks of the parliamentary baronage.[12] Even if in several of these instances this advance was assisted by military administrative and political as well as judicial service the wealth in land necessary for ennoblement (probably over £500 a year) must have been acquired largely through their judicial authority; although it cannot have resulted from their salary, their supplements, pay for additional duties, or fees as retainers. A fourteenth-century piece of writing known as the *Song on the Venality of the Judges* provides the explanation: the judges through their underlings were wont to induce gifts from prospective litigants on the understanding that their 'aid' would then be forthcoming in the suit; the litigant who was poor or who did not make gifts would meet with no success.[13] Thus the wealth of the judges must have derived largely from the perks provided by the private actions, mostly land cases, which came before them. Here the law was sophisticated, almost labyrinthine, and stimulating legal debate must have added to the interest of the cases, particularly as the judges were frequently involved in the land market themselves. Evidence from the later sixteenth century suggests the justices of gaol delivery/assize looked forward to hearing private actions and were suspected of failing to devote sufficient attention to the criminal cases.[14]

The paucity of professional judges may have been the result of royal parsimony, the king being aware he could associate with them other men trained in the law (serjeants at law and royal administrators) so as to ease the burden. It might also have been that he was reluctant to appoint to the bench any man of law who was not known to be in total agreement with royal objectives. Nor should we discount the possibility that the small number of puisne justices may also have been the result of their being in some way able to restrict entry to their highly profitable circle. Judges appear to have had the most amicable of relations with the magnates, both lay and ecclesiastical, being retained by them, invited to their residences, and sitting alongside them in the king's council.[15] They seem to have been less well-disposed towards the gentry, within whose ranks most of them had originated.[16] The professional judges did not have a monopoly of places on commissions of gaol delivery. A common practice in the later fourteenth and the fifteenth centuries was for three such commissioners to sit at each delivery, one being a judge, another a king's serjeant, and the third a member of the gentry, doubtless trained in the law, who held a non-local administrative position under the crown.[17] By the time of Elizabeth I the justices at any one delivery numbered only two, a judge and a serjeant or a law officer of the king.

It does not appear to have been the hope of sharing in the wealth accruing to the professional judges which provided the impetus for the English gentry to seek appointment as keepers, and later justices, of the peace and to demand in parliament the same powers in regard to criminal justice which the judges had. Since (after 1332) they could not try private actions effectively they were of little direct use to magnates in their litigation.[18] They were, however, of great value to them in another way. Litigation spurred land wars, land wars bred indictments for assault, forcible entry, riot, maintenance, illegal livery and retaining, and even homicide, larceny and rape on occasion. Since such indictments were largely the business of the justices of the peace they were in a position to interfere with due process in order to save a magnate's clients from the embarrassment of indictment and trial and make the same more likely for those of his enemy. They could also make life unpleasant for suspects by their control of manucaption. There can be no doubt that their legal authority gave justices of the peace substantial social power as well. It was probably a decisive factor in winning them positions as retainers of the nobility and offices from both the latter and the king. Indeed there may have been something of a bidding war to secure the services of these local justices at certain times.[19] The judicial powers of the justices of the peace doubtless allowed them to control strictly the lower class population on their own lands and on the lands of their patrons, even before they assumed the enforcement of the labour laws in the second half of the fourteenth century.

If the ability to take indictments and to determine cases of trespass made them a force to be reckoned with in county politics then being able to try felonies could have added to that power; homicide, larceny, and rape were not infrequent products of the land wars and the ability to reprieve a person convicted so he could seek a pardon must have been quite vital as the nobility saw it. To secure this authority they turned to parliament. In commons' petitions they pointed out that their knowledge of the locality made them better able than the judges to deter criminals, which may have been true; but then so was the rejoinder that their partiality was also the greater because of their land holdings in their area of jurisdiction.[20] Justices of gaol delivery were not supposed to hold property within their circuit. The several stages by which the justices of the peace achieved the power to determine felonies untrammelled have been carefully traced by historians. They appeared to have gained their objective in 1329, 1332, and 1338–44, but then were forced into a compromise: they might only try felons when men learned in the law (who might be justices of gaol delivery) sat with them. This restriction was lifted from 1361–4 and 1380–2 but thereafter, from the 1390s, felonies had to be tried at peace sessions before a quorum containing at least two local men of law and the justices of gaol delivery.[21] This continued to be the practice in the fifteenth century. Only in about the middle of the sixteenth, so it has been argued, did the justices of the peace begin to lose their power to try felonies. From around 1590 there is some evidence of efforts to prevent them determining serious cases, but they were still sentencing prisoners to death at the Devonshire quarter sessions at the end of the century.[22] In the fourteenth century the justices of the peace and the class they came from were able to secure the increase of their judicial powers, it seems now agreed, less through proving their juridical competence than through hard political bargaining in parliament: the king conceded their demands in return for parliament's granting of taxes.[23]

In the late fourteenth century and the early fifteenth the justices of the peace secured for themselves a prime position in managing the accusation and trial of most of the offences connected with the seamy side of bastard feudalism: forcible entry, embracery, maintenance, riot, and illegal livery and retaining. They even acquired the authority to employ summary methods of procedure in handling some of these offences, and in the later fifteenth century these powers were extended to include additional misdemeanours, a far cry from the occasions in the mid-fourteenth century when their class, the commons in parliament, were demanding that there should be no arrest without formal charge first.[24] As a result of this acquisition the political power of the justices of the peace must have risen still further. Yet it is also quite possible that these tasks, together with the undoubted burden of the many new statutes regulating commercial activity which they were given to enforce in the fifteenth century, reduced their ability to determine felonies even before the Tudor period.

How the key players among the justices of gaol delivery, the professional judges, viewed the trying of felons on circuit, and indeed the enforcement of the criminal law in general, is not a matter to which historians have given much attention, particularly in regard to the late medieval centuries. It has already been noted that the judges were more interested in the assizes part (i.e. the private actions) of their circuit work, but there must also be a strong suspicion they found the doing of criminal justice boring and distasteful. When additionally appointed to the peace commission they had the right to attend the indicting sessions, but we do not know how great was their inclination to do so. They seem to have wanted to get through the cases on the gaol delivery calendar at the greatest possible speed. Hence the way in which they compelled petty juries to consider verdicts for several cases at one time; and their refusal to allow severance, that is to say separate trials when several persons were tried on the same indictment.[25] It may well have been because of this haste that the method of forcing a prisoner to enter a plea changed from imprisonment of great severity to the much quicker method described by Thomas Smith: pressing with weights, which could quickly lead to the breaking of the spine of a recalcitrant accused.[26] Prisons produced 'gaol fever' and since the gaol delivery sessions were often held in close proximity to the place of confinement the justices must frequently have had to face the danger of contagion, which doubtless inclined them to keep the period when they were in contact with the prisoners as short as possible.

How good was the professional judges' knowledge of the criminal law and did they all interpret it in a similar way? It has been noted that in the early Tudor period expertise was fostered by readings on criminal justice at the Inns of Court, by discussion of difficult cases in the exchequer chamber, king's bench, or at Serjeants' Inn, and by interesting points of law being recorded by reporters in court and duly absorbed by all the other judges.[27] Yet not all of the puisne justices, in the late medieval period at least, appear to have been entirely sound in their legal knowledge. A lack of consensus on some of the knottier points of the criminal law can be explained by unwise promotions to the bench in a few instances, but more frequently by the lack of statutory definition of the chief felonies and process upon them. Thus the crime of burglary, although the main elements of its constitution can be recognized from plea roll cases and *Year Book* comments, was never defined with precision in the period under review, and rape was not dissimilar; nor were the judges certain if a thief could be hanged for stealing goods worth exactly one shilling; and there was uncertainty for a time whether a person whose property had been stolen could recover it by any means short of an appeal.[28] The problem was the absence of any machinery of supervision. In the middle ages the king's council appears to have had nothing to say on these matters, and unless the king or his chief minister had an appetite for the details of the law, and very few had, the only criticism which the judges were likely to encounter on the score of procedure and the scope of felony came from the commons in parliament.

Except when the case was of particular importance to the crown and the king's gaze fell in their direction the professional judges may have lacked enthusiasm for the administration of criminal justice. On the other hand among the keepers and justices of the peace there may well have been true zealots. Where the professional judges may have deserved some credit, from the humanitarian viewpoint at least, was for their acceptance of a low conviction rate for felony from the thirteenth century until probably some point in the reign of Henry VIII.[29] At least there is little in the records to suggest they attempted to pressure trial juries into verdicts of 'guilty'. A major reason for their moderation was probably the belief that a juror who followed his conscience was obeying the voice of God;[30] a second may well have been an acceptance that convictions should keep to a traditional level. The early thirteenth-century conviction rate by jury may well have been similar to that which was produced by trial by ordeal, which again would make the later rate seem divinely ordained.[31] The argument has been offered that the trial jurors sought at times to 'nullify' the charges produced by the crown, to protect their own and to convict as few accused as seemed deserving.[32] Yet if the role of the professional judges serving on gaol delivery was as has just been suggested and they found the relatively low conviction rate acceptable then surely 'consensus' is a better word to apply to the trial process and the conviction rate it produced. The statistical evidence tends to support this thesis in that jury 'nullification' of charges and evidence would surely have provoked confrontation with the crown from time to time and some sudden alteration in the level of conviction, yet in fact that rate remained remarkably constant according to region for decades at a time, and where the charges were brought by indictment it was virtually never out of the 10 to 30 per cent range between the reigns of Edward I and Henry VI. Indeed it was usually close to 20 per cent.[33]

The crown's acceptance of the low level of felony convictions in the late medieval centuries is thrown into relief by its obviously great concern to achieve the conviction of those accused of treason. Virtually all the important treason cases were tried not at gaol delivery but before commissioners of oyer and terminer, where efforts may have been made to ensure the jurors were compliant with the crown's wishes. The result, in stark contrast with felony, was that very few persons accused of treason were ever acquitted.[34] Whether, if the crown was set on the conviction of a particular person accused of felony, it could arrange for such a verdict to be returned is not clear; perhaps it could but probably only if the trial was before a commission of oyer and terminer and then with some effort. Such special attention must have been rare and thus those accused of felony or lesser offences may well have believed that the judicial system protected them from the animosity of the crown. This was in the later middle ages. In the sixteenth century the monarchs, their ministers, and their councils were ready to make greater and more frequent efforts to procure the verdicts they desired, yet the system of trial was still an obstacle to tyrannical rule. For a time, from the later fourteenth century into the sixteenth, it appeared that autocratic methods of trial might supersede the use of juries. From the reign of Edward III onwards statutes provided for the use of examination by justices as an alternative, or even as a replacement, for indictment. For some offences examination was made an alternative method of trial or even the sole method.[35] There were also statutes which allowed the record of justices (i.e. their personal observing of the crime) serve as an indictment or even provide a conviction. However, the crimes involved were those connected with the labour laws, commercial regulation, tampering with justice, and especially bastard feudalism (illegal retaining and livery, maintenance, forcible entry and riot) and thus were only trespass/ misdemeanour; none was felony. Not until the reign of Queen Mary was felony linked to examination in a mandatory way. Nor was it possible to arraign someone accused of felony merely on an information and without an indictment. Although the connection had never been sanctified by formal constitutional agreement felony had too long an association with juries of both types for the link to be broken.

The arrangement adopted for the subsequent sections of this book is one which generally follows the actual process of arraignment for felony. Thus the chapter on accusation is followed by one on trial, which in turn leads to the section on the juridical arrangements after the verdict had been delivered. However, between 'accusation' and 'trial' is placed an investigation on the nature, scope, and verdict history of the different types of felony which figure most prominently in the records: murder and manslaughter, robbery, burglary and felonious larceny. What might be called the lesser felonies, some of which were created by statute, have also been examined but because of their infrequent appearance in the plea rolls they are located in the appendices. Similarly rape as a felony, which appears only rarely in the court records of the period under review and does not on statistical grounds deserve inclusion in the main text, has been accorded, in company with the related offence of abduction, an appendix of its own.

In recent times the English criminal trial of the later medieval period, although not a topic entirely neglected, has failed to engage the serious attention of historians, and this is particularly true of the accusatory process. Yet accusation had an exceptionally important role to play in procedure in the centuries under review. The functioning of the jury of indictment was in practice like a jury trial within a jury trial, or even perhaps the first stage of a two-part trial. In the late medieval period appeal, the alternative mode of accusation, was still very much alive and was a potent instrument in securing convictions. However, the feature of surpassing interest in the accusatory field is the rise of the bill of indictment. These matters are the stuff of the first chapter. Actual trial, that is proceedings from plea to verdict, has attracted a greater number of commentators but much of their attention has been devoted to the membership of the petty jury. About the background of these men we now know a fair amount yet this illumination contrasts markedly with the limited returns from historical writing which touches on the procedural aspects of trial. Hardly recognized, and particularly deserving of investigation as a single topic, is the revolution in verdicts on felony which occurred between the early fifteenth century on the one hand and the later Tudor period on the other. The much greater likelihood of a felony suspect being convicted in Edwardian, Marian and Elizabethan times appears to be attributable to changes in procedure and particularly to the encouragement afforded to victims, and others with knowledge of the crime, to play a greater role in the trial process. Like the accusatory phase the aftermath of the felony trial has attracted little comment by historians in recent years. Benefit of clergy and the royal pardon affected an ever-increasing number of convicted felons in the later medieval and Tudor periods and reduced the work of the hangman enormously. How, and how frequently, these privileges were gained and the periodic shifts in their availability are the main themes in chapter four alongside the rise of punitive long-term imprisonment and some estimation of the percentage of arraigned felons who actually went to the gallows.

Notes

1   F.M. Pollock and F.W. Maitland, *The History of English Law before the Time of Edward I* (Cambridge, 1968), ii, 466–7.

2   *Placita Corone*, ed. J.M. Kaye (Selden Society, Supplementary Series, 4, 1966), pp. 1–31; J. Fortescue, *De Laudibus Legum Angliae*, ed. S.B. Chrimes (Cambridge, 1942), pp. 63–77; T. More, *The English Works of Sir Thomas More* (London, 1557), pp. 975–1003; T. Smith, *De Republica Anglorum*, ed. L. Alston (Cambridge, 1906), pp. 85–104.

3   *Year Books of the reign of Edward I, III*, ed. A.J. Horwood (Rolls Series, 1863), pp. 496–545.

4   *Bracton on the Laws and Customs of England*, ed. S.E. Thorne (Cambridge, Mass., 1968–77), ii, 374–437; *Britton*, ed. F.M. Nichols (Oxford, 1865), i, 1–125.

5   See chapters three and four.

6   E. Powell, *Kingship, Law, and Society, Criminal Justice in the Reign of Henry V* (Oxford, 1989), pp. 58–60, 250.

7   J.G. Bellamy, *The Law of Treason in England in the Later Middle Ages* (Cambridge, 1970), pp. 20–1, 45–7; *ibid.*, *The Tudor Law of Treason. An Introduction* (London, 1979), pp. 201–10.

8   *Letters and Papers, Foreign and Domestic, Henry VIII*, ed. J.S. Brewer, J. Gairdner and R.H. Brodie (1862–1910), i (ii), no. 2072.

9   Public Record Office, JUST 3/198, 202, 205, 211, and 213.

10   See *Proceedings before the Justices of the Peace in the Fourteenth and Fifteenth Centuries: Edward III to Richard III*, ed. B.H. Putnam, Ames Foundation (Cambridge, Mass., 1938), pp. xxxviii–liv, and E. Powell, 'The Administration of Criminal Justice in Late Medieval England: Peace Sessions and Assizes', in *The Political Context of Law*, ed. R. Eales and D. Sullivan (London, 1987), pp. 50–6.

11   *Selected Cases in the Court of King's Bench, V*, ed. G.O. Sayles (Selden Society, 76, 1958), pp. x–xi, xiv–xv.

12   PRO SP 12/242/16; M.R. Bloom, *The Careers of Sir Richard II de Willoughby and Sir Richard III de Willoughby, Chief Justice of King's Bench (1338–40) and the Rise of the Willoughbys of Nottingham* (D.Phil. thesis, Oxford University, 1985), pp. 284–92.

13 *The Political Songs of England from the Reign of John to that of Edward II*, ed. T. Wright (Camden Society, Old Series, 6, 1839), pp. 225–8. For such practice in an earlier period see *Chronica de Jocelini de Brakelonda*, ed. J.G. Rokewood (Camden Society, Old Series, 13, 1840), p. 25.

14 See J.S. Cockburn, *A History of English Assizes, 1558–1714* (Cambridge, 1972), p. 135.

15 *Political Songs*, pp. 227–8; J.R. Maddicott, *Law and Lordship: Royal Justices as Retainers in Thirteenth and Fourteenth-Century England*, Past and Present, Supplement 4 (Oxford, 1978), pp. 52–8.

16 As the activities of the Folville and Coterel gangs seem to suggest: see E.L.G. Stones, 'The Folvilles of Ashby-Folville, Leicestershire, and their Associates in Crime, 1326–41', *Transactions of the Royal Historical Society*, Fifth Series, vii (1957), 117–36, and J.G. Bellamy, 'The Coterel Gang: an Anatomy of a band of Fourteenth-Century Criminals', *English Historical Review*, lxxix (1964), 698–717.

17 Serjeants were given permission to serve as justices of assize (and thus of gaol delivery) in 1340: 14 Edward III st.1 c.16.

18 *Proceedings*, ed. Putnam, p. xxvi.

19 On the mechanics of the land wars see J.G. Bellamy, *Bastard Feudalism and the Law* (London, 1989), chapters one to three.

20 *Rotuli Parliamentorum* (London 1783–1832), ii, 174, 202.

21 Powell, 'Criminal Justice', pp. 50–5; Powell, *Kingship*, pp. 16, 56–8.

22 Cockburn, *English Assizes*, pp. 90–2.

23 G.L. Harriss, *King, Parliament, and Public Finance in England to 1369* (Oxford, 1975), pp. 512–15.

24 See Bellamy, *Bastard Feudalism*, pp. 19–23, and J.G. Bellamy, *Criminal Law and Society in Late Medieval and Tudor England* (New York, 1984), pp. 10–19.

25 See chapter three.

26 Smith, ed. Alston, p. 97. The earlier method is described in *Vita Edwardi Secundi*, ed. N. Denholm-Young (London, 1957), p. 128. Should a suspect not enter a plea he never came, technically speaking, under the common law and thus could not suffer its penalties of forfeiture.

27 *The Reports of Sir John Spelman*, ed. J.H. Baker (Selden Society, 93–4, 1977–8), i, 301–5.

28 See chapters two and three, and appendix one.

29 See chapter three.

30 The apparent reverence with which conscience was regarded by those in authority is well displayed in *Letters and Papers, Henry VIII*, xii (i), no. 777, and More, *Works*, pp. 998–9.

31 There are no statistics of verdicts at ordeal available for England but Hungarian cases of the thirteenth century provide a 37.5 to 62.5 conviction to acquittal ratio: R.C. Van Caenegem, *The Birth of the English Common Law* (Cambridge, 1988), p. 68.

32 See particularly T.A. Green, 'Societal Concepts of Criminal Liability for Homicide in Mediaeval England', *Speculum*, 47 (1972), 669–94; and *ibid.*, *Verdict according to Conscience* (Chicago, 1985), especially chapter three.

33 See chapter three.

34 Bellamy, *Tudor Law of Treason*, p. 171. In the later middle ages the only persons suspected of treason to be arraigned at gaol delivery in any number were counterfeiters of coins, whose chances of being convicted were about twice as great as the average for felons as a whole.

35 Bellamy, *Criminal Law*, chapter two (especially pp. 29–47).

1

ACCUSATION: BY JURY AND
BY APPEAL

While the functioning of the petty jury in cases of felony in the later middle ages has of late attracted considerable attention from historians, the role of the accusing jury has aroused much less interest.[1] This is unfortunate because of the manifestly great importance of jury accusation in the period under review. Reports of crime may well, for example, provide a better measure of criminal activity than the verdicts at trials, as criminologists frequently tell us. More importantly, at least for historians of the criminal law, there are indications that the nature and functioning of the jury of accusation may have had a substantial influence on the arraignment of felons and the verdicts pronounced upon them, and on the shaping of popular attitudes to felony also.[2]

Accusation by jury may have already been an ancient institution when it appeared in the laws of Henry II as a method of reporting a limited number of types of serious crime.[3] The Assize of Clarendon (1166) stipulated that twelve of the 'more lawful men' of the hundred and four from each township within it should report if there were in their locality any persons accused or notoriously suspect of murder, robbery, or theft, or receiving those who had perpetrated such crimes. If there were, they should be arrested until they could be tried before visiting justices. From a statute probably dating from early in the reign of Edward I, we learn how this 'presenting' jury was wont to operate at any eyre. The jurors of the hundred were twelve knights: two knights were nominated by the hundred bailiffs and they in turn chose the remaining ten jurors from men of their own rank.[4] These, as jurors, gave their information on the crimes not, so to speak, as the whim took them but in respect to a list of articles (the 'chapters of the eyre') to which the king demanded answer. The articles enquired not only about serious crimes but also such matters as whether there had been malfeasance by officials, defects in administration, or failure to meet feudal obligations since the last visit of the justices. In addition to specifying in their answers (or *veredicta* as they were called) the serious crimes committed, the knight-jurors were expected to arrest those they suspected of perpetrating the misdeeds. Those suspects whom they were unable to capture, says Bracton, were to be reported privately and in writing (*privata/privitez*) to the justices who would then alot the task of making the arrests to the sheriff.[5]

Legal historians have generally regarded the *veredicta* of the thirteenth-century eyres as the ancestors of the presentments of felonies and trespasses/

misdemeanours (i.e. the charges brought by juries of presentment based on their own joint knowledge), which figure so prominently in the records of the keepers and justices of the peace of the fourteenth and fifteenth centuries. The private reports (*privata/privitez*) have, in turn, been identified with the 'indictments', meaning in this instance the system by which bills (accusations by victims or interested individuals) were offered to the same juries of accusation so they might find them either true ('*billa vera*') or unsubstantiated. The bills found true were used as the indictment on which the suspect was to be put to answer. C.A.F. Meekings, the most recent advocate of this identification of *privata* with indictments, argued also for a difference in investigative aim between *veredicta* and *privata*. He regarded the former as being based on specific deeds while the *privata* were concerned with persons and reputations. We ought, perhaps, to be hesitant in accepting this opinion. It appears to have had its origins in part in Meekings' belief that the heading '*de indictatis*' in the rolls of the eyre referred to the confidential reports mentioned by Bracton when, in fact, it seems more likely they were concerned with suspects who had already become fugitives and outlaws: having been indicted they had fled.[6]

Although the records of the thirteenth-century eyre provide little assistance in clarifying this important matter of the nature of the *privata* further, there are hints in the legal treatise *Britton* which point in a quite different direction. In the part of his work where the author was concerned to give a careful description of procedure at the sheriff's biannual tourn there are two references to jurors (albeit township jurors whose job it was to provide presentments to the hundred jurors) having to communicate their presentments privately or secretly. One of the references provides the reason for this covert procedure: it was to be adopted when there was any danger to life or limb. When the hundred jurors, to whom the township jurors had offered their presentments, made their own in turn (to the sheriff) they should, says the author, exhibit the presentments for felony privately and other presentments openly.[7] The procedure at the tourn therefore suggests the *privata* were intended to ensure those suspected of serious crimes should not have advance warning of accusations being made against them. That these *privata* should be associated with felonies is also logical. Felons having already committed an offence carrying the death penalty might well be inclined to offer violence or threat of violence to those who had reported their crimes or were ready to assist in the prosecution.

More recently there has been advanced another theory concerning the antecedents of the late medieval bill of indictment. This thesis, which is more plausible than the foregoing one, argues that the rise of the complaint or bill (complaint in written form) procedure in the English courts can be traced back to the gravitation of cases of trespass/misdemeanour from the shire courts to the central courts from the middle of the thirteenth century onwards. Very significant, it is argued, was the use in the king's major courts of the informal complaint, the *querela*, promoted, so we may assume, like much of the less serious crime to the central courts from the shire court. *Querelae*, which were often informal complaints in French providing a fairly short account of the wrong, were put forward by complainants seeking redress for such mischief as assault, ejectment from land, asportation of crops or beasts, conspiracy, debt, the theft of deeds, and imprisonment by enemies. For some of these wrongs there was no writ of trespass available and thus informal bill procedure was the only avenue to redress. Sometimes the misdeed had been committed after the eyre had been summoned and thus process by writ was barred. On occasion the *querela* was also used at the eyre for starting an action of trespass to replace an appeal of felony made in the shire court.[8] The reason for this legal manoeuvre is not clear but it may have been that the *querela* was a less demanding (and less dangerous) procedure for the complainant. Furthermore the action which the *querela* initiated could provide damages, whereas appeals, the success rate of which was probably low at this time, would only, where the offence was theft, provide the restitution of the objects stolen.

From the beginning of the baronial wars in 1258 *querelae* were brought before the justices in eyre with increasing frequency and their major target was local office holders thought to have abused their authority or to have acted in a corrupt manner. In that the king permitted and even encouraged this development such complaints were probably regarded as being in his interest if not exactly at his suit. Although the *querela* is usually described as neuter in regard to the two basic fields of justice, civil and criminal, it has been argued strongly that it belonged much more to the latter than the former.[9] Significantly there is evidence that complaints in bill form were by the late thirteenth century finding their way into criminal presentments. For three years, from 1289–92, Edward I provided for hearers of complaints to receive at Westminster *querelae* against judges of high standing as well as against other royal officials. One of these judges, Salomon of Rochester, was charged with having at the Suffolk eyre of 1286 procured bills (written complaints) to be falsely and maliciously presented against a certain Henry, son of Nicholas of St Edmunds, and to have given one particular bill by his own hand to the jurors of one hundred for approval. In answer Salomon said he had not procured nor personally offered any bill against Henry but merely acted according to law and custom, which was that at the eyre, for the keeping of the peace, any person could offer a bill to any of the justices and that justice would receive it and hand it to a jury charged with answering the chapters of the eyre. If the jurors found it true they would present its contents in their *veredictum*; if not the bill would be quashed.[10] This is, of course, basically how Tudor commentators tell us the indictment system worked in the sixteenth century.

In Salomon of Rochester's response we have then that rare thing in regard to English medieval criminal procedure, a contemporary and unequivocal description of how the system worked. Were we to be in doubt about the veracity or accuracy of Salomon's statement there is other evidence pointing in the same direction. There is extant a township presentment of 1256 against the local abbot which is followed by a statement that the men of that vill are complaining (*queruntur*) about him; and there is a reference in the records of the Huntingdonshire eyre of 1286 to a man and a woman having been indicted by one Robert Scochere of Undele, the word form implying that a personal complaint or bill had been responsible for the indictment.[11]

Of particular significance was an Irish case in 1292 which was concerned with the misdeeds of the king's carpenter in Ireland, William de Prene. The record of this states that a bill was handed in to the justices of eyre by a particular person and that they delivered it to twelve jurors of county Dublin 'for examination'.[12] The jurors eventually found there was a valid charge in the bill and the accused was arraigned on it. Another section of the record states that 'if any person or persons should desire to indict . . . him' Prene should be put on trial, which shows, like the Scochere case, that it was assumed individuals as well as juries of presentment might be the prime movers in the indictment process even in the late thirteenth century. The eyre records reveal that the bills given to the justices were concerned essentially with misdemeanours. The evidence that the content of a bill might be a charge of felony is not substantial but neither is it entirely lacking. The man mentioned in the records of the Huntingdonshire eyre as having been indicted by Robert Scochere was eventually captured and hanged, but it may perhaps have been on account of a crime other than that laid against him by Scochere, so we cannot be sure. If it was on account of Scochere's bill and indictment then the charge he brought must have been one of felony as was, so it seems, the charge in the bill procured by Salomon of Rochester against Henry, son of Nicholas of St Edmunds.[13] The Prene case is tantalizing also, but it does take us a little further. The charges in the bill against Prene were said to be for both felony and trespass. In his complaint to the king Prene argued firstly and primarily that although no one in England or the parts of Ireland ought to be taken and imprisoned at the eyre for felony unless it was on the presentment of a jury, he had been so treated.[14] This might mean that at that time complaints of felony by bill as distinct from those for trespass by bill were totally unacceptable, but more likely the meaning was that any *querela* touching felony must first be passed to a jury of presentment and found true before it became an indictment and the accused arraigned upon it.

Thus by the middle of the reign of Edward I at the latest, and probably by a point in time decades earlier, the system of indictment referred to by Marowe, Smith, and Lambard in the sixteenth century, and indeed by a Worcestershire justice of the peace's manual of the early fifteenth century, namely one where presentments and indictments were based on bills offered by one or several persons to the justices who then put them before jurors of presentment, was well established.[15] At least this system was well established at the eyre at the end of the thirteenth century, but was it in place at the burgeoning sessions of the keepers of the peace and sessions held under other commissions like those of trailbaston and gaol delivery early in the fourteenth century? The answer is probably in the affirmative although the absence of legal treatises and a shortage of comment by contemporaries in general makes the fourteenth-century history of the topic somewhat indistinct.

The form of felony indictments in the extant proceedings of the fourteenth-century keepers and justices of the peace provides little help. The most common verbal formula used is that jurors present (*presentant*) X for such and such an offence. In a substantial number of cases, however, perhaps a quarter or a third of those extant, the word form is that an inquest has been taken (*inquisicio capta*) at which the jurors (*iurati*) say (*dicunt*) that X did such and such. In her exhaustive study of the proceedings of the justices of the peace in the fourteenth and fifteenth centuries Bertha Putnam noted only a handful of bills as such and the subsequent researches of her pupils and associates produced only a very few more. Despite this she was moved to argue that a good number of the indictments which she had studied must have been on bills offered by victims, a conclusion which, given the evidence for the thirteenth century already noted above, seems likely to be correct.[16]

Yet neither Putnam nor her successors in the field detected any difference in procedure lying behind the two different indictment formulae (i.e. *presentant* and *inquisicio capta . . . iurati dicunt*), that is to say they did not see one of these forms being particularly connected with bills of indictment. They even argued the two word forms were synonymous and interchangeable.[17] However, there can be little doubt that at the sessions of the peace from Edward I's reign onwards *presentant* usually signified the indicting jurors' response to a list of articles put to them by the keepers and justices.[18] As at the eyre such presentments may well have included accusations of crimes in bill form put before the jurors by third parties (i.e. victims) and found true, as well as the crimes which had become known to the jurors in more informal ways such as through gossip ('common fame' as it was called) or personal contacts. Such bills would have been for either felony or trespass. If the connection between the form *presentant* etc. and bills of indictment was occasional and certainly not exclusive, the relationship between such bills and the formula *inquisicio capta . . . iurati dicunt* appears rather stronger.[19] There survives a Suffolk bill of June 1362, which bears the endorsement 'inquisicio capta . . . qui dicunt in ista billa infrascripta sunt vera'.[20] Furthermore the fact that bills of indictment in their Latin form normally began *Inquiratur pro domino rege si . . .* suggests that their scrutinizing by the jurors would be at the taking of an inquest. The form *inquisicio capta . . . dicunt*, which appears to have been more prevalent at peace sessions after 1350, cannot be explained away as merely a regional or county variation or a clerk's affectation.[21] A Worcestershire justice of the peace's manual of about 1420 pays such close attention to bills and bill procedure that these appear to be the usual method of indictment.[22] By the end of the fifteenth century the most common indictment formula used in peace sessions records seems to have been *inquisicio capta* followed by an exact copy of each bill which had been put before the jurors and which followed the form *Inquiratur pro domino rege si* . . . etc. Peace sessions records for Hampshire and county court files and enrolments for Cheshire from the reign of Edward IV, most happily, provide us with a very clear demonstration of this.[23]

The indications, therefore, are that 'true bill' procedure started in the thirteenth century and never ceased, and that by the late fifteenth century and perhaps earlier the vast majority of the charges of felony offered by juries of indictment were based on bills.[24] Fifteenth-century correspondence where it mentions crime reads as if contemporaries saw indictments as originating from individuals rather than from the corporate mind of a jury of presentment; as being private accusations rather than communal ones.[25] We should also remember that since the indictments on which men and women were arraigned at sessions of gaol delivery, the main court for trying felons, were often sent up by the justices of the peace, then there also accusation was in essence by bill even if there is no trace of this in gaol delivery records because of lack of specificity.

The nature of the process by which a jury of indictment found a bill to be true, or made a presentment in answer to articles put to it by the justices, while crucial to our understanding of the medieval criminal trial, is still shrouded in mystery. It has failed to attract the serious attention of both historians of crime and historians of the criminal law. In the fourteenth and fifteenth centuries the juries of the hundreds, and the multi-hundred and county-wide grand juries also, expected to receive 'information' about local crime from the lower levels of the system, primarily the representatives of the vills.[26] Unfortunately we are not told in what form this 'information' came. This late medieval procedure is suggestive of that recorded in the thirteenth century whereby at the sheriff's tourn the representatives of the vills made presentments to the hundred jury, which sponsored those it thought true and passed them to the sheriff. It is also suggestive of the fact that the hundred jurors at the eyre were allowed to seek 'advisement' in cases of felony.[27] From the fifteenth century we learn of the grand jury receiving presentments from the tourn, some of which, like those of the hundred juries, were based on bills, and approving or rejecting them.[28]

In addition to receiving information, the raw material for presentments, from what might be called the official representatives of the townships – reeve, villagers and constables – the juries of presentment of each hundred in the fourteenth and fifteenth centuries learned about felonies and their circumstances from victims, informants, and from those who prosecuted the culprits by means of bills.[29] They even received information from the justices at whose sessions the case was being heard. Bills intended to indict felons would be handed to the justices who were to take the sessions or to their clerk. The task of the judiciary here was to see that the bills were in proper legal form, although on occasion the justices appear not to have limited themselves to this. A *Year Book* report of the 1340 trial for malfeasance of Chief Justice Richard Willoughby shows that in his defence he made the point, which was not rejected, that 'it is the custom for the justice to go to the indictors to encourage and inform them'. There is support for Willoughby's argument in a *Year Book* case of 1343. In this one judge said it was a duty of his office to inform people (*gens*) for the king, 'people' appearing to mean the indicting jurors.[30] Correspondence from the middle years of Henry VIII's reign reveals that on occasion justices might go to the indicting jurors to explain to them the circumstances behind the bill and this indeed may have been what Willoughby was wont to do. Justices obviously acquired much of their knowledge about the offence from the victim. A report from the reign of Edward IV says that when a man comes before a justice of the peace before the sessions to tell how he has been robbed, he names the robber, describes the circumstances, and the justice can put to him various questions to answer on oath. This is almost exactly what Sir Thomas Smith tells us about the same matter.[31]

By the fifteenth century bill bringers were probably well prepared to offer supporting evidence and indicting jurors well aware of how it should be presented if it was to sway them. On one occasion in 1450 Sir John Fastolf sent his legal advisers a forged acquittance he had acquired, to assist them in obtaining the indictment of the forger.[32] Even when indicting jurors were provided by local inhabitants with mere information rather than bills as the raw material for their presentments they might insist it was given to them on oath.[33] Very often in the late medieval period there must have been present at the indicting process witnesses offered by the victim. Exactly how frequent their appearance was is not clear although there are some clues. Thomas More, a very acute but much underrated commentator on the workings of the English criminal law, states that on some occasions no witnesses were present at the time of the indictment.[34] The point he was making was that in his time, the early sixteenth century, there usually were, at least in cases of felony. Indeed the lack of witnesses' evidence to the indicting jurors was believed to reduce greatly the likelihood of obtaining an indictment.[35] Witnesses may have been present occasionally at indictment even in the thirteenth century. From the time of the general eyres witnesses had been mainperned at coroners' inquests to appear at the indictment of the accused and it is hard to imagine that the use of witnesses could have been limited to the making of indictments for homicide and not for other serious offences.[36] Were the medieval plea rolls less laconic we might be able to estimate the frequency of witnesses at indictment from the mention of their presence at arraignment, since those who testified at indictment were likely to do the same at the trial. Unfortunately, except for one or two references in the early years of Henry III's reign, witnesses' appearances at trials are not recorded before the sixteenth century. Because witnesses appeared and good evidence was given at indictment, it did not necessarily mean a bill would be found true even, for example, when in the early sixteenth century the evidence was sometimes urged by the law officers of the crown (i.e. the king's prosecutors). More tells us that the nature of the offence might affect the jurors' decision. In his view juries of indictment were particularly likely to spurn the evidence when it related to riot or excessive apparel, which were only trespasses, or heresy, which carried the penalty of felony.[37]

Without 'politike serche and examinacions besyde . . . by . . . the iudges and iustices of peace . . . mischiefes by indightment never would be founden'. In this rather obscure passage of his writings More seems to have been suggesting that one way to ensure the finding of indictments was the use of examinations, that is to say to have the suspects, who had been arrested by constables in the course of their duties or as a result of information to the bench, questioned by justices.[38] The tenor of this examination was then, we may assume, offered to the indicting jurors as evidence. More does not tell us in what manner this was done. Very possibly in the period to which More was referring, that is to say about 1500–30, the salient points which emerged from such examinations the justices could communicate to the indicting jurors by word of mouth. To More's interesting comments on examination in relation to indictment other commentators of the Tudor period on the criminal law add almost nothing. This was probably because, as with witnesses and evidence, the subject figured, where the offence was felony, virtually not at all in the records of the major courts nor in the statutes before the middle of the sixteenth century. It should be borne in mind in regard to examination and the accusatory process in general that their connection had a long history. Legislation from the later fourteenth century onwards provided for the examination of those suspected of various different types of trespass to stand in place of a formal indictment.[39] In contrast, felony and examination did not appear together in legislation until the middle of the sixteenth century. In 1555 the justices of the peace were compelled by statute to examine suspect felons brought before them, and the bringers also; then to put the examinations in writing, and to certify them to the next gaol delivery sessions.[40]

What, it may be asked, do we know in regard to pre-trial investigation in the round about the activities and deliberations of the indicting jurors and the justices who took the indictment? About the work of the latter nothing survives from before the sixteenth century, but from the reign of Henry VIII we are able to garner one or two illustrations of justices of the peace examining suspected felons and those who might know about the crime, of the role of the bailiffs and even local residents who assisted them, and of the primitive detective techniques utilized. In the late sixteenth century contemporaries might at times expect exhaustive investigations by the indicting jurors themselves, as is demonstrated in a manual intended to advise them in cases of suspected witchcraft.[41] A chapter on the 'maner of examining witches' shows the writer expected the jurors first to question the 'injured' party (i.e. the supposed victim) and ask him or her why he believed his disease or injury came from witchcraft, whom he suspected and why. Then they were to question the victim's friends in the same manner, to ask 'indifferent neighbours' about the victim's life, to interrogate the 'adversaries' of victim and suspect, and finally question the supposed witch. The latter was to be interrogated with no one else present save the jurors, and urged to confess; then witnesses were called to give their evidence to the suspect's face. If this procedure was followed in felony cases generally then surely the truth must have been sifted as thoroughly (if not more so) at the indictment stage as at the actual trial. Very likely this was not common practice for indicting jurors but an ideal which might be attained where the crime was particularly notorious or heinous, or where outside pressure on the jurors was great. There is no reason to think that this had not been the custom in the late medieval period also.

By the sixteenth century there was a tendency for the hundred jury to be superseded by a grand jury drawn from several hundreds or the whole county as the main provider of indictments. That a grand jury possessed any special powers of investigation seems very unlikely, but it may have been more assertive and penetrating in its investigations because of its composition. Its members tended to be wealthier and of higher social status than the jurors of the hundreds. In some counties they seem to have been expected to handle socially sensitive crimes (those committed by wealthier inhabitants), and not simply substitute for the hundred jurors or indict the malefactors these had missed.[42] From the later fifteenth century there is some evidence that the crown was eager to have a man of substance and authority among the members of a hundred jury as well. The extant records of the Hampshire peace sessions of 1474–5 show that among the hundred jurors, serving indeed as jury foreman, was Sir William Sandes, a member of the county commission of the peace at that time. There are virtually no other similar sets of records surviving from the period and thus we cannot assess how common the practice was. It is well known, however, that constables sat on grand juries in the fifteenth century. Like William Sandes on the hundred jury they could do so without challenge for there was no rule which barred a law officer from serving as a juror.[43]

The relationship between the indicting jury and the petty jury is another juridical theme which has not attracted the attention it deserves. One obvious line of communication between the two juries was the jurors who sat on both. Putnam remarked that this 'overlap', as she called it, of indicting jurors serving also on petty juries, was not uncommon in Kent in the time of Edward II.[44] In the early 1340s the practice was clearly both common and acceptable. Concerning Chief Justice Willoughby it was complained by the commonalty of Lancashire that when he had procured some people to be indicted he had said to the indictors that no deliverance should be made (i.e. trial jury give a verdict) without them. Nevertheless he allowed the deliverance of those persons 'by others who were insufficient'. Robert Parvyng, who succeeded to Willoughby's position and before whom at this time Willoughby was on trial, observed that indeed an inquest (trial) should have been taken by the indictors (*enditours*) and others, a statement which at least seems to suggest that indicting jurors were not barred from petty jury service in 1340. Furthermore, when Willoughby said the trial jury which he used was a good (i.e. valid) one, Parvyng remarked that if indictors were not in attendance 'it is not well for the king', meaning no doubt that the crown wanted indicting jurors involved in the actual trial so as to increase the chances of the accused being convicted.[45] The only other construction which this verbal exchange will bear is that the indicting jurors might be used as prosecution witnesses at the trial. However, we have no evidence of such a practice.

The words of Parvyng and Willoughby are probably best taken as an affirmation that the crown favoured the use of indicting jurors on petty juries. Yet there must have been opposition to the practice among those who had the power to challenge the king.[46] In the parliament of 1351–2 an act (25 Edward III st.5 c.3) was passed which limited the usage. No indictor (*enditour*), it declared, was to be put on 'inquests upon deliverance' (petty juries) if he was challenged 'for that same cause' by the person indicted. Thenceforward a person being arraigned could, in theory at least, by claiming that a trial juror had served as a juror of indictment or was the original accuser, have him removed.[47] Since the Edwardian statute did not positively forbid indictors being on petty juries it is likely that the practice continued. Indeed some recent studies devoted to late medieval petty juries appear to indicate that such was the case, although there seem to have been only three or four such men on each.[48] The king and his judges were not likely to yield on the matter without a struggle for the practice was too valuable through its promise of more convictions and more forfeitures for the crown to abandon it. The practice of swearing a man to both an indicting jury and to one which would try the persons he had just indicted was still to be found on occasion in the late Tudor period.[49]

Some aspects of the nature of the indictment process can best be obtained by studying indictments themselves. The form of an indictment, as we have seen, may well have been altered, following its scrutiny by the justices when it was still a bill and had not yet been delivered to the indicting jurors. The crime mentioned in a bill of indictment might be diminished by the indicting jury, which eventually approved it, into a less heinous offence. It might also be altered when it was a presentment, that is to say when it was the product of a jury making presentments in answer to the justices' articles. In this case it might be altered by the clerk of the crown. Very few 'raw' presentments of felony (i.e. jury-composed without subsequent official amendation) have survived, perhaps because the jurors may have made their charges orally to the court clerk. Two, which by chance have been preserved, are in English but there survive also the Latin engrossments. The effect of the clerk's work is obvious. Apparently the clerk was supposed to ask the jury if it was content to allow the court to amend the form of the indictment and the Latin, although not the substance. However, in the instances mentioned the presentments have not been merely translated, they have been fleshed out into proper indictment form and the heinousness of the offence and the offender afforced. Whether these alterations derived from the clerk's or the justices' personal knowledge of the case, or, more validly, from their questioning of the jurors subsequent to the presentment, is not apparent. In the earlier sixteenth century there occurred instances where the crime mentioned in a bill of indictment was diminished in seriousness by the indicting jurors before approval. By the fifteenth century the 'pure' presentment, made in response to articles from the justices, were probably the poor man's end of the criminal accusatory system. We have no information about the cost of putting in a bill of indictment in the later middle ages but since legal expertise was needed it must have cost something. A presentment on the other hand, although dependent on others for its bringing forward, cost nothing. All one had to do was ensure the presenting jurors heard of the offence in such a way as to feel obliged to report it.[50]

Words and phrases of afforcement in indictments, through the suggested enormity of the offence and bad character of the accused, may well have been intended to influence the petty jurors towards a verdict of guilty. Yet this was not their only function. The bringers of bills of indictment and their lawyers were often intending to protect themselves and penalize those they accused even if there was no conviction. To say in an indictment that the accused was a known, common, or notorious criminal of some sort was, for example, a way of impeding an action of conspiracy should the accused be acquitted, for notoriety implied a wide reputation for infamy and what was common knowledge could not be conspiracy.[51] It might also deprive the accused criminal of his chance to purgate in court ecclesiastical should he successfully claim benefit of clergy, and it could make it more difficult for him to obtain a pardon.[52] In contrast with appeals it was never the practice to include in indictments any reference to the fact that the thief had been captured still bearing the mainour (loot). Whether words like 'common' or 'notorious' in the indictment were nonetheless intended to signify such an occurrence is a question which cannot yet be answered, although it cannot be denied that knowledge that a suspect was a repeat offender is a more likely cause. There is also some slight evidence that the acquittal of a 'common' felon by petty jurors might be to their future discomfort. Fitzherbert tells us of a case in Richard II's reign where Chief Justice Tresilian told the petty jurors that because they had acquitted a man whom the indictment described as a 'common' thief they would have to be responsible for his future good behaviour.[53] As a result they changed their verdict to 'guilty'. Proof that the employment of the adjectives 'common' or 'notorious' in indictments of felony increased the likelihood of conviction is provided by statistical evidence. A conviction against acquittal ratio for the early fifteenth century of about one to three has been found for common felons in contrast with a ratio of one to eight in cases where the accused was not so described. Another afforcement was the inclusion in the indictment of the word *noctanter* ('by night'). Medieval men were particularly fearful of criminals who operated under the cover of darkness. Jurors in the south-western counties in the earlier fifteenth century, an age of few convictions for felony, found 17 per cent of suspects guilty when the word *noctanter* or similar was included in the indictment, which was more than double the figure for cases where it did not appear 7 per cent).[54]

Afforcements of the indictments were but one way in which victims, indictors, justices, or the clerk of the court could signal to the petty jury the degree of suspicion existing against the accused. There were several other lines of communication possible with the petty jurors. Indicting jurors, as we have seen, must have served subsequently (i.e. in regard to the same cases) as trial jurors, although in what numbers we cannot say, except that an almost total complement of the former was not acceptable. Along with bills of indictment, presentments, and witnesses, information gleaned from victims and accused must have come within the purview of trial jurors. And so at times, but not every time, must have the victim. Victims, according to knowledgeable opinion of the Tudor period, often sought to indict the miscreants out of an early desire for revenge, a desire which faded in the extended period between the commission of the offence and arraignment.[55] It has been argued that in the fourteenth and fifteenth centuries the seeking of indictment was pursued as a method of simply frightening and harassing the felon, trial and conviction not being the prime intention.[56] The second of these explanations of the motives behind indictment seems less cogent than the first, although it must be admitted that incarceration in a late medieval gaol, which would follow indictment and arrest, cannot have been a pleasant experience. As well as endangering health it could also be expensive, as would be the precautions necessary, for those with the wherewithal, to ensure acquittal.

The rights and obligations of the victim, who sought the indictment of the felon from whose crime he had suffered in some way and the restitution of stolen goods, are lacking in medieval legal treatises. The latter were for the most part composed in the period between the late twelfth century and the early fourteenth, when charges were produced by the hundred juries in answer to the articles of eyre and the input by victims, in any formal way at least, was not very great. The only revealing comments are to be found in *Britton*. According to the author, who was probably writing in the late thirteenth century, the victim (*sakbere*) who was determined to recover goods stolen from him feloniously must freshly pursue and capture the taker. The latter would then be put on trial in the hundred court or that of the lord of the fee. There, with the coroner present, the *sakbere* would tell his tale and claim the stolen goods. If witnesses provided proof of his statement then the accused would be convicted and sentenced to death. Since a coroner was to be present we might assume this was process by appeal yet the word is noticeably absent.[57] What the writer says next proves the omission was deliberate. He states that should the culprit not be taken freshly but rather captured later, although still carrying the mainour, he should be imprisoned until the next gaol delivery when the victim must appeal him. The writer seems to indicate that for the victim there was also a third option. He might bring a personal action against the taker of the goods, although in such a case he could not seek the penalties of felony, only of trespass.

The first option for the victim of felonious theft or robbery may be characterized as instant pursuit, which if successful was followed by a summary or truncated trial of the mainour-carrying culprit. Probably because of the expanding jurisdiction of the king's courts it does not appear to have been available after the thirteenth century. Thereafter victims had to decide between appeal, which if successful would restore to them their stolen goods, or an action or bill of trespass (*querela*), whereby successful suit would bring not only restitution but damages as well.[58] As will be demonstrated below appeals remained fairly popular in the fourteenth and fifteenth centuries because of the good chance of success and perhaps because they could be brought against anyone found in possession of the goods. In expenditure of money and energy by the accuser an appeal must have been fairly costly. If it failed and damages had to be paid then it could be very expensive; furthermore the appellant might have to suffer a period of imprisonment. On the positive side, however, the likelihood of an appellant having to undergo trial by battle was extremely small.

If a felony suspect was indicted and subsequently convicted any loot which had been in his possession at the time of his capture, together with all his possessions, escheated to the king.[59] So did any goods of which he was the bailee. There has been some recent comment on the subject of victims having their property restored to them after a suspect had been convicted of felony on an indictment. Attention has been drawn to a small number of late fourteenth-century cases where this seems to have occurred, and it has been noted that Richard Littleton writing at the end of the fifteenth century states that a victim might recover his goods 'before an officer'. However, the fact that Thomas More in his *Utopia* (1516) and the author of *Diversite de Courtz et lour jurisdictions* (*c.* 1530) both state that there was no restitution of stolen goods after conviction on indictment, even if fresh suit had been made, has been rightly recognized as settling the matter.[60] When in the later middle ages a suspect was captured with what was thought to be mainour in his possession and there was no appeal, nor would a hundred jury produce an indictment against him, the victim might be allowed to purchase the goods he claimed were stolen. Presumably in this case the suspect did not, for some reason, say they belonged to him; but there is evidence of one particular suspect in such a situation claiming the supposed mainour as his own goods and doing so successfully.[61]

It cannot be denied there was a primitive logic in the rules governing stolen goods. The basic tenet seems to have been that the victim should make fresh suit and bring an appeal. If he did not do so he did not deserve to have his stolen goods back. If a jury of presentment had to discover the culprit it meant the victim had failed in his obligations. This logic, however, became somewhat flawed when, in the fourteenth century, victims began to put in bills of indictment for felony and provide testimony themselves and through witnesses, whom they persuaded to appear, as to the offence and the miscreant. It is difficult to believe victims found much satisfaction in doing all this a second time, before the trial jury at the arraignment, when there was no chance of recovering their stolen possessions, although admittedly where the offence had been against the victim's person he might feel differently. After achieving the indictment of the suspect in an asportation case the victim would most likely be seeking, if the miscreant had been captured but the loot was not yet in official custody, to make a deal with him. The basis of this arrangement would surely be the return of a good part of the goods stolen or their value. If satisfaction was offered then no doubt the victim would deliberately fail to give evidence at the trial or would give it in a half-hearted or negligent manner so that there would be no conviction. Where the felony had been homicide or rape the seeking of a deal such as this was doubtless also common but the victim's relatives would be demanding compensation.[62]

Not until 1529, it seems, was the anomaly ended which prevented victims, even those who had strenuously sought and achieved the indictment of felons, from regaining the goods stolen from them. The remedy was provided by the statute 21 Henry VIII c.11, the provenance of which we know little about. It was certainly a time when there was considerable discussion taking place concerning the English criminal law as the writings of Thomas More and Christopher St German demonstrate. The 1529 act stipulated that where a felonious stealer of goods was indicted and convicted on the evidence of the party robbed, or of the owner, or of witnesses they had provided, the owner might have the goods restored to him as if the conviction of the felon had been achieved by means of an appeal.[63] This was a very radical alteration to the law. In its legal novelty it was comparable to the establishment of the petty jury in criminal cases in about 1219 or Henry VII's experiments with summary and truncated procedure. It is, of course, quite possible that there had already been some 'bridging' cases where the justices, perhaps in ambivalent circumstances, had awarded restitution of goods to the victim. Unfortunately the loss of virtually all gaol delivery records of the period makes any search for pre-statute instances impractical.

In demanding the appearance of victim or owner and their witnesses before juries of indictment the statute demonstrates more clearly than anything else the vital nature of the indictment process in the later middle ages and shows that it was indeed a trial within a trial. The statute did not restore automatically stolen goods to owners and bailees who provided evidence. Their testimony had to lead to indictment, which was likely, and to conviction which, if the fourteenth- or early fifteenth-century rate prevailed in 1529, was unlikely. Furthermore it was left to the justices who determined the case to award writs of restitution to the victims 'from time to time': presumably, that is, when they thought the witnesses had made a good job of testifying. This new power must have increased the authority of justices of gaol delivery considerably.[64] As is demonstrated elsewhere the conviction rate in felony cases by the middle of the reign of Elizabeth was probably high enough to encourage most victims to believe the miscreants would be found guilty in their own cases.[65] It is, of course, quite likely that this increased percentage of convictions came from a rise in number of those giving testimony. To use the jargon of economics it was probably as much a case of victim 'push' as it was of jury 'pull'.

Service as a juror of indictment even more than as a petty juror carried with it certain hazards. Jurors of indictment could not produce accusations without some degree of fear for the safety of their persons. Many threats of revenge were made against them by those they had accused. Thus in a well-documented Somerset case of 1420 the indicting jurors refused to come to a verdict on the bills before them because an esquire, Richard Cheddar, threatened he would have them indicted in revenge.[66] There was also the possibility of what might be called disciplinary action against them by the crown, usually when they were thought to have failed to indict in the face of good evidence. The Statute of Winchester (1285) had announced that the king might establish a penalty against such negligence or concealment of felonies by indicting juries. However, this sanction was directed not against the jurors themselves but their communities. Hundreds which failed to name miscreants within forty days of the perpetration of the offence were to give satisfaction (i.e. damages) to the victim.[67] In the late fifteenth century the behaviour of indicting jurors was by statute (3 Henry VII c.1) made subject to the scrutiny of the justices of the peace. They were empowered to take inquests into concealments by juries which had indicted persons or presented offences before them. Here 'concealment' appears to have meant the ignoring of substantial evidence against the accused and the returning of an unwarranted decision of 'ignoramus' (meaning 'we know nothing of this', i.e. 'we cannot approve') on the charges in certain bills.[68] In a case in the next reign (February 1528) jurors who refused what the crown considered was a true bill were punished by council. The Kentish jury in question would not give its approval to a bill of murder despite what was called 'pregnant and manifest' evidence, which was presented in this instance by no less a person than the king's solicitor. As a result the jurors were dispatched to the Fleet prison on the orders of the council and new bills and a new jury were commanded.[69] There is no indication that the procedure laid down in 1487 was followed.

In addition to their accountability to the king, accountability of another sort confronted jurors of indictment occasionally. This was to persons whom they had indicted but who had been subsequently acquitted. From the number of references to the matter in the *Year Books,* we can assume it was not particularly uncommon in the fourteenth and fifteenth centuries for those acquitted of felony to bring actions of conspiracy against the jurors who had indicted them, and sometimes even against witnesses or justices who were at the indictment. In Edward II's reign it seems to have been a maxim that no conspiracy action lay against indictors, the word presumably embracing victims and jurors of indictment or presentment,[70] yet in the reign of his son writs of conspiracy were allowable if the conspiracy, such as a plot between jurors to indict X or Y, was supposed to have occurred before the sessions.[71] There are reports of cases in fourteenth- and fifteenth-century *Year Books* where those accused of conspiracy were justices. They were put to answer not for their actions in concert with other justices, but rather with bringers of bills or jurors of indictment, which demonstrates how ill-covered was the indictment process by law. In one such case in 1343, where a justice was said to have conspired with three jurors to indict a person of receiving and giving comfort to a felon, the justice defended himself by saying it was his duty to inform people (*gens*) for the king as best he could but he did not contest the matter further.[72]

To be found in most of the *Year Book* cases which touch conspiracy by jurors or justices is the argument that these could not, by the nature of their office, commit that offence, although the judges who are recorded as making comments were noticeably vague on precedents and law. What made justices and jurors of presentment and indictment safe from actions of conspiracy, so seems to have been judicial opinion of the mid-fifteenth century, was their oath that they would discover felonies for the king. Once sworn they were compelled by law to assist in accusation.[73] The bringer of a bill of indictment also, so long as it was his own (or his lawyer's) concoction and not in collaboration with others, could not be the subject of an action of conspiracy. Yet a person who merely informed the justices about a felony seems to have been at some risk if he then obtained assistance from a justice or a clerk in turning his information into a bill of indictment. A particularly revealing *Year Book* case of 1456 shows individual judges arguing for freedom from action of conspiracy for any person who assisted in the prosecution of felons.[74] They protested that a person who would discover felony should be free from any punishment for so doing; furthermore if he actually witnessed a felony he was obliged to report it to the justices and such compulsion totally excused the reporter in law. Ashton, a judge of the common bench, pointed out that at every sessions it was customary for the justices to make proclamation that anyone who wished to come and 'show anything for the king' would be listened to. This, he argued, was proof that those who gave evidence or informed the justices could do so with legal immunity. Yet Ashton obviously recognized this immunity was limited. It was available after such a proclamation, it was available where the person was compelled by law to accuse or indict, and it was available if the victim of a felony had raised the hue and cry. This last point was emphasized by two other judges, Laicon and Moile, who stressed that an informer, and presumably a person who brought a bill of indictment also, was immune from an action of conspiracy if he could show that 'the common voice' or 'common fame' likewise accused the felon he named.[75] This comment helps to clarify why those seeking an indictment liked to be able to include the adjective 'common' and 'notorious' in reference to the miscreant.

Because actions of conspiracy must have been quite an expense for the plaintiff they cannot have been brought in great numbers despite the frequency of acquittal in the courts. Most suspected felons were no doubt satisfied with being found not guilty and set free, while others had made private deals with their victims to restore property stolen in return for 'faint' evidence at the trial. Persons who brought actions of conspiracy against those who had indicted them of felony must have been of substantial status and wealth. Writs of conspiracy were not likely to be sought by the average thief or those who robbed along the highways or in the fields. The crimes in bills of indictment which later gave rise to conspiracy actions were probably homicide and rape, offences where the hostility of families was assuaged only very slowly, and the felonious taking of animals where the value was considerable and ownership genuinely hard to ascertain. The rise of actions of conspiracy was clearly connected with the rise of the bill of indictment, but there is no evidence of connection with presentment in answer to articles; and it is from *Year Book* reports of such actions that we acquire a fair amount of what we know about bills of indictment. The reports show quite clearly how important it was for the bringer of such a bill, who wished to avoid an action of conspiracy to be seen to consult only with a lawyer and not with sympathizers. They also show that the bill should not have originated as an information. As to limitations on who might proffer bills of indictment there seems to have been only one of general application. They should be by victims or by lawyers on their instruction. However, where the offence was homicide the bill bringer was supposed to be a kinsman of the deceased or his servant, a practice vaguely suggestive of the rules governing appeal of felony.[76] Finally in regard to indictments we should ask if the finding of the bill as true had to be by a unanimous decision of the jurors or by something less, as, for example, by a minimum of twelve jurors. Modern scholars have had little to say on the matter. The only contemporary comment seems to have been by a Venetian visitor in Henry VII's reign, who says a mere majority was sufficient.[77]

An accusation of felony, if it was to be heard before the courts and was not brought forward by means of the indicting process, had to be made in the form of an appeal. An appeal was a formal charge, from about 1300 usually in written form, put forward by an individual in the vast majority of cases although more than a single appellant was not unknown. The appellants were usually the victims of the felonies or, in the case of homicide, the victims' next of kin.[78] The appeal was the appellant's own suit and not, as indictments were, the king's. Appeals could be brought for all the ancient 'common law' felonies, that is to say those in existence before the age of statutes, and theoretically although not in practice for the felonies created by statute in the late medieval period. There were also appeals which were brought against their confederates and associates in crime by confessed felons. These were known as appeals by approvers, and are sometimes referred to by historians as approvements. The plea rolls demonstrate that appeals by appellants did not, as was once believed, shrink to a very small percentage of the total of all accusations before the king's courts in the later medieval period. For the first three-quarters of the thirteenth century, so it has been shown, appeals of homicide accounted for about 35 per cent of all persons accused of that felony who appeared in court.[79] Very probably if all types of felony were taken into consideration the percentage would be considerably lower. Gaol delivery records of the period 1329–35 and 1399–1407 suggest appellees amounted to between 8 and 13 per cent of the persons arraigned according to county. The gaol delivery records of the south-western circuit for the years 1416–30 show appellees totalling about 11 per cent of those arraigned.[80] Appellees who appeared before the gaol delivery justices on the eastern circuit in 1437–41 comprised about 12 per cent. Thus for over a century the percentage had remained roughly constant. The records of the northern circuit for 1439–60 show that in Yorkshire in that period, however, appellees comprised about 23 per cent of those arraigned, which was almost double the earlier rate.[81] As to the types of felony which were the subject of appeal no clear pattern is evident. Appeals of homicide seem to have been few, at least before gaol delivery juries, around 1300, whereas soon after 1400 they appear to comprise about 20 or 30 per cent of all appeals. The greatest number of appeals at gaol delivery were undoubtedly for larceny, although appeals of robbery and burglary were not infrequent; there were very few indeed for rape.[82]

The reasons for the persistent resort by felony victims and their associates to appeal are not difficult to discover. From the thirteenth century to the sixteenth contemporaries regarded the appeal as a method of seeking vengeance rather than mere justice. The appellants frequently sought to embarrass, impoverish, and mentally exhaust the perpetrators of the crimes. The late medieval appellant, even if he lusted for blood, had little chance of getting the appellee to face him in trial by battle rather than trial by jury since it was the appellee who had the right to decide.[83] Should the appellee prefer trial by battle he was likely to be frustrated also. If there was an indictment against him for the same offence, or if he had been captured carrying the mainour, or if he made a cash payment in order to have the charge tried by jury, then battle would be denied. A procedural reason for a person to resort to appeal, rather than rely on the offender being brought to trial through the indicting process, was probably the realization that in an age in which local pressures and politics often subverted that process, indictment of the felon might never occur. If the victim of the crime was a known opponent of a magnate from whose part of the county the indicting jurors were drawn, a bill of indictment was unlikely to be found true and no presentment was likely to be made. There is a suspicion therefore that from the fourteenth century appeal was to some degree the preferred process of the outsider in local politics, of a person with either no patron or a patron who would not back him on that occasion.[84]

Along with the near certainty of arraignment the appeal of felony produced something of almost equal value: the strong likelihood of the accused being convicted. In the period from the end of the reign of Edward I to the middle of the fifteenth century the conviction rate of those who were indicted of felony fluctuated between about 10 and 30 per cent, as will be demonstrated. In contrast, appeals, as will be shown in more detail below, produced a strong conviction rate of between 50 and 75 per cent (according to county) of those arraigned in the fourteenth century, and a quite startling one of 70 to 90 plus per cent by the mid-fifteenth century.[85] The vast majority of appeals in the fourteenth and fifteenth centuries were for larceny, robbery, and burglary, the felonies of asportation, rather than for homicide or rape, which rarely provided as much as a third of the total in any gaol delivery roll and usually a great deal less. It seems a reasonable deduction therefore that many appellants employed the appeal procedure because they saw it as a way to regain stolen property. In contrast with conviction on indictment, when the proceeds of the theft forfeited to the king, the mainour which the appellee had asported was, on his conviction, nearly always the subject of a writ of restitution in the appellant's favour.[86] With the strong likelihood of the appeal being successful and the appellee found guilty, and thus a writ of restitution being awarded, there can have been little incentive for the appellant to seek or accept an out of court settlement with the appellee, although there obviously was where the offence was homicide or rape.

In the fifteenth century there flourished the practice of appeal on indictment, the bringing of an appeal against a person who already stood indicted for the same felony. In these cases the victim-appellant may well have been prompted to bring an appeal because he heard of the existence of an indictment or presentment in regard to the offence. If the victim did nothing the loot would be retained by the thief on acquittal, or forfeit to the king on conviction. In either case the victim lost his property. Where no stolen goods were involved he might be persuaded to bring an appeal by what appeared to be a golden opportunity for revenge. This was because the existence of the indictment or presentment made a subsequent appeal for the same offence virtually certain of success. At Yorkshire gaol delivery sessions for the period 1439–60 in cases of appeal on indictment the appellee was found guilty in every instance.[87] There were also a number of appeals on indictment, by the late fifteenth century at least, being brought in the king's bench. Whereas the Yorkshire cases were very largely (84 per cent) for felonious larceny almost half of the cases in the king's bench in the period 1485–95 were for homicide. It has been suggested that the appeal was made in the king's bench, whither the case would be removed, when the appellant came to believe that the indictment of the miscreant was not likely to bring about conviction at the gaol delivery sessions.[88] Acquittal was expected presumably because of the known inclinations of the petty jurors. Why these king's bench appellants should not have made their appeals at the gaol delivery sessions is not clear, but it might possibly have been because of shortage of time or of mistrust of the local petty jurors even in regard to an appeal. The appeal in the king's bench ensured proceedings on the indictment would be suspended and that therefore the appellee would be receptive to the suggestion of an out of court agreement such as the restitution of part of the stolen property, or, in the case of homicide, some financial compensation, in return for the appellant non-suiting. The appellant in these king's bench cases was unlikely to recoup his losses entirely because his bargaining position was not the strongest. He might be able to arrange for the suit to drag on for a considerable time without coming to trial but his chances of having the appellee convicted should attempts at an out of court agreement founder were not good. Apparently in the period 1485–95 in the 167 cases (against 312 persons) in which appearance was recorded there were only twelve verdicts of guilty (2.24 per cent),[89] a startling difference from the conviction rate of appellees at the gaol delivery sessions. It may be, of course, that the relatively small number of appearances by appellees means that many of the appeals persuaded them to come to an early agreement. No doubt there were others who concorded after making an appearance.

Appeals of felony continued to be heard before justices delivering gaols in the Tudor period, although very likely in diminishing numbers. The relevant records for the reign of Elizabeth I (the home circuit only) contain a mere five.[90] Earlier in the sixteenth century, very probably up to about 1530, appeals of felony must still have been reasonably popular. This is suggested by the fact that there were two statutes, 1487 and 1529, which touched appeals, as well as a number of relevant cases in the *Year Books*. In addition, some legal writings such as those of Spelman, Fitzherbert, and Staunford refer to appeal procedure in terms so detailed they imply personal acquaintance with more than a few instances.[91] The statute of 1487, 3 Henry VII c.2, was intended to address the practice of delaying the arraignment of persons indicted of homicide for a year and a day. This had been originally stipulated in the Statute of Gloucester (1278), in order that an appellant would have the opportunity of bringing his suit first. It had become customary, if the appellant then allowed his appeal to abate, for the king to seek the truth of the matter by means of an inquest. Such an inquest, the *Placita Corone* tells us, did not necessarily have the same effect as a jury verdict in a normal trial on a felony indictment.[92] If the accused was found guilty he might merely be fined for trespass. The 1487 statute radically amended the existing rule. It noted that because of the period allowed for the private prosecution of an appeal before the matter was determined at the king's suit, the party was wont to prosecute only sluggishly or to seek a compromise so that by the end of the year 'all is forgotten, which is another cause of murder'. Reference was also made to the fact that bringing an appeal was expensive both in time and money which made 'the partie appellant wery to sue'. Therefore the act commanded that indicted murderers and their accessories should be arraigned within a year of the committing of the misdeed without awaiting any appeal. This was a complete reversal of what the judges of the two benches had said was the proper policy only four years earlier;[93] it was a *volte-face* of striking proportions even if it was in regard to only a single type of felony. The 1487 act was not intended to be the death knell of appeal of felonious homicide. It was to be preserved and in a most novel way. As the statute put it, if the person indicted of the murder was acquitted he was to be bailed or gaoled for a period of a year during which time the wife or the 'next heir' of the victim might bring an appeal against him.

Whatever its precise cause an act which must have had the greatest of repercussions on the bringing of appeals of felony was passed in the parliamentary session which began in November 1529. Except in its final sentence the new law made no direct reference to appeal procedure: that was an effect. It was designed simply to make the process of indictment more efficient by offering, as we have seen, restitution of goods to the indictor who testified successfully at indictment and trial or provided witnesses to testify on his behalf. The act must have caused many victims of felony, who in earlier years would have been inclined to bring an appeal, to turn instead to indictment, although we must admit that the level of the conviction rate in the period subsequent to 1529 would probably have been influential in determining the victim's decision.[94] Those who might not opt for indictment would probably be the relatives of homicide victims and women who had been raped and their husbands. Perhaps also there were a few persons who had been beaten when robbed or burgled and who were bent as much on revenge as on the recovery of their possessions.

As well as what might be referred to as private appeals there appear in the late medieval plea rolls numerous appeals brought by approvers (king's approvers as they were called). Approvers were men or women, taken on suspicion, indictment or even appeal, who, while in custody and before a verdict was given at arraignment, confessed to their felonies and offered to appeal on the king's behalf their erstwhile accomplices in crime. It was up to the justices to decide whether they should allow the prisoner to become an approver. Those who were the subject of their appeals were supposed to have participated in committing a felony with the approver, or have acted as his receiver; they could not be felons whose criminal activities he merely knew about, or former associates now branching out into a type of felony quite alien to the approver's preferred field.[95] Approvers' appeals (approvements) appear only rarely in the records of the thirteenth-century eyre but the gaol delivery records of Edward I's reign seem to contain a good number.[96] Thus the extant rolls for Wiltshire for the years 1275–1306 mention 34 persons who turned approver. In total they appealed 122 accomplices, about one-seventh of all persons accused before those justices in that period. In contrast there were only 24 persons appealed by non-approvers. Of the 122 accomplices two approvers accused 17 each while another two accused 8 each. In the fourteenth and fifteenth centuries very few of those appealed by approvers, when they were tried by a petty jury, were found guilty. The Wiltshire records noted above, however, provide a guilty/not guilty ratio of 3:5, which was a higher level of conviction than was produced by the indictment of felons at that time. The felonies attributed to those the approvers accused were of all types, although robbery (55 instances) and larceny (30 instances) predominated and were very often in conjunction. Homicide was less common (16 instances) but by no means negligible, but burglary (9 instances) and arson (1 instance) were rare.[97] It has been suggested that most of those appealed by approvers were accused of receiving but this was not the case in the records under discussion. That offence was attributed to only thirteen such appellees.

Gaol delivery and coroners' records of the first half of the fourteenth century provide a picture of approvements and their effects which differs substantially from that offered by those of the late thirteenth century. The Norfolk records extant for 1308–16 mention a good number of approvers (94) and some 200 persons whom they appealed. They also yield a guilty/not guilty ratio, startlingly different from the Wiltshire one, of approaching 1:50. A gaol delivery roll covering eight counties for the period 1329–35, which contains fifty-nine approvers' appellees, confirms that their conviction had become infrequent since only four of them were found guilty.[98] By the beginning of the fifteenth century approvers appear only rarely in gaol delivery records. The Yorkshire rolls and files for 1399–1407, which show just under 400 persons as arraigned, reveal that only nine had been appealed by approvers. The records of the south-western circuit for 1416–30 (431 arraigned) contain the name of only a single approver, who appealed but two accomplices.[99] The gaol delivery records for the eastern circuit from 1437–41 mention a mere four approvers although admittedly they appealed a large number of accomplices (49). The same records for Yorkshire for 1439–60 (463 persons arraigned) refer to eleven persons put to answer on appeals brought by a total of seven approvers. There were no successful approvements on the south-western or eastern circuits in the periods mentioned or in Yorkshire 1399–1407, but the seven Yorkshire approvers in the records of 1439–60 achieved the conviction of five of those they had appealed, three for felonious larceny and two for receiving.[100]

The most common explanation of why a felon became an approver is that when arrested and in prison he came to believe his conviction was very likely. Therefore he sought to save himself from the gallows for the moment by accusing his accomplices after making a confession of his own guilt. A second explanation is that the harsh conditions which a strongly suspected felon might experience in gaol, particularly a starvation diet and being lodged in the foulest part of the gaol, persuaded him to appeal his erstwhile associates in crime because this would provide immediate improvement in the necessities of life. An approver would know that at least one of his appellees must go to trial before he met death himself and he no doubt hoped to escape in the interim or perhaps have someone of influence intercede on his behalf. Although contemporary writers are generally uninformative about the attitudes of medieval felons there is one fourteenth-century chronicler who provides some useful information about approver motivation through his interest in a particular robber's career.[101] He tells us that at the time of a spate of robberies committed against churches and wayfarers in 1367 one Hugh de Lavenham was persuaded by threats, but also by a desire for profit, to join the miscreants and came to know them and their routes well. Indeed through his criminal expertise Hugh became a leader. However, he began to fear for his personal salvation if he persisted in this occupation and decided to reveal to the authorities his fellow misdoers and their receivers. He surrendered, became an approver, and served the king thereby most effectively. Seven of those he appealed were convicted by jury and hanged, two others he killed in trial by battle. While in gaol at the time of these events he was given by the crown an allowance of sixpence a day 'with royal favour' and was allowed food 'at the servants' table' whenever he wanted it. Lavenham was pardoned, and his career flourished. He was made a sergeant at arms of the king and later became the keeper of Ilchester gaol.[102] One valuable aspect of this tale for the historian of criminal accusation is that it shows what a windfall at times for the maintenance of public order was the felon who became an approver, and how, if he was successful, he would be not only pardoned but rewarded. Indeed we may suspect he was deliberately tempted to approve by talk of rewards. It was important, given the likelihood that some appellees would opt for trial by battle, that the approver should be a man of considerable strength or martial skills, and no doubt Lavenham, a robber leader, was one. It seems unlikely men would have become approvers if they doubted their prowess in combat, for the king only granted pardon when several accomplices had been convicted, some usually by battle. Formerly historians doubted the veracity of approvers' appeals but recent research has tended to emphasize the likelihood of their general accuracy.[103]

In the later fifteenth century appeals by approvers seem to have become increasingly uncommon but they did not cease entirely as two *Year Book* cases of 1472 and a parliamentary petition of 1468 testify.[104] Another *Year Book* reference from the beginning of Henry VIII's reign suggests the procedure was still acceptable although a coroner was not provided for the would-be approver in that particular case.[105] Legal commentators of the Tudor period, especially Staunford, give considerable space to approvers. In fact Staunford devoted about 7 per cent of his whole treatise on the criminal law to 'l'appel al suit le Roy' as he called it. In his extensive commentary on relevant *Year Book* cases he shows that the finer points of approvement were of great interest to him, perhaps because he was bent on making an exhaustive record of all the rights of the crown in the area of criminal law.[106] After Staunford there is very little. Historians have discovered no approvers or approvements in extant sixteenth-century court records, but this does not necessarily mean the process had ceased. There is a reference in Stow and another in the records of the council which suggest men might still turn approvers even in the reign of Elizabeth I.[107]

In gaol delivery records of the fourteenth and fifteenth centuries, alongside cases where accusation is by indictment, appeal, or even *querela*, are to be found others where men and women appear before the court although not charged in any of these formal ways. Such a suspect is recorded as being *captus*, that is to say 'taken' or 'arrested', or more fully 'taken on suspicion', but not 'arrested because he is indicted' or 'arrested at the suit of X' (i.e. on appeal) as is the standard form in the majority of gaol delivery record entries. The plain arrest form of the late medieval period, *captus*, or even *captus pro suspicione*, was clearly not an abbreviation for 'arrested because indicted' nor for 'taken at the suit of'. The use of this *captus* formula is of considerable importance in the history of the accusatory process and worthy of our close attention.[108] It is quite apparent that in the later thirteenth century there were many persons put to answer for felony who had been neither indicted nor appealed. Wiltshire gaol delivery records of Edward I's reign contain a large number of 'taken' or 'taken on suspicion' cases and indeed, provide few instances of arraignment on indictment. London trailbaston records of the last year of the same reign contain 'taken' and 'taken on suspicion' cases mingled with indictment cases roughly in the ratio of one to three.[109] There is nothing in the details of any *captus* case which suggests why the suspect should not have been indicted. The best explanation of this truncation of accusatory procedure, or rather of what later came to be normal accusatory procedure, is perhaps that the persons 'taken' were arrested in circumstances where their guilt was obvious: as, for example, just as they were committing a felony, or because they were seen with evidence of their misdeed (a weapon or loot) in their hands. Where these were not the circumstances then they may have been arrested because they were recognized as criminals of notoriety, 'repeat offenders' in modern parlance. It has been suggested that in some cases the key reason suspects were taken and subsequently arraigned without a formal charge was simply that they had the misfortune to encounter in suspicious circumstances an officer of the law.[110]

The indications are that *captus* cases, that is where persons were arrested and arraigned without formal accusation, became fewer as Edward I's reign progressed although there were conflicting opinions in the government and the judiciary about their continuing legal acceptability. While the Statute of Winchester (1285) appears to have increased the likelihood of arrest without formal accusation by its permitting the taking of strangers travelling at night, the Statute of Westminster II, promulgated the same year, forbade sheriffs to arrest suspects who had not been indicted and instructed them to proceed by indictment first in the future.[111] A case in the king's bench in 1290 suggests the latter statute had some effect. John de Brampton, who was suspected of forging the king's seal and writs in Norfolk, argued, when he eventually appeared in that court, that he had no need to make a response since there was no suit of the king against him for he had not been indicted or appealed. Nor, said Brampton, had he been arrested while carrying mainour. This appears to have been the first instance where the validity of an arraignment which lacked accusation by indictment or appeal was questioned. Furthermore the challenge was successful for the king's council, despite the notable gravity of the offence, ruled in Brampton's favour.[112]

At the close of Edward's reign, a time when according to contemporaries public order was in singular jeopardy, the crown decided that for the moment at least the new policy of indictment before arrest needed amendment. In the summer of 1306 orders were given to the sheriffs for the provisions of the Statute of Winchester to be thoroughly implemented while at the same time they were to ignore the clause in the Statute of Westminster II which forbade arrest before indictment. They were to arrest persons suspected of felony, but not indicted, without delay and to see bailiffs acted similarly. Yet despite this measure there is some doubt that arrests without prior indictment increased at that time. Indeed it has been suggested that the reverse occurred and that it became increasingly the practice to secure indictment first.[113]

Nevertheless arrest without indictment continued to flourish in the early fourteenth century and the suspects so taken continued to be arraigned without there being indictment or appeal to respond to. A Kent gaol delivery roll of July 1317 shows that in one-tenth of the cases tried the suspect had been arrested while carrying mainour but had never been indicted. A roll of gaol delivery cases of the same period, which were tried in Northamptonshire, contains seven (out of a total of 75) where the suspect was simply stated to have been taken with mainour, and another four which likewise have no reference to indictment or appeal. The latter group, while having no mention of mainour, contain the phrase 'taken on suspicion'. A Yorkshire gaol delivery roll covering the years 1317–27 shows that at that time cases where the suspect was called a common felon, or was arrested carrying mainour, or had been discovered committing the crime by a law officer (usually a bailiff), might still go to trial without there being an indictment or appeal against him.[114] By the 1330s there seem to have been only one or two mainour, common criminal, or arrest by a law officer cases at each gaol delivery sessions. The extant gaol delivery records of Essex and Hertfordshire for the period 1332–6 suggest, furthermore, that such cases would not usually be allowed to go to trial without the suspect being indicted or appealed. The evidence for this is the references to a procedure, for cases where the suspect was arrested with the mainour, which was to become standard in later years. When the person taken came before the court the justices ordered a proclamation to be made that anyone who wanted to accuse him should do so. A variant, sometimes an addition, was for the sheriff to be instructed to enquire about the person arrested at his next tourn in hopes an indictment would be forthcoming.[115] This adoption of the shrieval inquest seems to have been the result of the statute 5 Edward III c.14, which also stipulated that the sheriff should return the findings of the inquest to the justices of gaol delivery together with the cause of arrest. We should notice that this less summary procedure may have been put into the act to balance its extension of the arrest process mentioned in the Statute of Winchester in order to now permit the immediate taking of suspect robbers and burglars by constables of vills and bailiffs of franchises by day as well as by night. In the middle of the fourteenth century arresting powers were being confirmed and even extended, notably in the statute 34 Edward III c.1, which allowed justices of the peace to take men on suspicion and imprison them but there was a rising reluctance to arraign without a formal charge.

Arraignment without indictment or appeal was still a possibility in the 1350s and the early 1360s although examples in gaol delivery records by that time appear to be few and to occur almost entirely in cases where the suspect had been arrested in possession of mainour.[116] By the end of Edward III's reign even this remnant of trial without formal accusation was gone.[117] Any mention of the suspect being a common thief appears to have been merely to afforce a normal indictment for felonious larceny, while references to being taken with the mainour are usually followed by an appeal of felonious larceny.[118] By the last decade of the fourteenth century even arrest before indictment had become an issue of some sensitivity and, if we judge by the form of gaol delivery records, the crown was on the defensive in the matter. Where a person had been arrested without first being indicted it was common for the entry to state he had been taken on suspicion in accordance with the Statute of Winchester.[119] Perhaps this is why there is little evidence from the fifteenth century to suggest that arrests by officers of the common law, without formal accusation made, ever came to be regarded as being to the prejudice of the custom and law of the land and thus a potential constitutional issue.[120]

In the second decade of the fifteenth century there were a good number of *captus* cases at gaol delivery sessions. The extant records of the south-western circuit contain 241 instances of arrest on suspicion without formal charge laid for the period 1416–30 as against 384 persons indicted and 47 appealed, a ratio of those formally charged to mere suspects of a mere 1.8:1. The gaol delivery records of Yorkshire for the years 1439–60 provide a similar picture. There were 463 persons indicted or appealed as against 199 appearing in court who had been simply arrested on suspicion without being formally accused (a ratio of 2.33:1). The records of the eastern circuit for 1440–1 yield a ratio of those formally charged to mere suspects, who appeared in court, as low as 1.42:1.[121] We should probably not be much in error if we assumed that approximately one person out of every three appearing before justices of gaol delivery in the reign of Henry VI had been arrested on suspicion without being indicted or appealed first. This new high level of *captus* cases is by no means self-explanatory. Perhaps constable and bailiffs were becoming more efficient and beginning to assume the role of the modern police officer a little. Certainly it appears that the arrests were made by law officers rather than by incensed victims, although, of course, the latter may have persuaded or assisted the constable or bailiff to make the arrest, a situation which would not be recorded in the records.

While the forms of the various types of *captus* cases are identifiable, and the prevalence of arrest on suspicion of felony where those taken were produced in court is assessable, there are aspects of the *captus* phenomenon which call for further consideration. Although it is easy to conceive why there should be arrest on suspicion without formal charge it is less easy to find a reason why such persons should appear before a gaol delivery court without being indicted or appealed from the mid-fourteenth century, when arraignment in such circumstances was not possible. We might surmise it was because they had been arrested too close to the time of the gaol delivery sessions for a formal charge to be made. The records only rarely provide an indication of when the felony of which the arrested person was suspected had occurred, but where the date can be recovered it is usually well before the time of the sessions and thus the shortage of time hypothesis cannot be sustained. A much better argument is that those arrested on suspicion had already, before they appeared at a gaol delivery sessions, been the object of attempts at indictment or at appeal and that those efforts had come to nothing. Now a second attempt was to be made at indicting them.

The procedure adopted by gaol delivery justices in the handling of *captus* cases is also not entirely clear. It seems that in the course of the late fourteenth and the fifteenth centuries either it was subject to change or the recording formulae of the clerks who kept the records altered drastically. By the middle of the fifteenth century, so the gaol delivery records seem to tell us, the procedure usually amounted to making a proclamation to the effect that if anyone wanted to prosecute the suspect he should come and be heard.[122] From other records we discover that prosecution meant giving information which might lead to an indictment, putting in a bill of indictment, or making an appeal.[123] Except in a very few cases no one came to prosecute and this lack of an informant/accuser is recorded. There often follows a note that it was then testified in court that the suspect was of good fame and that he had taken an oath of good-bearing and been set free.

This, on the face of it, is considerably different from what the gaol delivery records of the earlier fourteenth century have to tell us. In the 1330s, when a mere suspect was brought into court, the sheriff was instructed to enquire at his next tourn as to whether anyone wished to indict him. By the middle of the century the justices of gaol delivery were ordering the sheriff to hold an inquest on the person arrested immediately, but this procedure was probably ended by the statute 28 Edward III c.9.[124] In the 1370s and 1380s there appear in the records references to proclamations which invited anyone who wished to prosecute the suspect to now do so, the form which was to become standard. Also provided sometimes is information which does not figure in later files and rolls. The sheriff, for example, might report he has enquired but found no one who wishes to indict the suspect, and occasionally we are told that men worthy of credence have vouched for the good fame of the *captus* and that X and Y (and even Z) are the pledges for his good bearing.[125] Whether the sheriff's inquest and the testimony about good or bad fame were mutually exclusive or complementary is not clear.

Those who testified to a suspect's reputation are not identified but they may well have included the reeve and four men of the township where the suspect had been arrested; for these were expected to attend the gaol delivery sessions and their vill was fined should they fail to appear. The purpose of their presence is explained in an early fifteenth-century Devon gaol delivery record: they were there to testify and to inform the court what suspicion of felony there was against the person taken.[126] It is not clear in what manner or to whom they testified. It may have been to the gaol delivery court itself or perhaps to a vestigial shrieval inquest, which may have survived although no longer appearing in the records. An interesting mid-fifteenth-century peace sessions record shows a *de gestu et fama* inquest, as they were called, being taken by several grand juries of a county.[127] The 'trial' of a person's fame, good or bad, it should be noted was not a proper arraignment. Those found to be of good fame went free, those of evil reputation were remitted to gaol with the intention of trying to obtain an accusation against them at a later date. In essence the findings were those of a jury of indictment and the proof of this is that when a person's fame was thought to be bad the fourteenth-century sheriff's inquest endorsed the order to enquire with the word 'ignoramus', the traditional way of refusing to find an indictment true.[128] An investigation into the early fifteenth-century records of one gaol delivery circuit has shown that the vast majority (85 per cent) of persons taken on suspicion and not indicted were allowed to go *sine die* following proclamation, a few (8 per cent) were released on sureties, and a very small number (3 per cent) were remitted to gaol.[129] Of those released on surety or remitted only one or two appear again in the records either to be the subject of another proclamation or as eventually indicted.

If we now leave the particular parts and consider English late medieval criminal accusation in the round it is clear that the most important aspect was not the continuing windfalls for the crown provided by appeals or approvements, nor arrest without prior formal charge, but the development of the indictment, process through the rise of the bill of indictment. This form of accusation seems to have progressively superseded those produced by juries of presentment from their own knowledge and local gossip. The plea rolls, as we have seen, provide only opaque evidence of this but there is a considerable amount of more positive proof, albeit largely circumstantial. Thus fifteenth-century correspondence shows that men believed the hand of an individual was behind virtually any indictment, not the group discussions of twelve or so jurors.[130] It even tells us courts kept lists of individuals who had handed in or were responsible for the bills of indictment. Particularly valuable as a yardstick of the rise of the bill of indictment was the popularity of the action of conspiracy. Such actions, brought by those who had been acquitted of felony, could not be used against jurors of presentment, since what these men discovered was considered common knowledge; but they could and were brought against those responsible for bills of indictment. This occurred from the reign of Edward III onwards and, if we judge from the space devoted to the matter in the *Year Books*, not infrequently.[131]

The active role of justices in regard to indictment is another very noteworthy aspect of late medieval accusation. In the late thirteenth century they were said to be receiving information about crimes and passing it to presenting jurors so it could be turned into indictments. In the mid-fourteenth century justices were advising such jurors about crimes reported to them (the justices). In the fifteenth century they were examining the victims of felonies when they reported their misfortune, and maybe even sending on to the trial their own views on the cases. Another pre-trial task for the justices, so thirteenth- and fourteenth-century sources tell us, was to enquire how juries of presentment had acquired their knowledge about the crimes they presented. Presumably this was done in order to warn them about the dangers of following hearsay evidence.[132] Justices of gaol delivery were more involved with the handling of felonies than any other type of justice yet were they concerned with the production of indictments to the same degree as were, for example, justices of the peace and justices of oyer and terminer? Justices of gaol delivery cannot have been present at sheriffs' tourns or at indicting sessions before bailiffs and stewards of liberties. Whether members of the gaol delivery commission were present at indicting sessions of the peace in their capacity, where they possessed it, as justices of the peace in that county is not clear.[133] They were unlikely to have been present in the periods between gaol delivery sessions but were probably able to participate when indictments were taken immediately before or at the time of those sessions. In these instances, which seem to have been frequent by the early fifteenth century, the evidence concerning the felonies would be already known to the justices of gaol delivery when they came to preside at the arraignment.[134] There can have been no monopoly of background knowledge about the crime for the trial jury. The justices of the peace before whom the indictments had been taken (and who were not justices of gaol delivery) were probably also present at the trial, although we have no record of them giving evidence before the early sixteenth century.

With the dominance of the bill of indictment the late medieval indicting process assumed the form of a preliminary trial, or a trial within a trial. Often the victim appeared before the jurors to tell his tale, witnesses told theirs, evidence was offered, and the jurors were able to put questions. A bill had to be properly supported in this way, so it seems, if it was to have a good chance of being found true. From the victim's viewpoint a bill of indictment, although an expense, offered a better chance of getting the accused indicted than did awaiting the deliberations of, or even labouring, a jury of presentment. Provided the jurors, or the clerk of the court, did not tamper with his bill the tenderer through the verbal format could exacerbate the sanctions leviable against the suspect should he be found guilty on arraignment. With legal expertise to pay for, a victim was likely to take it ill if his bill did not produce an indictment. It is possible such chagrin was partly responsible for the proclamation system at gaol delivery sessions whereby a second opportunity was provided for indictment.

There can be little doubt that the production of indictments was of great concern to society at large, not simply to victims and accused. Frequently indicting sessions must have been the scene of tests of political strength between magnates of the shire. In a society with a clearly defined hierarchy and where patronage and its counterpart clientage were the sinews, most serious offences were likely to affect some member of the upper class even if only indirectly.[135] If the suspect felon, or the victim, was in some degree connected with a member of his affinity the magnate had to decide whether he should try to influence the indictment process, reserve his tampering for the arraignment, or allow the criminal process to work without interference. He would know that when a life was at stake, and stolen goods and possessions were forfeitable, there might well be interference by lordship on the other side. With patrons involved and with the danger for one of them of loss of face (and future influence) if there was a clear-cut victory at either indictment or actual trial there must have been a tendency among the upper classes to give their blessing to surreptitious deals between victim and criminal of the kind mentioned above.

We must now move on from the accusatory part of the criminal process. The next stage in proper sequence is the trial, but its features are the more clear if, beforehand, some examination is made of the major types of crime, that is to say the different categories of felony, which dominate in the records of arraignment. To this end the nature and scope, and the verdict history of the crimes of murder, manslaughter, robbery, burglary, and serious larceny are investigated in the following chapter.

Notes

1 The best outline of the early years of the jury of accusation is still Maitland: see F.M. Pollock and F.W. Maitland, *The History of English Law before the Time of Edward I* (Cambridge, 1968), ii, 641–8.

2 See below.

3 N.D. Hurnard, 'The Jury of Presentment and the Assize of Clarendon', *English Historical Review*, lvi (1941), 374–96, but compare R.C. Van Caenegem, *The Birth of the English Common Law* (Cambridge, 1988), pp. 79–80. Van Caenegem argues strongly that under Henry I, Stephen, and in the early years of Henry II the crown employed the 'systematic prosecution of suspected criminals by individual officials acting on their own authority'. As proof he offers the *Leges Henrici Primi* which refers categorically to a royal judge, acting with the authority of his own jurisdiction, without another accuser, without an informer, and without the culprit being caught in the act, impleading a person: R.C. Van Caenegem, 'Public Prosecution of Crime in Twelfth-Century England', *Church and Government in the Middle Ages*, ed. C.N.L. Brooke et al. (Cambridge, 1976), pp. 52–5.

4 *Statutes of the Realm* (Record Commission, 1810–28), i, 232.

5 *Henrici de Bracton de Legibus et Consuetudinibus Angliae*, ed. G.E. Woodbine with revisions and a translation by S.E. Thorne (Cambridge, Mass., 1968), ii, 329–31. *Veredicta* may have included appeals: see R.D. Groot, 'The Jury of Presentment before 1215', *American Journal of Legal History*, 26 (1982), 11–12.

6 *Crown Pleas of the Wiltshire Eyre, 1249*, ed. C.A.F. Meekings, Wiltshire Record Society, xvi (1961), pp. 92–4. M.T. Clanchy, *The Roll and Writ File of the Berkshire Eyre of 1248* (Selden Society, 90, 1973), pp. lix–lx, points out the 'de indictatis' heading 'was evidently used to introduce lists of fugitives rather than indicted persons as such'. He suggests this may have been merely a peculiarity of the Berkshire roll but it seems to me it was general practice. See also A. Harding, *The Law Courts of Medieval England* (London, 1973), p. 66.

7 *Britton*, ed. F.M. Nichols (Oxford, 1865), i, 178.

8 See A. Harding, 'Plaints and bills in the history of English law, mainly in the period 1250–1350', in *Legal History Studies, 1972*, ed. D. Jenkins (Cardiff, 1975), pp. 66–75; *Select Cases in the Court of King's Bench, IV*, ed. G.O. Sayles (Selden Society, 74, 1957), pp. lxxix–lxxx.

9 Harding, 'Plaints and bills', pp. 686–9, 72–5.

10 *State Trials of the reign of Edward I, 1289–1293*, ed. T.F. Tout and H. Johnstone (Camden Society, 3rd Series, 9, 1906), pp. 67–70.

11 *Select bills in Eyre, AD 1292–1333*, ed. W.C. Bolland (Selden Society, 30. 1914), p. 74; *The Roll of the Shropshire Eyre of 1256*, ed. A. Harding (Selden Society, 96, 1981), pp. 236–7; E.B. DeWindt, *Royal Justice and the Medieval English Countryside* (Toronto, 1981), i, 348.

12 *Select Cases in the Court of King's Bench, II*, ed. G.O. Sayles (Selden Society, 57, 1938), pp. 125–35.

13 DeWindt, i, 348; *State Trials of Edward I*, p. 68.

14 *Select Cases in King's Bench, IV*, pp. 125–7.

15 See *Early Treatises on the Practice of the Justices of the Peace in the Fifteenth and Sixteenth Centuries*, ed. B.H. Putnam (Oxford, 1924), pp. 237–9, 383–4; Smith, ed. L. Alston, pp. 87–8; W. Lambard, *Eirenarcha, or, of the Office of the Justices of Peace* (1581), pp. 383–426.

16 See *Proceedings*, ed. Putnam, pp. c–cii.

17 *Ibid.*, p. ci.

18 Thus five Kent hundreds in their presentments to the keepers of the peace in 1316 gave separate and specific answers to the 'first article' and 'second article' as well as to 'all articles touching the statute of Winchester': *Kent Keepers of the Peace, 1316–1317*, ed. B.H. Putnam (Kent Archaeological Society, Records Branch, xiii, 1933), pp. 24–5.

19 The distinction is sometimes confused by use of the word form '*inquisicio capta . . . presentant*', but there is no doubt that '*inquisicio capta*' are the key words and that bills of indictment are involved. See D.J. Clayton, *The Administration of the County Palatine of Chester, 1442–1485* (Chetham Society, 3rd Series, 35, 1990), p. 217.

20 *Proceedings*, ed. Putnam, p. 344.

21 It seems possible the '*inquisicio capta*' formula may have derived from the form ('*inquisicio facta*') used in the early thirteenth century to record inquests by hundred bailiffs into felons who were at that time the subject of appeals: see the short tract 'De criminalibus placitis coram iusticiariis itinerantibus' in *Select Cases of Procedure without Writ under Henry III*, ed. H.G. Richardson and G.O. Sayles (Selden Society, 60, 1941), p. ccii.

22 *Early Treatises*, pp. 237–42.

23 *Proceedings*, ed. Putnam, pp. 237–69; B.E. Harris and D.J. Clayton, 'Criminal Procedure in Cheshire in the Mid-Fifteenth Century', *Transactions of the Historic Society of Lancashire and Cheshire*, 128 (1979), 163–4.

24 This development could almost be described as the re-privatization of much of the system of public prosecution.

25 See *The Paston Letters*, ed. J. Gairdner (Edinburgh, 1904), nos. 117, 175, 214.

26 In the summer of 1373 the wapentake jury of Wraghowe (Lincolnshire) reported to the justices of the peace that five townships had failed to come and give information: *Records of some Sessions of the Peace in Lincolnshire, 1360–1375*, ed. R. Sillem (Lincoln Record Society, 30, 1936), pp. 20–1. A *Year Book* case of Henry VII's reign shows the reeve and village officials would be called before the justices of the peace to inform and give evidence and that the justices of the peace would order them to make a bill (for the indicting jurors to consider); *Year Books* 20 Henry VII Mich. pl.21.

27 See *History of English Law*, ii, 643; *The Eyre of Kent, 6 and 7 Edward II, A.D. 1313–1314*, ed. F.W. Maitland, L.W.V. Harcourt and W.C. Bolland (Selden Society, 24, 1910), i, 20.

28 *Select Cases in the Court of King's Bench, VII*, ed. G.O. Sayles (Selden Society, 88, 1971), p. 142.

29 Justices of the peace at fifteenth-century sessions, when they had asked the indicting jurors for charges in response to the articles, invited information in regard to the same articles and on the king's behalf from anyone present at the sessions. This was done by proclamation: PRO KB 9/263/ 19d. See also below.

30 *Year Books of the reign of Edward III, V*, ed. L.O. Pike (Rolls Series, 31, 1889), p. 260; *Year Books, Liber Assisarum*, 12 Edward III, pl. 12.

31 *Letters and Papers, Henry VIII,* iv (ii), no. 4835; *Year Books,* 21 Edward IV Mich. pl.49; Smith, ed. Alston, p. 87. Bracton suggests justices might enquire into the background of a presentment; if they have any doubts about its accuracy they should enquire from which persons the jurors obtained their knowledge; Bracton, i, 404. *Placita Corone* (p. 18) shows a justice very knowledgeable about a man arrested for having possession of lost or stolen cattle, his background and behaviour.

32 *Paston Letters,* no. 160.

33 We read of jurors of presentment (1420) trying to ensure the veracity of those who brought them information by insisting they should tell their tales on oath: *Calendar of Patent Rolls, 1416–1422,* p. 266.

34 More, *Works,* p. 976. The suspect, it should be noted, did not have to appear at indictment. Indeed some seem only to hear they had been indicted a fair time after the event.

35 *Letters and Papers, Henry VIII,* xii, no. 416.

36 See, for example, *The Eyre of Northamptonshire, 1329–1330,* ed. D.W. Sutherland (Selden Society, 97–8, 1983), i, 196.

37 More, *Works,* pp. 992–3.

38 *Ibid.,* p. 990. Marowe says justices of the peace could not examine witnesses offered by the accused: *Early Treatises,* p. 409.

39 On the early history of examination see chapter two of my *Criminal Law in Late Medieval and Tudor England* (Gloucester and New York, 1984).

40 See *ibid.,* pp. 25–5. The statute was 1/2 Philip and Mary c.13.

So far as I can see the *Year Books* (which extend only to 1536) contain no mention of examination of felony suspects, which is not surprising. There is, however, at least one clear mention of the examination of a victim on oath. In a case of Edward IV's reign (21 Edward IV Mich. pl.49) it was stated that when a victim of felony comes to the justices of the peace before the sessions and tells his tale, naming those he suspects, the justices can put to him various questions and he must answer on oath. Definite proof of prisoners' examinations by justices being offered to indicting jurors is only to be found at the end of the sixteenth century: see J.S. Cockburn, *Calendar of Assize Records, Introduction* (London, 1985), p. 93.

41 R. Bernard, *Instructions for Grand Jury Men* (1592), pp. 228–40. For an earlier example of detective work in rural England, notably by a bailiff and constables (although perhaps on the instructions of a justice of the peace), see my forthcoming study of the Witherick 'murder' case in Suffolk, 1538.

42 On the ancestors of the grand jury in the form of the multi-hundred triers of the eyre see *Eyre of Northamptonshire,* i, xxvii–xxviii, but compare D. Crook, 'Triers and the Origin of the Grand Jury', *Journal of Legal History,* 12 (1991), 112–13, who points out eyre triers were elected at the end of the eyre to check and supplement indictments and were not therefore involved in the original indicting process like later grand juries.

43 *Proceedings,* ed. Putnam, pp. 241–2, 245–9; E. Powell, *Kingship,* pp. 68–9.

44 *Kent Keepers of the Peace,* p. xxxv.

45 *Year Books of Edward III, V,* pp. 258–61. Presumably the indicting jurors wished to be members of the petty jury so as to ensure a conviction. Thereby the accused would not be able to take reprisal against them.

46   In what seems to be an exemplar of a criminal trial (perhaps for instructional purposes) set down in the reign of Edward I, the accused, indicted for rape, objected to the petty jury on the grounds they were his accusers: *Year Books of the reign of Edward I, II*, ed. A.J. Horwood (Rolls Series, 1863), pp. 531–2.

47   *Stat. Realm*, i, 320. The word 'enditour' both here and in the *Year Book* case of 1340 merits close attention in that although it is best translated as 'indicting juror' it could just possibly mean the accuser who brought the bill of indictment, or who gave information to a jury of presentment. It might even have been a term which embraced both these persons and the members of the presenting juries. The general nature of the word 'enditour' hints at the fact that there was more than a single path to indictment.

48   See E. Powell, 'Jury Trial at Gaol Delivery in the Late Middle Ages: The Midland Circuit, 1400–29', in *Twelve Good Men and True: The English Criminal Trial Jury, 1200–1800*, ed. J.S. Cockburn and T.A. Green (Princeton, 1988), pp. 92–3.

49   Cockburn, *Assize, Introduction*, p. 50.

50   Nottingham City Library, Nottingham Sessions Files, CA 26B/9 and M. Bateson, 'English and Latin versions of a Peterborough court leet in 1461', *English Historical Review*, xix (1904), 527–8 (the Nottingham presentment [17 Henry VIII] in its original English form simply states 'we present Thomas Sutcliff for an accessory [to murder]', nothing more; the handwriting is that of a novice); *Calendar of the Caernarvonshire Quarter Sessions Records, 1541–1558*, ed. W.O. Williams (Caernarvon Historical Society, 1956), p. xcvi; *Letters and Papers, Henry VIII*, xiii (i), no. 1411.

51   For actions of conspiracy against indictors see below. 'Common' felons came in all varieties: for example 'a common slayer of men', 'common plunderer', 'common ambusher', and even 'common depopulator of fields': *Cal. Pat. Rolls, 1338–40*, p. 340; *ibid., 1370–74*, p. 378. Such 'notoriety' may even have blocked actions of defamation against indictors in ecclesiastical court (i.e. pre 1 Edward III st.2 c.11).

52   A. Fitzherbert, *La Graunde Abridgement* (1515), f. 255r; *Cal. Pat. Rolls, 1381–85*, p. 399. There is a good plea roll example in PRO JUST 3/167 m.7. The statute 17 Richard II c.10 may be read as meaning that notorious or mainour-bearing thieves should not be remitted to gaol as pardon was out of the question.

53   Fitzherbert, *Graunde Abridgement*, f. 250r. Elder found 60 per cent of those called 'common' felons in some manner were indicted of more than a single felony; 'common' or multiple offenders comprised a quarter of all accused: C. Elder, *Gaol Delivery in the Southwestern Counties, 1416–1430* (Carleton University, M.A. thesis, 1983), pp. 275–6.

54   This statistical evidence for the years 1416–30 is from Elder, pp. 168, 275–8.

55   Bracton, ii, 429–34.

56   See Powell, 'Jury Trial', p. 112. Certainly a fifteenth-century land wars indictment was one method of retaliating to legal action by the opposing party: *Paston Letters*, nos. 502, 510.

57   *Britton*, i, 56–7.

58   Many complaint-by-bill (*querela*) cases are to be found in the records of oyer and terminer sessions (which include the so-called 'trailbaston' sessions). These exist in abundance for the fourteenth and fifteenth centuries in the 'Ancient Indictments' (PRO KB 9).

59   There was one exclusion: land which the convicted felon held of others than the king; this

latter might only 'waste' for a year and a day before it passed to the felon's immediate feudal lord: see *Tractatus de legibus et consuetudinibus regni Anglie qui Glanvill vocatur*, ed. G.D.G. Hall (London, 1965), p. 91; T.F.T. Plucknett, *Edward I and the Criminal Law* (Cambridge, 1960), p. 81.

60   See C. Whittick, 'The Role of the Criminal Appeal in the Fifteenth Century' in *Law and Social Change in British History*, ed. J.A. Guy and H.G. Beale (London, 1984), p. 61n. It is worthy of notice, however, that two cases in the Cornwall eyre of 1302 seem to indicate an earlier custom to allow victims, who had pursued mainour-bearing thieves, to have their goods returned to them, even if they made no appeal, so long as the suspect was not arrested by an official while carrying the loot. The victims would, however, have to prove ownership. By the time of the Cornwall eyre the crown opposed the practice and would not allow such restitution: *Year Books of Edward I, III*, pp. 513–15, 526–7. The two cases and the commentary on them are reminiscent of *Britton*'s explanation of the *sakbere*. Littleton presumably drew his reference from these.

61   PRO JUST 3/209 mm. 9d, 14.

62   To postulate that the accuser-victim used the pressure of an indictment to force the accused to come to terms seems to be one of the very few satisfactory ways of explaining how the conviction rate on indictment of felony was so low in the thirteenth, fourteenth, and earlier fifteenth centuries. On 'faint evidence' see the comments of Edward Hext in the late sixteenth century: F. Aydelotte, *Elizabethan Rogues and Vagabonds* (Oxford, 1913), p. 168. Also *Letters and Papers, Henry VIII*, xv, no. 241.

63   *Stat. Realm*, iii, 291–2. For comment on the influence of this statute on rates of conviction see chapter four.

64   How well this rule was implemented in the subsequent decade or so we do not yet know.

65   See chapter three.

66   *Select Cases in King's Bench, VII*, pp. 253–4.

67   *Stat. Realm*, i, 96–7.

68   The statute 3 Henry VIII c.12 is worthy of notice here because it was designed to combat not failure to indict but deliberate indictment of the wrong persons by the presenting jurors. So that this should not happen in future justices of the peace and justices of gaol delivery were empowered to remove potentially malicious jurors from indicting juries.

69   *Letters and Papers, Henry VIII*, iv (ii), no. 3926. See also A.F. Pollard and C.H. Williams, 'Select documents, IX, Council memoranda in 1528', *Bulletin of the Institute of Historical Research*, 5 (1927–8), 26.

70   *Year Books*, 13 Edward II Mich. f. 401 and, particularly, 17 Edward II Trin. f. 547 (where Scrope argues that if writs of conspiracy were granted against indictors they would refrain from indicting). The rule is first mentioned in 32 Edward I: *Year Books of the reign of Edward I, IV*, ed. A.J. Horwood (Rolls Series, 1864), p. 462. The so-called ordinance against conspirators of 33 Edward I included within that category those who sought falsely and maliciously to indict others, but it did not mention jurors as such.

71   *Year Books*, 21 Edward III Pasch. pl. 19. However, *Year Books*, 47 Edward III Mich. pl. 30, shows that some judges were none too happy at the time about this position. In the 1390s the abuse arose whereby indictees who had been acquitted brought actions of conspiracy against their indictors claiming falsely the conspiracies had been made in some other county, a county where they had alliances and friends: *Rot. Parl.*, iii, 306, 318.

72 *Year Books, Liber Assisarum*, 27 Edward III pl 12. Presumably in this case and others like it (see, for example, *Year Books*, 12 Edward IV Mich. pl. 23) the justice sued had passed a bill to the jury of indictment with comments which the accused considered unfair, or had instructed the bill bringer to support his accusation with oral evidence of a particular sort: see *Year Books*, 7 Henry VI Mich. pl. 21.

73 *Year Books*, 21 Edward IV Mich. pl. 49.

74 *Year Books*, 35 Henry VI Mich. pl. 24. There could be no writ of conspiracy where the indictment was for trespass: see *Year Books*, 7 Henry IV Mich. pl. 15.

75 This point is also well brought out in the report touching the famous Kebell-Vernon suit of 1502. See *Year Books*, 20 Henry VII Mich. pl. 21.

76 See *Select Cases in King's Bench, VII*, pp. 190–1.

77 See *A Relation . . . of the Island of England*, ed. C.A. Sneyd (Camden Society, Old Series, 37, 1847), p. 33; however, *Paston Letters*, no. 747, seems to imply the opposite.

78 Appeals of robbery and larceny might be brought by bailees of the owner of the goods stolen, who were usually their servants.

79 J.B. Given, *Society and Homicide in Thirteenth Century England* (Stanford, 1977), p. 98. The courts were those of the general eyre.

80 N. Gadbois, *The Willoughby Roll: PRO JUST 3/123 mm. 1–16. An analysis and commentary* (Carleton University, M.A. Research paper, 1982), p. 5; K.E. Ellis, *Gaol Delivery in Yorkshire, 1399–1407* (Carleton University, M.A. thesis, 1983), p. 92; Elder, p. 25. Unfortunately, except in regard to appeals by approvers, B.A. Hanawalt, in her book *Crime and Conflict in English Communities, 1300–1348* (Cambridge, Mass., 1979) appears to incorporate appeals with indictments and thus provides no separate statistics.

81 These are my calculations based on PRO JUST 3/210–13.

82 The sources are those in footnotes 80 and 81 above with additional calculations based on cases in *Wiltshire Gaol Delivery and Trailbaston Trials, 1275–1306*, ed. R.B. Pugh (Wiltshire Record Society, 33, 1978) and *Crime in East Anglia in the Fourteenth Century: Norfolk Gaol Delivery Rolls, 1307–1316*, ed. B. Hanawalt (Norfolk Record Society, 44, 1976).

83 *Britton*, i, 87.

84 Ways in which an appellee might avoid trial by battle (in this case in the twelfth century) are conveniently listed and explained in R.D. Groot, 'The Jury in Private Criminal Prosecutions before 1215', *Am. Journ. Legal Hist.*, 27 (1983), 116–25.

Late medieval men regarded appeals as being a particularly harassing form of procedure in an age of legal harassment. Where it was not intended simply to obtain restitution of property, the appeal of felony was probably seen as the recourse of those of a wild or violent character.

85 See chapter three.

86 This is first stated clearly in Edward I's time: see *Year Books of Edward I, III*, p. 512.

87 PRO JUST 3/211 and 213.

88 Whittick, pp. 55–72.

89 *Ibid.*, p. 63.

90 *Calendar of Assize Records, Surrey Indictments, Elizabeth I* (London, 1980), pp 34, 103, 166, 217; *ibid., Kent Indictments, Elizabeth I* (London, 1979), p. 243.

91 See *Spelman*, ed. Baker, *passim*; Fitzherbert, *Graunde Abridgement*, passim; W. Staunford, *Les Plees del Coron (1557)*, pp. 58v–83v, 167v–71v, 181v–2v.

92 *Placita Corone*, p. xxvii.

93 See *Year Books*, 22 Edward IV Hil. pl.1.

94 See below.

95 *Year Books*, 21 Henry VI Hil. pl. 12; *ibid.*, 21 Henry VI Pasch. pl. 1; *ibid.*, 25 Edward III Pasch. pl. 3.

96 It has been argued there were official drives to turn felons into approvers in the fifth, fourteenth, and eighteenth to twentieth years of Edward I: see R.B. Pugh, 'Some Reflections of a Medieval Criminologist', *Proceedings of the British Academy, 59* (1973), 96.

97 These are my calculations from *Wiltshire Gaol Delivery*. The Wiltshire ratio of conviction to acquittal was somewhat higher than that achieved at the deliveries of persons appealed by approvers at Newgate gaol in 1281–91.

98 *Crime in East Anglia* (the calculations are mine); Gadbois, pp. 27–36.

99 Ellis, pp. 39–41; Elder, p. 31.

100 PRO JUST 3/191, 210–13.

101 *Chronica Johannis de Reading et anonymi Cantuariensis, 1346–1367*, ed. J. Tait (Manchester, 1914), pp. 178–9. The statute 5 Henry IV c.2 implies that men turned approvers when it became obvious at their arraignment they would be convicted. Thereby they obtained a respite in which they could get their associates to arrange their pardon.

102 *Cal. Pat. Rolls, 1370–74*, p. 309; *Calendar of Fine Rolls, 1368–77*, p. 312. Another celebrated approver of the time was John Mawer, a Boston cook. He appealed 21 accomplices and conquered four of them in battle: *Cal. Pat. Rolls, 1367–70*, pp. 166–7, 402. See also *ibid., 1370–74*, p. 297.

103 See J. Rorkasten, 'Some problems of the evidence of fourteenth-century approvers', *Journal Legal Hist.*, 5 (1984), 14–19; also Pugh, 'Some Reflections', pp. 98–9 and J.B. Post, 'The Evidential Value of Approvers' Appeals: The Case of William Rose, 1389', *Law and History Review*, 3 (1985), 98.

104 *Year Books*, 12 Edward IV Pasch. pl. 26. The petition was to the effect that justices of the peace should be given the power to assign a coroner in order to take approvers' appeals: *Rot. Parl.*, v, 620–1.

105 *Year Books*, 2 Henry VIII Mich. pl. 8. Thomas More, who notes that felons sometimes tried unsuccessfully to become approvers after conviction, shows that approvements were by no means unknown in the criminal courts of his day: *Works*, p. 976.

106 Staunford, pp. 42–50.

107 J. Stow, *Annales* (London, 1605), p. 1176; *Acts of the Privy Council of England*, ed. J.R. Dasent et al. (London, 1890–1964), x, 202.

108 This interesting topic has somehow escaped proper study by legal historians, although T.F.T. Plucknett made some brief comments on it (see 'The origin of impeachment', *Trans. Roy. Hist. Soc.*, 4th Series, 24 (1942), 60–1) and R.B. Pugh separated *captus* cases leading directly to arraignment when he categorized types of accusation (see *Wiltshire Gaol Delivery*, p. 13, *Calendar of London Trailbaston Trials under Commissions of 1305 and 1306*, ed. R.B. Pugh (London, 1975), p. 13, and also *Procs. British Academy*, 85–6). See also J.B. Post, 'Jury Lists and Juries in the Late Fourteenth Century', *Twelve Good Men*, pp. 75–7.

109 *Wiltshire Gaol Delivery* and *London Trailbaston*, *passim*.

110 *London Trailbaston*, p. 14. The *captus* was allowed bail universally from the reign of Richard III (1 Richard III c.3).

111 *Stat. Realm*, i, 81, 97.

112 *Select Cases in King's Bench, II*, pp. 25–6.

113 *Calendar of Close Rolls, 1302–07*, pp. 396–7; *London Trailbaston*, p. 14.

114 *Kent Keepers of the Peace*, pp. 81–103; *Rolls of Northamptonshire Sessions of the Peace*, ed. M. Gollancz (Northamptonshire Record Society, 11, 1940), pp. 55–79: PRO JUST 3/76 mm. 4, 5d, 14, 15, 17d, 18, 20, 41d.

115 PRO JUST 3/126 mm. 11, 12, 24d, 25d, 26.

116 For example see PRO JUST 3/136 mm. 20, 21, JUST 3/149 mm. 8, 12, and JUST 3/145 m. 36. See also *Year Books, Liber Assisarum*, 17 Edward III pl. 5 and 27 Edward III pl. 19.

117 In felony cases that is. Arraignment in the king's courts in cases of trespass without formal accusation was just beginning: see Bellamy, *Criminal Law*, especially pp. 8–31.

118 For example PRO JUST 3/164 mm. 37d, 38.

119 PRO JUST 3/180 mm. 7d, 9, 13d, 14.

120 K.E. Garay, '*No peace nor love in England': An examination of crime and punishment in the English counties, 1388–1409* (University of Toronto Ph.D. dissertation, 1977), pp. 230–2. The northern circuit was not included in Garay's calculation for the period 1399–1409.

121 Elder, pp. 27–8; PRO JUST 3/211, 212, 213.

122 The commission to the justices of gaol delivery when, by 1360, it included a reference to such a proclamation, might imply this should be made by the sheriff throughout his bailiwick rather than just at the sessions themselves: see PRO JUST 3/163 m. 1.

123 PRO KB 9/262/19, KB 9/267/37.

124 PRO JUST 3/126 m. 24d; JUST 3/136 m. 19.

125 PRO JUST 3/163 m. 1; JUST 3/164 mm. 9, 50.

126 Elder, p. 158 (quoting PRO JUST 3/198 m. 18: 'ad testifiandum et informandum curiam . . .').

127 'Grand' juries in the sense of containing jurors from several hundreds; PRO KB 9/262/98.

128 PRO KB 9/263/46; KB 9/267/66, 68; KB 9/268/88; KB 9/269/30a.

129 Elder, pp. 156–9.

130 See for example *Paston Letters*, nos. 176, 180.

131 See above.

132 Above note 31.

133 By the mid-fifteenth century one at least of the trio of justices who held a gaol delivery sessions was on the bench of the county being visited.

134 Post, 'Jury Lists', p. 109; Powell, *Kingship*, p. 58.

135 See J.G. Bellamy, *Bastard Feudalism and the Law* (London, 1989), especially chapters two and four.

2

MAJOR CRIMES

MURDER AND MANSLAUGHTER

The history of homicide in England between the fourteenth and sixteenth centuries is not easily analysed, even if it is not as obscure as some commentators have suggested. The greatest problem is to distinguish murder, which is best described as morally wicked slaying, from other forms of killing, which are embraced within the generic term of 'homicide'. To this end we must go back as far as the Norman period. In the *Leis Wilhelmi* of the later eleventh century, murder (*murdrum*) was one crime and homicide (*homicidium*) another, in a list of five common offences for which, when he was accused, an Englishman might defend himself by either ordeal or wager of battle.[1] The *Leges Henrici Primi*, which date from the second decade of the twelfth century, made, in two places, murder one of several unamendable crimes; and that murder at this point in time was not simply a synonym for homicide is shown by the latter word also making appearance in the same sections.[2] Neither of these collections of laws made any attempt to define homicide or murder, but it seems probable that at the beginning of the twelfth century those crimes amounted roughly to the general definition suggested above. The legal tract *Glanvill* written later that century was more precise. The author held there were two kinds of homicide. The one he called murder (*murdrum*) was slaying done secretly, that is to say out of sight and knowledge of all but the killer and his accomplices.[3] The other, he said, was in ordinary speech called 'simple homicide' (*simplex homicidium*). We are not informed of the dimensions of this offence but very likely it was a residual category comprising all killings not amounting to murder. Perhaps it was even while *Glanvill* was being written that murder and 'simple homicide' began to lose their clear distinction, at least in legal terminology. Maitland argued for a twelfth-century change whereby homicide came to absorb murder through becoming a capital crime with the kin of the slain person losing their right to the *wer* and to any sort of compensation: homicide became unamendable like murder.[4] The word 'murder' made what was to be its last appearance for a long while in official documents in the Assizes of Clarendon (1166) and Northampton (1176), where it was to be found among a group of common felonies which were to be presented by the men of the vills and hundreds to the justices and sheriffs. There was no reference to homicide at all.

By the early thirteenth century, in the earliest surviving plea rolls, the word 'murder' does not appear. At least it does not appear as the noun 'murder' or the verb 'to murder'. There were, it is true, a good number of occasions when the word *murdrum* occurred but the meaning here was 'murder fine', not reprehensible killing. A vill where a secret slaying had taken place, if it failed to discover the offender, might be adjudged to pay *murdrum* under the practice known as presentment of Englishry, but this was the sole usage. The verbs utilized by the justices and their clerks throughout the thirteenth century to express the deed of killing were *occidere* and *interficere*, almost entirely.[5] Yet although not evident in thirteenth-century legal records, the term 'murder' was not forgotten, certainly not by the popular mind and seemingly not by the lawyers either.[6] Bracton was mindful of it and, following the author of *Glanvill*, wrote that murder was secret slaying unknown to all save the slayer and his accomplices, so that no public hue and cry pursued them. For him murder (*murdrum*) was one species within that category of homicide which he described as *voluntarium*, that is to say, wilfully done or intentional, which he distinguished from *casuale* or accidental homicide.[7] In regard to wilful killing Bracton referred to deaths occurring 'in assultu praemeditato' although this was not a description he used frequently. *Praemeditatus*, *precogitatus*, and *excogitatus* were, however, adjectives which had become attached in records to certain slayings from early in the thirteenth century. From that time, so Hurnard suggests, justices were asking jurors to explain how they had come to say that such and such a killing was not a felony. The jurors soon discovered that to excuse themselves successfully they must in reply use the formula that the slaying was 'non aliqua malicia vel felonia excogitata' or was 'per infortunium et non ex malicia excogitata'.[8] Sometimes the justices put the question to the jurors directly: did the killer act 'aliquo insultu premeditato vel aliquo felonia?' It is likely these phrases were meant to show the victim died by misadventure or was killed by someone acting in self-defence, and not from attack prompted by malice. But did the words *praemeditatus* and *excogitatus* amount to the modern word 'premeditated' and did the phrase *ex malicia precogitata* mean 'with malice aforethought' or was it something less sinister?

Drawing attention to the use of the phrase *ex assultu praemeditato* in appeals of several different types of felony, not only homicide, Kaye argues the meaning was 'attack deliberately, wickedly or wilfully made', the adverbs providing attributes which were nothing more than those which felonies were always deemed to possess. 'Whatever the precise significance of the phrase', concludes Kaye, 'it had nothing to do with actual premeditation' and he holds the same was also true of the words *ex malicia praecogitata*, which should also be taken as meaning 'deliberately', the simple attribute of any felony.[9] Slaying with malice aforethought was not therefore, according to Kaye, a separate category of homicide; indeed, because he could see no examples in the thirteenth century of killing by poison 'or other modes of killing taken at a later time to be copybook instances of premeditation', he has argued it was not even a legal notion at that time. Although this thesis has undoubted attraction it is difficult to accept without reservation. Bracton's employment at one point of the phrase 'occidit hominem sine odii meditatione' (i.e. slaying unmotivated by contemplation of hatred) suggests that malice aforethought was nevertheless a concept current in his period.[10] Sure judgement on the matter must be delayed because of the lack of unequivocal evidence.

As to the word 'murder', where it did appear in the late thirteenth century it served, argues Kaye, as a word to describe a slaying in popular parlance, as a rare word meaning 'secret killing', and as an uncommon synonym in official records for the verb 'to kill' but no more.[11] These usages were current, so the argument continues, until about the year 1380. If we examine the records of the century prior to the accession of Richard II to test these theses, we notice various Latin forms of the word *murdrare* appearing in a considerable number of official documents, as well as the Norman-French form 'murdre' in one legal treatise dating from the reign of Edward I. This was *Britton*, whose author when referring to outlawry talked of enquiries into the activities of murderers as well as into homicides.[12] The legal formulae of the fourteenth century containing the word 'murder' were in part to be found in judicial commissions. Thus the articles of trailbaston of January 1305 were intended to reveal those who committed 'homicide and murders by day and night secretly or openly and their abettors'.[13] A commission of oyer and terminer of December 1335 was directed against those who, at Ipswich, had formed unlawful assemblies, committed murders and extorted ransoms. In January and February 1341 there were commissions of oyer and terminer issued for the majority of the counties of south and central England in regard to homicides, murders, larcenies and other felonies committed both in the current reign and the previous one. In October of the same year a commission was issued for Northumberland, in addition.[14] In 1348 another oyer and terminer commission was designed explicitly to cover both 'murdra' and 'homicidia'.[15] Other official instruments which specifically mentioned murder at this time were an appointment of William Carles to attach a monk of Buildwas indicted in Salop of the death of his abbot (September 1342), the findings of an inquest into riots in Montgomery (April 1332), a commission of June 1342 to enquire and certify to the king if in Edward I's time one Ralph le Porter of Bamborough murdered Robert de Fletham and under what circumstances, and a good number of pardons issued in March 1338 to those who accompanied the king on his military expedition overseas.[16] There are also several references to murder in the Public Record Office Chancery Miscellanea relating to Yorkshire in the earliest years of Edward III's reign.[17] Less official in origin, but still reflecting to some degree the legal thought of the period, were entries in the rolls of parliament. In 1347, as Kaye has noted, the commons complained that the too frequent issue of pardons had much encouraged 'murderers, embleours des gentz, roberies, homicides et autres felones'. A petition presented in the parliamentary session of 1353 used the word *murdre*, although without mention of any other felonies.[18]

The overall impression then is that the word murder, referring to certain types of homicide, not the *murdrum* fine, was in quite frequent use in official documents until the 1340s, and that its meaning was usually killing by stealth, or killing when the victim was taken unawares and could not retaliate. After that time it still appeared, but until the mid-1370s only rarely; then it began to occur more often again.[19] In particular there were two notable instances of its use just before the reign of Edward III ended, both involving gentry. In March 1377 a pardon was granted to Sir John Clifford, at the special request of the lords and commons in parliament, of the king's suit for the 'death or murder' of John de Coupland in 1363.[20] The other instance concerned the slaying of Sir William de Cantilupe in 1375. One indictment stated that two of his servants *sedicione precogitate . . . interfecerunt et murdraverunt* their master, although others omitted the verb murder.[21] Here was perhaps the first use of the common fifteenth-century formula 'killed and murdered'. In both examples, which were obviously quite notorious, the killers could be said to have plotted their misdeed well in advance and then to have carefully awaited their opportunity. It is not impossible that these celebrated cases revived the verb *murdrare*.

An inspection of the period from the accession of Richard II to 1390 shows the term 'murder' appeared with considerable frequency in official records at that time. Apart from those granted to individuals excusing one particular murder, there were a number of pardons from the year 1378 which excused all felonies committed except for treasons, murders or rapes, which was novel.[22] General pardons granted after the great insurrection of 1381 might be drafted in the same form.[23] There were also pardons to individual offenders suspected or indicted of homicide which were phrased in the conditional sense: they were valid only if the would-be recipient had not committed the particular crime of murder.[24] In addition there were pardons for *pre facto* accessories to murder, or for receiving and harbouring murderers.[25] Inquests, some taken before coroners, also provide examples of the persistent use at this time of the word 'murder', although such instances cannot be called frequent.[26] There was also one appeal of murder. More significant still was the use of the word by parliament. There was a statute containing the verb 'to murder' promulgated early in Richard's reign: this was 2 Richard II st.1 c.5.[27] It was directed against those who in routs seized land and lay in wait to beat or murder, and it required gentry to be commissioned in each county who might arrest such malefactors without waiting for them to be indicted. The act was soon repealed, but certainly the word 'murder' was now more reputable in legal and official circles. In the next parliamentary session (1379) the commons asked that justices of the peace should be given the power to hear and determine *larcynes, notoirement comiz et de murdres et gents tuez par malice prepense*.[28] No doubt it was as a result of this that on 26 May 1380 a commission was issued to the justices of the peace empowering them to enquire into larcenies notoriously or openly committed, mayhems, the killing of men through ambushcades or by *malicia praecogitata*, murders, and other felonies.[29] This was seemingly the first occasion the word 'murder' had appeared in the wording of a judicial commission for several decades, but it stood alone at this period in time, for subsequent peace commissions returned to the verb *interficere*. The word *murdrare* did appear in commissions in the decade subsequent to May 1380, but only in those of a special nature, as for example to enquire who had murdered a particular person or who had received the misdoers.[30] Thus it is evident that the word 'murder' was used by lawyers not infrequently from 1377 and right through the 1380s. It did not have an official rebirth in 1380, as has been argued, nor did its use then lapse until just before 1390.[31] As to the meaning of the word 'murder' at this time, there seems little doubt that it was understood to amount to killing by stealth or in secret as it had in Bracton's day and in the intervening period.

The argument has been made in extensive fashion by Kaye and, more recently, by T.A. Green that it was only after about 1380 that the category of homicide was divided by the judicial authorities into murder and other types of culpable slaying.[32] However, the use of words like *murdre, murdrare,* and *ex malicia praecogitata* suggests otherwise, and so too and even more strongly than the evidence we have already noticed does the employment in legal documents of an adverbial phrase which is their antonym. Thus in a number of pardons for homicide dating from the years 1358, 1359, 1360, 1362, 1367, and 1371 the phrases *ex malicia praecogitata, per maliciam excogitatam,* and the like stand alongside and in contrast with the word *impetuose*. We have, for example, 'Johannes Horspath de Walyngford interfecit Johannem Chaunce de Ryngmere impetuose et non per malitiam excogitatem' and 'Thomas Symond interfecit Willelmum Caly, capellanum, impetuose et non per malitiam precogitatam'. The phraseology of the other pardons is very similar. The adverb *impetuose* clearly meant 'in hot blood', which demonstrates that in the official mind there was also the antonym, namely, killing with cold deliberation or slaying which had been carefully planned. Another of the pardons demonstrates this even better. It referred to John de Redgrave the younger, who had killed John Neel of Melford 'impetuose et non per insidiam aut malitiam precogitatam'.[33]

It seems therefore virtually certain that at least thirty years prior to 1390, and probably well before that, legal authority recognized as distinct categories of homicide those later referred to in law tracts as planned, cold-blooded killing (murder) and slaying in hot blood (killing in chance medley, manslaughter). Yet if during much of the fourteenth century government circles made a clear distinction between murder and slaying in hot blood, why was it that the accusations in court, the indictments and the appeals, failed to distinguish between the two categories of offence before 1390? Not beyond the bounds of possibility is the thesis that coroners' inquests and presenting jurors forbore to use the verb *murdrare* because of its connection with the *murdrum* fine.[34] More plausible is the argument that the crown, once it had in the twelfth century made simple homicide (i.e. non-murderous culpable slaying) an unamendable crime, was determined to keep it so; which it achieved by using the same verbs in most court and official records to cover all types of culpable slaying. Relatives of slain persons persisted in seeking compositions from the slayers into the sixteenth century which shows the continuing vitality of the 'amendable' tradition. The potential loss of escheats and forfeitures should the crown reverse its stand must also have been an important factor. Furthermore kings must have been well aware that chance medley killing/manslaughter was a crime which figured frequently in the fourteenth-century land wars of the upper classes, which exacerbated the feuding and which might imperil public order throughout the whole shire.[35] To distinguish simple homicide and diminish the penalty which this type of slaying carried must have seemed to encourage this evil. An alternative, to increase the penalty for murder, does not seem to have ever been considered. The later medieval English kings eschewed such barbarities except in the case of treason. To the modern mind the equal punishment of murder and manslaughter may seem grossly unfair but medieval men of law did not tend to visualize particular types of crimes in terms of the judicial penalties they incurred. Nor did the system lend itself to fine gradations of punishment.[36] Quite as 'unfair' as the death penalty for those convicted of manslaughter was the use of the same punishment for relatively petty theft. Men and women were hanged not infrequently for stealing goods of only eighteen or twenty pence in value while highway robbery involving a large sum of money and, as we would say grievous bodily harm, was not and could not be punished any more severely even if the likelihood of conviction was greater.

Failure to distinguish between the different categories of homicide could also be explained by the fact that pardons were more easily obtainable for manslaughter, thus mitigating the apparent inequity of the penalty involved.[37] That is not to say pardons for murder were very difficult to obtain. Yet to do so may have become somewhat harder as the fourteenth century progressed. The king in response to parliamentary pressure began to show more reluctance to pardon persons accused of murder.[38] This in turn seems to have been the signal for those responsible for indictments (not necessarily the juries but the relatives of the slain or their legal advisers, who primed them with information, brought in bills, or sued appeals) to seek to insert words which made clear to the dispenser of the pardon, the king or his minister, that the slaying was a murder. Hence the use later in the fourteenth century of the verb *murdrare* and the rising frequency of such phrases as *ex malicia praecogitata* and *per malitiam excogitatam*. The aim must have been to stop, hinder, or at least raise the cost of the pardon. Even kings short of cash were reluctant to pardon in cases of murder which were truly heinous, and the phrases of afforcement in the charges might cause them to enquire into the facts of the offence. Also pardons to be acceptable to the bench when they were produced in court had to annul all aspects of the charge in the indictment in exact terms; and the use of words of afforcement would therefore cause additional legal expenses for the accused.[39]

Another possible explanation for the failure of indictments and appeals before the late fourteenth century to distinguish between murder and manslaughter lies in the fairly clear differentiation already being made on equitable grounds in the verdicts of the petty jurors. Green has argued at some length that petty juries, applying what he refers to as the principle of 'merciful nullification', were wont to acquit those accused of a homicide which fell within the category later to be manslaughter, but produced what for the later middle ages was a high rate of conviction where murder was concerned. Also in some of the 'manslaughter' cases the accused seem to have argued they had slain in self-defence, and this plea the jurors readily accepted. As a result they were able to procure *de cursu* pardons. For Green the justices were unable to thwart such fabrications, so often fictitious, because the petty jurors alone had access to the facts of the case.[40] The latter supposition, we may rejoin, seems, on the evidence adduced in the previous chapter, to be unlikely.[41] More probably there was an element of truth in the asseverations of self-defence, which allowed the justices who quite often knew this, to accede happily to the jury's verdict.

With the divisions of homicide being already, in all probability, connected with royal pardoning it causes little surprise to find that in 1390 murder was given some degree of definition in a statute (13 Richard II st.2 c.1), which was essentially concerned with pardoning. The intent was to ensure pardons were not accepted by the justices for murder, treason or rape, unless they specifically covered one of those offences. There has been much debate amongst historians of the meaning in the act of the words 'pur murdre, mort de homme occys par agayt, assaut ou malice purpense'.[42] Precision in language and meaning was rarely achieved in fourteenth-century legislation in matters to do with the criminal law and the 1390 act was no exception. Nonetheless there can be little doubt that since the act was aimed at murder not other homicide the words 'mort de homme occys par agayt etc' stood in apposition to 'murdre' and were not other types of culpable slaying.[43] Manslaughter, therefore, was not mentioned in the statute of 1390 but that it was a separate yet fully fledged category within the felony of homicide, even if not yet referred to in court records by that name, we have already noticed. Confirmation of this view is afforded by an extant justices' charge to juries of indictment dating from the early years of the reign of Henry IV. By this justices were to instruct their hearers to enquire 'de toute maniers homicides cibien de ceulx quy gisent en guaite par malice devant pourpense en pais, maison et aultres lieux mourdrent les gens et de ceulx quy tuent hommez par chaude melle'.[44] Here murder by ambush, that is taking the victim unawares which was cold-blooded killing, stands in contrast with slaying in hot conflict, killing, as the modern term is, 'when the blood is up'. There can be little doubt that killing 'par chaude melle' was the same thing as the killing *impetuose* of the 1360s. Furthermore this category of crime was being referred to as manslaughter before the end of the fourteenth century. This was, however, in popular rather than legal parlance. John Gower, writing about the same time as the 1390 pardon statute, referred to 'moerdre and manslawhte', the latter word taking in, so it seems, all non-murderous culpable homicide.[45]

The word 'manslaughter' seems to have first appeared in a legal tract in the *Boke of Justyces of Peas*, which dates from about 1506. There its identification with *chaude melle* in its English form of 'chance medley' is incontrovertible. 'Manslaughter', states the *Boke*, 'is where two men or mo mete and by chaunce medely fall at affray so that one of them sleeth an other.'[46] The reign of Henry VIII provided several other definitions of manslaughter by lawyers, each stressing the chance medley element. Sir Richard Elliot, chief justice of common pleas, is reported to have said, perhaps during the early years of Wolsey's ascendancy, that if a man in chance medley without malice prepense killed another, it was manslaughter. For a legal writer in 1538 manslaughter was 'a thynge felonously don by chaunce medley' and occurred fortuitously.[47] The standard charge for 'inferior courts of inquisition', which dates from the same period, referred to manslaughter as being where 'by chaunce two mete and by large communication fall to fighting whereby thone killeth thother'.[48]

After 1390, as historians of the law have been wont to point out, there are to be found in the records of the courts which handled felonies indictments specifically of murder as well as indictments in regard to other types of felonious slaying. In the former the use of the verb *murdrare* became common, although often within the phrase *felonice interfecit et murdravit*. Manslaughter/killing in chance medley was noted by the single verb form *interfecit*, the word used to describe all types of slaying hitherto.[49] Because of the 1390 statute the use thereafter in indictments of *murdrare* was probably essential if the accused was to be seriously hindered from obtaining a pardon from the king. To the same end we find *ex malitia praecogitata* and similar reinforcing *murdravit*, whereas before 1390 such words had sometimes been used alongside the catch-all verbal form *interfecit* so as to imply murder. Neither the words 'chance medley' nor 'manslaughter' appeared in commissions to justices in the fifteenth or early sixteenth centuries. In proclamations the English word 'murder' seems to have been used to cover all forms of culpable homicide.[50] In statutes 'chance medley' and 'manslaughter' made their first appearance at the same time (1530). This was in the act 22 Henry VIII c.14, which permitted the privilege of sanctuary to those who had already enjoyed it once if the second offence was 'manslaughter by chance medley' but not where it was 'murder of malice prepensed'. Two years later, in the statute 24 Henry VIII c.5, chance medley killing was noted as involving the forfeiture of the miscreant's moveable property.

Apart from virtually all general pardons, there were promulgated during the reigns of Henry VIII, Edward VI, and Mary no fewer than twenty-two statutes which mentioned murder.[51] One (4 Henry VIII c.2), which has been much quoted, did, it is true, by removing from murderers the privilege of benefit of clergy where the offence was committed in church, on the highway, or in the victim's home, effect a distinction in regard to punishment between some murderers and those who committed manslaughter. Yet in none of these statutes were the proposers and drafters really intent on defining the different types of culpable homicide. This deficiency had to be made good largely through judicial decisions made in particular cases and by subsequent discussion of them by the writers on the law.[52] Not until the middle of the sixteenth century does it seem that lawyers' attention was focused seriously on the dividing line between murder and manslaughter. This was in homicide cases where the party slain was not the one against whom the malice was precogitated and where a number of persons participated in an illegal act and one of them perpetrated murder during its commission. Attention was drawn to the first of these problems by the trial of George Herbert in 1558. Herbert had taken forty men to the house of Sir Robert Mansfield, intending to cause an affray and fight with him. While the two sides were still engaged in verbal altercation a woman, who was trying to pacify the parties, was killed by a stone hurled by one of Herbert's servants bent on injuring Mansfield or his men. In a meeting of the judges of the two benches, serjeants, and law officers of the crown at Serjeants' Inn to discuss the matter, it was pointed out that the law already called it murder when a person was killed by another who intended only to hurt him, and secondly that according to the Lord Dacres case of 1541, when a number of persons decided to commit an illegal act and to kill anyone who should resist them, they were all guilty of murder as principals should in fact any of them slay someone.[53] Neither of these two cases was totally relevant to the Herbert case, since there was no malice directed against the woman victim, nor had Herbert's group decided in advance to kill all opposers, and in any case the woman was not opposing them. In making their decisions as to Herbert's guilt the judges and their colleagues divided. The attorney-general, the solicitor general, two serjeants and five judges argued he was guilty of murder because a man who enters on an unlawful act is responsible for all the consequences, however unlikely, and of a type never intended; that in doing a wrong 'il sera adiuge par la ley en le plus extreme tort'. However, four judges, Brooke, Staunford, Dyer and Morgan, and a serjeant (Prideaux), argued that Herbert and his accomplices were guilty only of manslaughter, because there had been no intent to hurt the woman. As a result no decision was reached. The debate was adjourned until more information on the role of the woman had been elicited, but there is no suggestion it was renewed.

For Kaye, one particular importance of this case is the light it shed on manslaughter: was it deliberate slaying, accidental slaying in criminal circumstances, or did the suddenness of a fatal encounter lessen the crime from murder to manslaughter? Kaye states the case showed that 'the mere fact that a killing had taken place in a "sudden encounter" without premeditation did not of itself reduce liability from Murder to Manslaughter'. Another importance, he argues, was that to Brooke, Staunford, and their three supporters, chance medley, which was what the incident amounted to, meant 'an accidental killing in the course of an unlawful act of violence not directed at the party slain or any member of his company'. Furthermore, said Kaye, we should notice the possibility that this was an opinion held generally at the time by all lawyers, and not peculiar to the five. All this, he argued, goes to show that, in 1558 at least, 'the authorities do not support an identification of chance medley with a deliberate killing done in the course of a sudden encounter'.[54]

The thesis is not particularly convincing. To the first argument (that a killing in a sudden encounter without premeditation was not automatically manslaughter rather than murder) we may respond that the judges did not see the Herbert affair as a definite case of sudden encounter without premeditation. They had first to examine if there might have been a prior intent to kill any opposers and consider if the slain woman came within that category. To the second argument (that in 1558 the term chance medley was not used to cover deliberate killing done in the course of a sudden encounter) we may answer that the early history of that offence points very much in that direction, as we have seen, and furthermore a case from July 1553 confirms it. In this instance Richard Salisbury and two other men had lain in ambush to kill a Dr Ellis. It seems that when he came, they attacked him, but only succeeded in killing one of his servants. One of the three ambushers' servants, a John Vane Salisbury, had apparently joined in when he saw the fray and had been responsible with the others for the death. However, very probably he had not been told beforehand of their intent by his fellow miscreants. At the trial, therefore, after the evidence had been given, the jury asked if John Vane Salisbury, since he had taken part in the crime 'of a sudden' and without malice prepense, was guilty of murder or manslaughter.[55] The court said that as John Vane Salisbury had had no malice prepense the crime he committed was the latter.[56] Now, it is clear that since John Vane Salisbury was not privy to the plot the ambush was for him a sudden encounter, a chance medley; therefore in 1553 the latter, contrary to Kaye, could indeed be a deliberate killing when the parties had met suddenly, and did not have to be a slaying done accidentally in such a situation.[57] In all likelihood then, by 1558 chance medley was not still in process of definition but a category of homicide already well marked out, as it probably had been throughout the previous century and a half, and it meant slaying in a chance encounter, whether committed accidentally by an unlawful act or deliberately. However, these definitions, we should remember, were in the minds of the lawyers and not in the statutes or clearly observable in the indictments. For the jurors there were still only two forms of indictment when the offence involved was homicide. Either the slayer murdered (*murdravit*) his victim, or he had feloniously slain him (*felonice interfecit*). That the killing was manslaughter because it had occurred in chance medley would not be stated, although occasionally (for example in coroners' inquests post 1550) it was inferred in additional wording which might say that the killing took place following assault provoked by a sudden quarrel or opprobrious words.[58]

With the distinction between murder and manslaughter/chance medley being found increasingly in premeditation or lack of it (i.e. the suddenness of the affray) it is worthy of comment that there were in the later sixteenth century several types of homicide classified as murder, yet where malice aforethought was lacking. One of these was where the victim was an officer of the law, a constable, watchman or similar doing his duty. He might, for example, be seeking to make an arrest or to disperse rioters. The victim might not be known to the assailant at all, and the encounter in which the blow was given might have been of the utmost suddenness. Nevertheless such a killing was held to be murder from the middle years of Elizabeth's reign, and later the rule was extended to cover the slaying of officials engaged in duties not strictly involving the keeping of the peace.[59] When one man suddenly attacked another without any warning and killed him, there being no known evidence of premeditation (and no mêlée), it was also held to be murder at this time. Clearly that old category of murder, killing a man while off his guard, still existed. It is also likely that jurors were keen to categorize as murder any homicide where the killer had had a great advantage in weapons, strength or tactical position over his victim.

There was, it seems, one other extension of murder in Elizabeth's reign which was of a different category. The details of the Saunders case, decided at Warwick assizes in 1573, were that a father, John Saunders, intending to kill his wife, gave her a poisoned apple which she in turn gave to their three-year-old daughter. The child ate it, there being no attempt to stop her by the father (who was present), and died. The justices decided the wife could not be a principal since she was ignorant of the intended crime. The difficulty in finding Saunders himself to be a principal was circumvented by declaring his wife to be only an agent. The more important issue of whether it was murder if someone other than the person against whom the malice was intended died was decided in the affirmative, the reasoning being as that by the majority of legal experts in the Herbert case, namely that those committing a violent act are responsible for all the consequences of that misdeed, however unexpected.[60]

There was no further definition of murder or manslaughter in the Tudor period, but the history of the two crimes had also another side, one which showed very little in the comments of the treatise writers, in the statute book, the rolls of parliament and chancery, or the debate of the lawyers. This aspect comprised the frequency of those offences, and the number of convictions and acquittals of principals and accessories. If we consider the number of cases of homicide of all sorts (killing in self-defence, suicide, and accidental slaying excluded) to be found in the total of all felonies tried at various times in the period under review we get evidence of a decline in incidence even if it was not a decline at a steady rate or without sporadic reversals. From examination of the records extant for eight counties for the period 1300–48 Hanawalt concluded accusations of homicide comprised just over 18 per cent of all felonies charged. The gaol delivery records for Yorkshire for 1359–63 show, similarly, homicide cases providing 20 per cent of the calendar.[61] However, towards the end of the fourteenth century homicide figured noticeably less frequently. The extant gaol delivery rolls for all the English circuits for the years 1388–99 yield the low rate of around 14 per cent of all felony cases. Furthermore for the first decade of Henry IV's reign, 1399–1409 (the northern circuit excluded), the level was only about 11 per cent. Thereafter the rate may have risen, again slightly: for the south-western circuit for the years 1416–30 homicide cases have been calculated at about 13 per cent. By the early fifteenth century, as we have noticed, a distinction began to be made in the plea rolls between murder and manslaughter, which can therefore be counted separately. The gaol delivery records for Yorkshire for the period 1439–60 reveal that murder accounted for 8.4 per cent of cases and manslaughter 6.6 per cent.[62]

Because of the failure of the records to survive no satisfactory figures are available for the century after this. Only with the accession of Elizabeth I does the picture become clearer again. The extant assize files, quarter sessions files, and coroners' inquests for Essex for the years 1558–1603 show culpable homicide cases of all sorts amounted to about 4.5 per cent of the total of felony indictments. The assize files for Sussex tell us that culpable homicide cases in that county for the same period were as high as 11.5 per cent of felonies as a whole. The Cheshire assize records for the period 1569–97 give a total homicide percentage of 7.25. If murders are examined as a separate class they are found to amount to a mere 1.07 per cent of all felonies in Essex, 4.71 per cent in Sussex and 5.6 per cent in Cheshire. When homicide cases other than murder are examined, the order is found to be quite different. In Essex they comprised 3.5 per cent of the felony total, in Sussex 6.9 per cent and Cheshire about 1.7 per cent.[63] The decline in the number of cases of culpable homicide between the fourteenth century and the late sixteenth century was, therefore, pronounced. However, for the long reign of Elizabeth the diminution was more apparent than real. This was because the small percentage which homicides comprised of the total number of felonies was rather the result of a great and continuing increase in the number of other types of felony (i.e. non-homicidal) which came to trial rather than an absolute decrease in the number of murders and manslaughters. Thus in Essex in any five-year period of Elizabeth's reign about six cases of murder came before the courts, and similarly in Cheshire.[64]

To complete this profile of homicide we need to notice the rates of conviction among the accused. Of the more than two hundred cases of homicide tried at deliveries of Newgate gaol in the period 1281–90 a verdict of guilty was returned in 21 per cent. In comparison, for grand larceny, which amounted to half of all the cases, the conviction rate was 39 per cent. In the first half of the fourteenth century the rate of homicide convictions over eight counties was about 12.5 per cent, and there seems to have been an average of about 20 per cent in the reign of Richard II.[65] By the middle of the fifteenth century convictions were becoming noticeably more frequent. The Yorkshire gaol delivery records for 1439–60 provide a murder conviction rate of about 21 per cent and for felonious killings of the manslaughter variety one of about 19 per cent. For felonious larceny, by way of comparison, convictions were at about 43 per cent.[66] In Essex in the reign of Elizabeth convictions were recorded in 35 per cent of murder cases and in 37 per cent of manslaughter cases, the latter being a notable increase on the fifteenth-century Yorkshire figure. The Sussex Elizabethan records show more severity on the part of the jurors. In half of the murder cases a verdict of guilty was returned while of the manslaughter cases 42.5 per cent resulted in convictions. In Cheshire the juries were draconian. Murder cases resulting in a verdict of guilty totalled 70 per cent, while other culpable homicides provided a conviction rate of almost 73 per cent. Not very different was the county of Kent where the rate of conviction for murder was 63 per cent and for other homicide a remarkable 78 per cent.[67]

LARCENY, ROBBERY AND BURGLARY

Larceny, or theft as we call it more frequently, was distinguished from robbery from early Anglo-Saxon times. While it is true that the laws of Ethelbert of Kent seem to imply that to rob meant to thieve and vice-versa, those of Ine indicate that by the beginning of the eighth century robbery was seen as amounting to seizing the goods of another person with violence.[1] Larceny, on the other hand, although none of the laws of the Anglo-Saxon kings says as much specifically, was the taking of goods when the owners were unaware. It was thus a secret rather than an open crime, or so at least the perpetrator intended it to be. From the middle of the Anglo-Saxon period larceny, despite the element of secrecy, seems to have been held less reprehensible than robbery. Until probably the twelfth century persons who were suspected of committing larceny which had gone at the time unobserved seem to have been allowed the opportunity of paying compensation to the victim and thereby escaping trial and punishment. From the reign of Canute one particular type of larceny, 'theft which cannot be disproved' which was very likely when the suspect was caught in the act or with the loot, barred the payment of compensation and necessitated arraignment. If a person accused of larceny went to actual trial he could take comfort from the fact that, according to the laws of Athelstan, he had to have been convicted on several occasions before he was in danger of being executed. Even then he might escape if his kinsmen paid the value of his wergild and stood surety for his future good behaviour. The thief who confessed his crime, or was convicted of it, had to pay a fine of 120 shillings if the goods taken were worth 60 shillings or more. If he was put to death the value of the stolen goods was taken from his possessions.[2]

So far we have referred only to theft of a serious nature, or, as some modern historians would say, grand larceny. The dividing line between grand larceny and lesser, or petty, larceny was set in Saxon times as in the period following the Norman conquest at twelve pence (one shilling). If the object stolen was valued at over one shilling the offence was held a major one. The division into two categories had been established by the middle of the tenth century. Among Athelstan's early laws there is one which stipulates that no one should be spared from punishment if caught in the act of stealing goods worth more than eight pence. A later law of the same king states, perhaps in amendment, or perhaps where no mainour was found, that no one shall be spared for theft if the value of the property taken is more than twelve pence. The punishment intended here for the miscreant is death. A third law of the same monarch gives instruction that no thief is to be put to death where the object stolen is worth less than twelve pence. The punishment to be meted out to the miscreant who takes goods valued at under this amount is not suggested in any of the Saxon laws, but we know there was mutilation, the loss of a hand or foot, for an unidentified form of theft in the eighth century and that imprisonment was also a permissible penalty.[3]

The Norman period provided no substantial alteration in the general tenor of the law concerning theft but royal jurisdiction over that crime became more apparent. Thus the *Leges Henrici Primi* tell us that manifest thefts were not to be amendable by the payment of compensation in the future. Theft which was not manifest, however, might still be satisfied by the giving of money or the loss of a limb. Henry I seems to have been intent on bringing cases of serious theft before his own courts; he reserved to himself the right to deal with theft punishable by death.[4] This category, we might imagine, must surely have included manifest grand larceny, but Maitland was moved to argue to the effect that such manifest larceny was 'still within the manor' and the jurisdiction of the infang-thief seigneurial courts in the thirteenth century.[5] This argument probably derives in large part from *Glanvill* and the *Dialogue of the Exchequer*. In the former the author states that since his aim is to consider only the king's court it is not appropriate for him to deal at this point with theft and other pleas belonging to the sheriff, which are heard and determined according to the varying customs of different county courts. The *Dialogue of the Exchequer* appears to indicate that in the late twelfth century serious theft came before the local courts within the sheriff's jurisdiction, and either at his instigation because he thought the case an important one or because of the personal pursuit of the party injured, before the king's courts as well. The writer of the same treatise supplies the additional information that in contrast with robbers whose goods when they are captured go to the king, those of thieves go to the sheriff in whose bailiwick the arrest has been made. *Glanvill* tells us in similar vein that the land of the convicted thief goes straight to the lord of the fee in contrast with that of other sorts of felons where the forfeiture goes first to the king for a year and a day before reverting to the immediate lord.[6] All this suggests that at the end of the twelfth century theft was still treated somewhat differently from other felonies.

The thirteenth century was important in the history of illegal taking because of the fairly lengthy definitions of larceny, and attempts to analyse the nature of that crime, which appeared in legal treatises. Bracton, *Fleta*, and the *Mirror of Justices*, the second and third probably drawing on the first, each emphasizes the need for an *animus furandi*, that is to say a deliberate intent to deprive another of his property, on the part of the thief. The *Mirror* makes the additional and valuable point, probably prompted by the *Institutes* of Justinian, that it is not larceny to take another's goods believing them to be one's own, nor if the taker believes it is agreeable to the owner, so long, that is, as he has good reason for this belief. Such 'eloining', as *Fleta* calls it, is to be dealt with only by an action of trespass. The *Mirror* alone among the contemporary commentaries brings out the point, clear enough in the Saxon laws, that theft, in contrast with robbery, is usually done secretly, often by a pick-pocket or cut-purse, the possessor who is deprived being unaware of the exact point in time when the offence is committed. The same work tells us it is also theft to defraud by means of false measures, to keep treasure trove, to levy outrageous tolls, or to take the fish, conies, pheasants, or deer of others. Extortion, disseisin, distraint, rape, the taking of property on the orders of a lord, on the other hand, can amount to robbery, so the *Mirror* would have us believe; the distinguishing feature of these offences being that they usually involve the use or threat of force and the abuse of might or authority.[7]

Among the treatises Bracton, *Fleta*, and *Britton* were those most concerned with legal procedure against thieves. Bracton and *Britton* state that commonly the miscreant who committed manifest theft (i.e. was observed committing the crime or captured carrying the pelf) would be sued by the victim either through an appeal of felony or an action of trespass. The only way in which the mainour-carrying thief might escape trial was to vouch to warranty the person from whom he claimed to have purchased the stolen object. If this was done successfully then the accuser should appeal the warrantor instead. As to secret theft, that is to say where there were no observers or mainour involved, Bracton implies in one place that the suspected thief is to be indicted and tried in a royal court. If, however, the suspect was not in frankpledge, nor had a lord to vouch for him, he might equally well be the subject of an appeal, appeals being justiciable in both seigneurial and royal courts at this time. For one important aspect of how the law treated theft Bracton is our only thirteenth-century informant. He points out that, when it comes to laying charges against a thief, whether in fact the goods were stolen from the actual owner or from someone entrusted by him with their custody is of no consequence; it is quite in order for the custodian-bailee to bring an appeal of larceny. This makes it quite clear that to steal from one who had been entrusted by the rightful owner with the keeping of goods was considered to be in no way different from taking from the owner himself.[8]

The distinction between larceny as a felony and larceny as a trespass (the latter usually called 'petty larceny') was most important because to many thieves it meant the difference between living and dying. Both *Britton* and *Fleta* contain substantial comment on the matter and agree that petty larceny amounted to the illegal taking of goods valued at under twelve pence; it should be punished by imprisonment in the pillory at the least. *Britton* has it that a person convicted of this offence should no longer be oathworthy and that if perchance he bore a bad character and had stolen for profit, so to speak, and not just in order to eat, he should in addition lose an ear and be made infamous. For a second such offence he must lose another ear or be executed; for a third the punishment could only be death. To cut a purse by stealth but, because of lack of opportunity, without taking any of its contents, a crime apparently common enough to call for special comment, was, according to both *Britton* and *Fleta*, punishable by the pillory. To commit this offence and take contents of under the value of twelve pence was to result in the loss of an ear; to cut a purse and take more than twelve pence carried the death penalty.[9]

The thirteenth-century writers of legal treatises do not tell us very much about robbery, its nature, or the procedure associated with it. The definition of a robber had not changed from Saxon times, that we do know. Such a miscreant was still one who seized the goods of others by force, and it was considered to be the vicious element in the misdeed which distinguished the robber from the thief. In the late thirteenth century a successful appeal of robbery or an action against the misdoer was likely to provide the injured party with four-fold damages, twice the amount stipulated in the laws of Canute. This is stated in the *Mirror*, which also tells us that King Edward commanded that no one should be sentenced to death for robbery (as with larceny) if the goods taken did not exceed twelve pence in value.[10] Such information is particularly useful because in the later middle ages the judges generally held that for an offence to be robbery there was no need for the actual taking of goods: the use or threat of force to that end itself amounted to robbery whether the attempt brought profit or not.

It is the *Mirror* which tells us that the twelve-penny rule applied also to hamsocn, a contemporary term for burglary. It says that King Edward ordered that no one should be sentenced to death if he or she took less than twelve pence when they broke into a house. Elsewhere, however, the writer says something quite different, to the effect that it is sufficient merely to break in through a door or window of a house or an out-house for hamsocn or burglary to be committed.

He gives no indication here that for burglary to be perpetrated anything must be illicitly taken; rather he implies that burglary or hamsocn is the breaking into a house or the committing of felonious assault on people in houses with intent to rob, kill, or beat. Without the reference to assault these words are not far distant from what came to be the accepted definition of burglary in the sixteenth century. Burglary, we should notice at this point, was not regarded at the end of the thirteenth century as being a nocturnal crime. Bracton refers very clearly to burglars and thieves who operate by day, and the *Mirror* specifically states the offence may be committed by either day or night. However, Bracton, although his imagery is not particularly clear, does seem to imply that to commit burglary by night is an offence of greater heinousness than the same crime by day.[11]

From the late thirteenth century to the fifteenth the history of burglary, robbery, and larceny can be traced more clearly than at earlier times because of the greater sufficiency of surviving court records and also because of reports of particular cases in the *Year Books*. Nevertheless legal historians have been wont to discover difficulties in ascertaining the exact nature of late medieval burglary in particular. They have warned against seeking to give this offence precise definition, noting for example that it is unclear whether breach or theft was the essential element and whether the words 'by night' were a vital part of any charge. The varied definitions of the crime to be found in the legal treatises of Tudor commentators have been taken as affording support for this thesis. Furthermore the infrequency of the word for burglary (*burglare/burgare*) in contemporary records, so it is implied, supports the argument that this crime was not separate and distinct in the later medieval period.[12] This last contention is not, on examination, a weighty one. The verbs *burglare/burgare* or the rarer noun *burgaria* appear in the records of gaol delivery, of commissions of the peace, and of king's bench for the whole fourteenth century and the first half of the fifteenth, even if they do not show a uniform incidence in each decade.

The gaol delivery and peace sessions records of Kent for 1316–17 provide as many as 38 cases (in a total of 268 instances of theft) where some form of the verb *burgare* is used. This profusion is not found anywhere later in the century but a small number of cases appear in the Yorkshire peace rolls for the years 1361–4, 1383, and 1390–2, in those for Lincolnshire for 1373–5, and in those for Cambridgeshire for 1338–9.[13] There are similar appearances in gaol delivery rolls for Nottinghamshire and Derbyshire for 1329–30, and in the Yorkshire gaol delivery rolls of the 1440s and 1450s.[14] There seem to be other instances as well; for a full picture we must await a thorough examination of the mass of fourteenth- and fifteenth-century gaol delivery records. Even from a sampling of the records examples of *burglare* and similar do not appear to be lacking for any decade between 1270 and 1460; on the other hand we cannot say they are plentiful. Except in the case of the Kent rolls referred to above the frequency in appearance of the phrase *domum felonice burglavit* is much surpassed by instances of *domum felonice fregit et intravit* or similar, which give every indication of meaning the same thing, namely to have broken into a habitable building with intent to commit a felonious act.

Bertha Putnam noticed an interesting phenomenon in regard to certain burglary indictments in the Kent peace rolls which later appeared in the records of gaol delivery. In the latter they changed their form. In the peace rolls the *fregit* form was used but in the gaol delivery records this was replaced by some part of the verb *burgare* or by nouns from the same stem. Presumably these alterations were the work of the clerks of the professional judges who held the gaol delivery sessions. Thus they represent what Plucknett liked to call the view of 'Westminster Hall', that is to say the opinion of the experts on the criminal side of the common law. The choice in the rolls of the Kent peace sessions of *burglavit* or *fregit* seems to have been made by the juries of individual hundreds, or their 'interpreters', the clerks of the peace sessions. Virtually all of these opted for one phrase or the other consistently. Indeed in no instance do we find one of these juries offering *burglavit* in one of its indictments and *fregit* in another. Those which come nearest were the jurors of the hundred of Larkfield, who placed alongside two *burglavit* cases one of *intravit in grangia (et asportavit)*, and those of Lanbridge who reported alongside a *burglavit* case one containing the words *fregit molendinum (et asportavit)*.[15] Neither, it will be noted, was concerned with breaking into a house. The indications are that *burgare/burglare* in most parts of Kent was the word form preferred to indicate breaking into a house, although in a smaller number of localities the synonymous *fregit* was in favour. Why this should be so is not easy to discover; perhaps the traditions of the hundred had something to do with it. Alternatively the jurors may have had access to some copy of the articles of the sheriff's tourn or those of the general eyre. Both of these sets made use of words from the *burgare* stem: one of the articles of the eyre was 'de burgatoribus et malefactoribus et eorum receptatoribus tempore pacis' while an article of the tourn, according to *Britton*, was 'de burgesours'.[16]

The decline in the popularity of *burgare*-based words in indictments may well have followed closely on the decline and eventual demise of the general eyre in the first half of the fourteenth century, even if the sheriff's tourn still continued to flourish in the late fifteenth century. The rise and ascendancy of the justices of the peace may also have had an effect. An extant justices' charge to the jurors of about 1403–4, in Norman-French, nowhere uses a word akin to the 'burgesours' of *Britton*. It refers rather to 'ceulx qui debrusent maisons et robbent le people de leur biens' and thus shows a connection with *domum fregit*.[17] Nor was there any popularization of the *burgare* word-form through its use in fourteenth-century statutes or in the rolls of parliament. The Statutes of Westminster I (1275) and of Winchester (1285), which clarified a great deal of existing criminal law, mentioned robbery and larceny but not burglary. The later statutes which rehearsed or confirmed these two, such as 5 Edward III c.14 and 28 Edward III c.11, were similarly omissive although the former did name a category of felon called a 'draghlacche'. Other statutes touching the criminal law, such as 9 Edward II st.1 c.6, 10 Edward III st.1, 1 Henry IV c.18, 2 Henry V st.1 c.9, when they made a list of the major felonies, were wont to talk shortly of thefts, robberies, homicides, and ravishment of women, but never mentioned burglary.

The less frequent use of forms of the word *burgare* as the fourteenth century progressed, it might be argued, could have been connected with a desire on the part of presenting jurors or their clerk to afforce or aggravate their accusations; they may have sought to suggest a greater heinousness in a crime by using a more emotive word like *fregit* in order to influence the deliberations of the petty jurors later on. However, the verdicts in the plea rolls do not indicate, for this period at least, any greater incidence of conviction when *fregit* appeared in the indictment: the two word forms produced about the same percentage. Neither is there a case to be made that one of the word forms was more successful than the other in blocking those two common ways convicted felons cheated the hangman, namely successfully claiming benefit of clergy or acquiring a pardon. There is no shortage of cases where the clerical privilege was successfully pleaded by persons accused of either *domum burgavit* or *domum fregit*, and burglary in either form never seems to have figured as an exception in general pardons in contrast with treason, rape, murder, mainour-bearing theft, and robbery and larceny where the perpetrators were noted as being common felons of that type.

While the use of the verb *burgare* in indictments taken by the justices of the peace was less frequent by the middle of the fourteenth century, the professional judges appear to have been in little doubt as to the validity of that word form. The manner in which the clerks of gaol delivery justices changed *domum fregit* to *domum burgavit* has already been noted but well worth our consideration is the manner in which the word burglary appears in the *Year Book* reports from the middle years of Edward III's reign. 'Burglar' or 'burglary' as a word appears at least twice in reports of cases of 1348 and in one of 1353. Particularly important is the clear definition of burglary which the judges had to offer. Burglars, they said, were those who broke houses or churches, their walls or doors, intending to take goods. By so doing they became felons whether or not they actually stole, or, as one report colourfully had it, they put nothing in their sack.[18] There is nothing imprecise here; the scope of the crime seems clearly delineated and the definition water-tight, as if the judges had come to it through consideration of a large number of cases over many years. Doubtless this was why the issue of the scope of burglary only made one later appearance in the medieval *Year Books*. The case in point was discussed in the exchequer chamber in 13 Henry IV. It concerned breaking into a close (*clausum fregit*) and one judge felt obliged to ask if this was felony like *domum fregit*. The general opinion seems to have been that it was only trespass and that burglary meant breaking into a house. The case which caused the debate has not yet been identified in the plea rolls but there is an indictment which runs *felonice fregit clausuram et asportavit* in a Hampshire peace roll of May 1391 suggesting there had been a problem for some time prior to 1412.[19]

In the sixteenth century Marowe, the author of the Yelverton tract, and Staunford defined burglary as breach by night.[20] This has been a great legal mystery. Neither the *Year Books*, nor plea roll or chancery evidence of the fourteenth and fifteenth centuries give the slightest indication that an essential element of burglary was the committal of the offence by night. The adverbs *nocte* and *noctanter* appear not infrequently in *domum fregit* indictments and are not unknown in *burgavit* indictments. Unless their appearance in the latter was an idiosyncracy of a particular clerk or locality it is a bar to any theory that the verb *burgare* contained within itself the implication that the crime was nocturnal. The evidence from the fourteenth and fifteenth centuries, we may say, shows that if the burglary was by night then *nocte* or *noctanter* was likely to be included in the indictment although it was not strictly necessary. The intention was probably to aggravate the charges by adding an extra degree of heinousness and thus, hopefully, to make the conviction of the accused by the petty jury the more likely. The addition of *nocte/noctanter* was, of course, not peculiar to accusations of burglary. They were particularly frequent when the offence was felonious larceny.

The history of robbery from the thirteenth to the fifteenth centuries poses fewer problems than burglary. The character of the crime was quite clear to contemporaries and its key elements not in doubt. Furthermore its description in the plea rolls never varied in essentials. The verbs indicating robbery were admittedly three, *spoliare, expoliare* and *depredare*, but they were in use in roughly the same volume throughout each decade of the later middle ages in all parts of England. They always referred to the taking or attempted taking of money or goods from a person by use of violence or causing fear. To lie in wait intending to rob and achieving nothing was as much robbery as taking at sword point the valuables in a person's purse. Indeed, as the remarks of Chief Justice Gascoigne in a case at Michaelmas term 1411 demonstrate, the crime of robbery had been committed even if the intending robber was instantly overcome by his intended victim. This was no more than confirmation of a case of 1348–9 in which the judge, William Thorpe, said a man could be hanged for robbery even if he took but two pence, and one of 1353–4 where 'Sharde' (probably Shareshull, chief justice of the king's bench) stated that a man could be hanged for robbery even if he took no loot at all. There are indications that the point had also been made by judges in the early 1340s.[21]

Unlike burglary robbery secured specific mention in a fair number of later medieval statutes. This was mainly, one suspects, because of its several appearances in the first two sections of the Statute of Winchester, an act which was drafted in such a way as to imply that the whole spectrum of serious crime was made up of robberies on the one hand and the remaining felonies on the other. Statutes of Edward III's reign concerned with the criminal law in general such as 2 Edward III cc.1 and 7, 5 Edward III c.14, 10 Edward III st.1, and those concerned with the pillaging of merchants in particular like 27 Edward III st.2 c.13, 28 Edward III c.11, and 34 Edward III c.1, utilized the words robber or robbery in a prominent way. When, in the fifteenth century, a number of criminal offences were listed in remedial statutes 'robbery' was a word which was rarely absent whereas larceny was a periodic appearer and burglary a perpetual absentee. The word's popularity was not confined to the statute book. It figured in the articles of the general eyre between 1280 and 1321, and it appears in the first section of the charge to jurors at peace sessions which dates from the early years of Henry IV's reign.[22] In the later medieval period the word 'robbery' was possessed of what we now call a 'high profile'. The reason for this, apart from its emotiveness, may well have been that the word was very similar in Latin, Norman-French, and English. It also had a tendency to become in popular language a generic term for all forms of illicit taking.

The committing of felonious larceny was commonly described in the plea rolls of the later medieval period by the words *furavit* or *furatus fuit*. Frequently these were accompanied by the adverb *felonice*, occasionally by *furtive*, but neither was essential, as a judgment in Richard II's reign clearly demonstrates.[23] In some indictments we meet the phrase 'furtive (or felonice) cepit et asportavit', but this alternative was less common. The difference between larceny and robbery as they appear in these rolls was exactly as it appeared in the definitions of the thirteenth-century treatise writers: larceny was a surreptitious crime, robbery was an open one. Having pointed to the consistency of jurors and lawyers in one important field we must immediately qualify our categorization: there exist a fair number of indictments where the word *furavit* (or *furatus fuit*) was used only to be followed a little further on in the charge by a statement which shows that the victim was not only relieved of his goods but also assaulted and perhaps injured. Such a crime ought surely to have been described as robbery and the verbs *depredavit* or *spoliavit* used. They were not and the reason for this is unclear. We can only surmise that a sneak thief was detected while committing his mischief, resisted apprehension, and caused or threatened injury to his discoverer.

In neither burglary nor robbery was the value of the goods stolen of any relevance to the charge. To have taken nothing at all was immaterial; the mere attempting to rob, or simply breaking into a house with that or another felonious intent was sufficient, if proven, to warrant a sentence of death. Larceny, however, was quite different: the value of the goods taken decided whether a convicted accused was hanged or received relatively minor punishment. The division was at the one shilling mark as in Saxon times, as we have noticed. If a thief stole to the value of more than twelve pence, even if it was only to the value of a shilling and a half-penny he would be hanged on conviction: such was the weightier opinion in the fourteenth century. To take illicitly to the value of only twelve pence was thus only trespass, or at least such was the meaning of the first Statute of Westminster and the opinion of the justices in eyre in Kent in 1315.[24] There were, however, some dissentient opinions at that period. At the trial in 1348 of a woman who had slain her husband, Thorpe, a justice of the king's bench, is reported to have stated that theft of objects worth exactly twelve pence was punishable by death, not, as some laymen would have it, only if the loot was worth more than twelve pence half-penny.[25] If the line distinguishing grand and petty larceny ('petit briberie' the latter was sometimes called) was not fully agreed on, all commentators seem to have considered that when a felonious theft was committed by more than a single person it was felony in all of them; that is to say whether the perpetrators numbered two persons or twenty they might all hang if, collectively, they had taken objects worth more than a shilling or a shilling and a half-penny, or wherever the line was reckoned to be by the justices in charge.

Perhaps the most noticeable feature of the history of felonious larceny in the fourteenth century was the more precise definition of that crime which developed. A case was discussed by the judges in 22 Edward III which concerned the killing of doves and fishes.[26] The judges apparently agreed that to take savage beasts, as they were called, in their natural state was not normally felony. It could only become such if they were feloniously stolen from a house where they were kept, that is when they were in the possession of the householder who had taken them out of their natural environment. Another relevant case occurred ten years earlier and concerned a forester who was indicted for feloniously cutting down and carrying away a tree. The justices, so the report tells us, refused to accept the indictment because 'the felling of a tree which is so annexed to the soil cannot be called a felony' regardless of who did it.[27] Here we have something akin to the doves and fishes case. The taking of an object in its natural state or habitat could not be felony because it was not in anyone's possession, as it would be if cut down, harvested, or quarried, and then stored. In 27 Edward III the judges had to consider a case where a man took linen and other goods from the chamber of an inn. While passing through the hall of the hostelry en route to the stable to get his horse, he was discovered by the inn-keeper with the articles in his hands. Although he had not left the house the miscreant was found guilty of felony.[28] The felonious larceny lay not, as some have surmised, in the mere intent to carry the articles off (the accused had not broken into the building, he was apparently a guest) but in moving them from their proper place with intent to steal at a later time. This must have meant that a person who did not break into a house but somehow entered it peacefully, having in his mind an intention to steal which then became known, must actually steal some article before he could be held to have committed felony. However, such stealing in these circumstances might amount to merely taking an object from its resting place with felonious intent. This was quite a reasonable doctrine and it closed the gap between burglary and felonious larceny.

These decisions about the scope of larceny make quite good sense but this was less true of other *dicta* a century and a quarter later. The situations causing concern at that time were in essence where a man delivered goods or chattels belonging to him to another, a bailee, probably his servant or a tradesman, to keep or carry for him; and the latter then, with larcenous intent, fled with them. Such absconding with goods or chattels was not rated as felony until the passing of the act 21 Henry VIII c.7,[29] although the unsatisfactory nature of the doctrine of bailment, as it was called, was moderated by a decision of the judges in 1473. The debate on the matter in the latter year was clearly lengthy and it was complicated through doubt as to the status of the guilty party. Was one who had made a bargain with an owner to transport merchandise for him technically a bailee, as was for example a butler who had charge of his master's plate? The point was a crucial one since a person entrusted like a butler, should he flee with his master's valuables, was reckoned to be committing no felony. This was because in the medieval mind a bailee was temporarily vested with ownership, which a person who through a bargain acquired possession for the purpose of transportation or selling did not. In the case of 1473 the judges eventually decided the transporter of the goods was a bailee rather than a party to a bargain, but that nonetheless in the case in point, he was guilty of felony. This was because, after taking the bales, he broke them open and took some of the goods they contained. Thus the judges were able to say that the things taken were not the things baled to the accused but others, and the rule was made that it was a felony for a carrier to 'break bulk'.[30]

There was another judicial debate which concerned the scope of larceny at about the same time. At Michaelmas term 1470, when Henry VI had been readepted, the judges considered a theft of a number of boxes containing land charters. They agreed that the offence was not felony because charters were without monetary value. They were, it was stated, not personal chattels but real property like land. One of those present, Choke, justice of common pleas, pointed out that if a man was convicted of felony he did not forfeit his charters to the king: like his lands these went to his immediate lord.[31] If this was indeed the practice Choke's was a better argument than the one based on the lack of monetary value. The suggestion that the land law may have affected the scope of larceny is particularly interesting.

While the clarification of the scope of felonious larceny in these areas cannot be deemed unimportant there was one aspect of that crime concerning which judicial debate resulted in a decision of the greatest notoriety. The matter in question was the receiving of stolen goods. Giving shelter to (i.e. 'receiving') persons known to the receiver as perpetrators of felony had always been felonious and was to remain so. However, the receiving of goods, as distinct from the miscreant, which were the loot from a larceny or robbery was another matter. Once such receiving was thought to have been rated as felony only from the end of the seventeenth century, but Plucknett suggested it was felony in the early fourteenth century and changed to misdemeanour in the middle of Edward III's reign.[32] We can now add to Plucknett's thesis. Gaol delivery records demonstrate that the felonious receiving of stolen goods appeared occasionally in indictments from at least 1275 and that some of those indicted were convicted and received judgment of death.[33] What makes the history of the law concerning receiving of particular interest to the historian is a dramatic change in the law which occurred in about 1352. This was a rarity: interpretation and the substance of the law touching criminal matters would change over a period but infrequently, I think, to such a degree and so quickly.

In the first half of the fourteenth century there was no shortage of cases where persons were indicted or appealed of feloniously receiving goods *tout court* with no mention of receiving the thief himself.[34] In a good percentage of these instances the charge was laid by an approver who was appealing his confederates in a desperate attempt to save himself from the gallows. There were also cases where the accused had purchased stolen goods from the approver rather than receiving them as a gift, and there were others where the person arraigned had bought some of their loot from thieves who never turned approver. Such purchase appears to have been regarded as equivalent to receiving. The change in judicial attitudes to receiving, alluded to above, must have occurred around the middle of the fourteenth century. Two reports concerned with this issue appear in the *Year Books*, one dated 25 Edward III, the other 27 Edward III; they probably referred to the same case. Apparently an approver had appealed a man of receiving some of the approver's loot, but the appeal made no reference to his receiving the approver or anyone else who had been involved in the commission of the crime. Because of this counsel for the defendant demanded acquittal. In the event the charge was quashed by Shareshull, at that time probably chief justice of the king's bench.[35]

Whether this was intended to demonstrate there should henceforward be no such felony as receiving loot without the person of the miscreant when the charge was laid through the appeal of an approver, or whether there was to be no such felony in any circumstances (i.e. on appeal of the person robbed, on appeal of an approver, or on the indictment of jurors) is not clear. That it was a startling departure, however, is undoubted. The *Year Book* reporter found the decision an amazing one and said so in as many words. Cases where the offence was simply the receiving of loot are rare in the plea rolls of the later fourteenth and earlier fifteenth centuries but the few which have been noticed are of both varieties, i.e. where the charges were brought by approver and where they were laid by an appeal of the party robbed, or by indictment.[36] The impression we get is that Shareshull and those on the benches who thought like him had made a decision which had long-lasting effects, being forgotten or ignored in a relatively few cases. The reason for the decision is not apparent. Milsom has argued that receiving of goods was not generally felony in the later middle ages because the receiver did no 'taking', which was essential for the crime to amount to theft.[37] Perhaps the reason was a more practical one. Should a person accused of the felonious receiving of stolen goods be acquitted the goods were kept by the accused; but if the accused was charged with receiving both loot and miscreant, knowing the latter had perpetrated a felonious theft, and the receiver was then acquitted, the king would receive the loot as forfeit provided the thief was convicted of the original theft.

The history of larceny, robbery, and burglary in the later middle ages is not, of course, to be derived only from literary sources. It can be made a good deal clearer by calculations based on numbers of like cases to be found in the plea rolls. One of the most noticeable features of the court record evidence is the relative incidence of the different types of felony. In most rolls the number of persons accused of felonious larceny is greater than that of those accused of burglary, which in turn is greater than that of those charged with robbery. In Wiltshire gaol delivery rolls of the reign of Edward I those accused of grand larceny amounted to approximately 44 per cent of the total of persons charged with felony of any sort. Those charged with burglary on the other hand totalled just over 18 per cent (the same as for homicide) and those accused of robbery under 13 per cent.[38] The eight counties whose extant gaol delivery records for the period 1300–48 were investigated by Hanawalt show a similar pattern. Felonious larceny amounted to between 45.7 per cent (Northamptonshire) and 32.4 per cent (Essex) of all felony charges, burglary to between 31.5 per cent (Norfolk) and 7.5 per cent (Huntingdonshire), and robbery to between 16.5 per cent (Herefordshire) and 5.2 per cent (Yorkshire). The medians were 39.14 per cent for larceny, 23.93 per cent for burglary, and 10.28 per cent for robbery.[39]

The evidence from later in the fourteenth century provides us with a picture only slightly different. The rolls of the Lincolnshire justices of the peace for the years 1360–75 yield a total of 281 charges of felony of which serious larceny accounts for 52.7 per cent, burglary 7.1 per cent and robbery a mere 2.13 per cent. The extant peace rolls for Coventry and Warwickshire for the period 1377–97 contain 190 indictments for felony of which eighty (42.1 per cent) were for larceny, twelve (6.3 per cent) for burglary, and eight (4.2 per cent) for robbery. The Shropshire peace rolls for 1400–14 show 171 felony cases of which eighty-three (49.5 per cent) were for larceny, twenty (11.7 per cent) for burglary, and thirteen (7.6 per cent) for robbery.[40] The evidence from the reign of Henry VI, a period commonly believed to have been particularly lawless, tells virtually the same story. Before the justices of gaol delivery in Yorkshire in the years 1439–53, 45.3 per cent of those arraigned were accused of felonious larceny, 20.7 per cent of burglary, and 10.8 per cent of robbery. Between 1454 and 1460 in the same county and before the same justices 60.1 per cent were charged with larceny, 18.0 with burglary, and a mere 2.18 with robbery.[41] Nearly always, so it seems, felonious larcenies greatly outnumbered burglaries, which in turn usually substantially surpassed robberies. The century between 1360 and 1460 was notable particularly for the considerable decline in violent theft, i.e. robbery, one of the most common forms of which had always been by ambush or confrontation on the highway. Whether this was because of a decline in 'infra-local' trade and market-oriented production in agriculture in the later middle ages, which some economic historians consider a distinct possibility, or whether it was because of greater reluctance to use force or threat of force on the part of the miscreant is not clear.[42]

What might have persuaded would-be miscreants to eschew violence in committing their crimes was some awareness of relative conviction rates, if, that is, they differed significantly between different types of offence. Wiltshire gaol delivery records of the reign of Edward I yield a conviction rate for felonious larceny of 26.3 per cent, and for burglary of 25.3 per cent. In contrast, when the crime was robbery those found guilty amount to 31.5 per cent of the total number of accused. This may, it could be argued, have persuaded a criminal to steal by stealth. In her study of gaol delivery records of the first half of the fourteenth century Hanawalt found a conviction rate for robbery which was very similar to the one in late thirteenth-century Wiltshire (30.6 per cent); the incidence of burglary convictions was slightly increased (31.0 per cent) whereas those for larceny had diminished to 22.4 per cent. The trend, however, was not maintained, or at least not maintained consistently. Mid-fifteenth-century gaol delivery rolls, those for Yorkshire, show a much higher conviction rate for larceny (43.8 per cent) than is to be found a century or so earlier, whereas that for burglary had declined to 24 per cent and that for robbery to 21.9 per cent. In contrast the rolls of the eastern circuit for the years 1440–1 reveal a 31 per cent conviction rate for both larceny and burglary and one as high as 59 per cent for robbery.[43] These eastern circuit records may have been the result of changing public attitudes towards felony in general, a belief that more of those accused had to be sent to their deaths if public order was to survive, or perhaps a greater revulsion at the felonious act. More likely, however, as will be demonstrated below, it was connected with the revival in popularity of the old process of appeal whereby the victim of the felony personally charged the suspect with the crime and a jury of indictment did not have to participate. The attractiveness to the victim of the crime of proceeding in this manner was that the result was a conviction in a very high percentage of cases, and that furthermore the successful appellant was likely to be awarded by the court the restitution of his stolen goods, neither conclusion being at all likely where the trial was on indictment.[44]

The history of felonious larceny, burglary, and robbery in the Tudor period shows only modest amendment in regard to the definition of the scope of those crimes. In regard to robbery the writers of legal treatises, namely Marowe, the compiler of the *Boke of Justyces of Peas*, Fitzherbert (or whoever wrote the *Newe Boke of Justices of the Peas*), the drafter of the charge in the Yelverton manuscripts, and William Staunford each emphasized that the value of the goods taken might be only a pennyworth or less.[45] This of course had been declared by the judges in the fourteenth century. The other aspect of robbery which always received comment was, as the *Boke of Justyces of Peas* had it, the 'jeopardy' to the person, that is to say the danger and fear created for the victim. Again this was a traditional part of any definition of robbery, but the references are sometimes so emotive, as for example Staunford's emphasis on that crime's implicit 'menace of death', that they cannot be dismissed lightly.[46] What is not clear is whether this concern with force and danger to the person sprang from a new sensitivity caused by the maturing of society or whether robbery (and burglary also in that it might engender fear) was particularly frequent in the earlier Tudor period. The problem may never be solved because very few records of the courts which handled felony in this period have survived. What is not in doubt is that the Tudor treatise writers saw these two offences as being 'greater than theft', and when they talked about robbery were prone to mention ambush and emphasize the precogitative yet at the same time random nature of the illegal doings of highwaymen. The obsession with robbery in the form of highway ambush lasted to the end of the sixteenth century at least. It shows clearly in the *Boke of Justyces of Peas* published in the first decade of the sixteenth century, and although one recent commentator, noting the way in which those giving readings in the Inns of Court in the early sixteenth century stressed the element of fear, has argued that this association had not long to live and that in fact the reign of Henry VIII saw its demise, the evidence is by no means unequivocal.[47] We notice, for example, that the justices' charge in the Yelverton manuscripts, which dates from the 1530s, defines robbery as lying in wait on the highway in order to take men's goods, and more particularly that fifty or so years later magistrates in the north midlands were still describing the crime to indicting jurors in words which were very similar.[48] The Tudor writers on criminal law were keen to emphasize that a highwayman did not have to use actual violence against his victim for the deed to be robbery; mere verbal threat was sufficient. Again this had been the view of the late medieval judges. It was even robbery, wrote Staunford, drawing on a *Year Book* case of Edward III, where the victim was permitted to depart from the scene of the crime so as to collect his goods and deliver them to the robber, provided he had been threatened with death if he failed to do as instructed.[49]

When they came to define and discuss burglary Tudor writers on criminal law followed medieval assumptions less closely. One area which was of particular concern to them was burglary and the night-time. For virtually all of them burglary was a nocturnal crime: entering a house with intent to commit a felony must be by night if it was to be properly called burglary. The compiler of the *Boke of Justyces of Peas* had been the first to make this point but most of the later Tudor commentators said something similar. Staunford and the compiler of the charge which appears in the Middleton manuscripts supply the intriguing information that while an indictment for burglary should contain the adverb 'by night' (*nocte/noctanter*) this did not necessarily mean the offence had been committed in the darkness; it had simply become accepted practice to insert the word.[50] How and why this came about are great mysteries. As we have seen there is no suggestion that *nocte/noctanter*, although it did appear occasionally, was an essential component in indictments of burglary in the century and a half prior to 1460, the date to which gaol delivery records have survived. The new rule, if such it was, must have developed in the period 1460–1500, but it is odd there is no reference to it in the *Year Books* of that time. The best clue as to why *nocte/noctanter* became essential is Spelman's belief that the word *burgulavit* in indictments meant exactly the same as *noctanter fregit*, that is to say it carried the meaning of breaking in at night without any need for the adverb.[51] What may have happened was that some lawyer of distinction or a notable judge of the Yorkist or early Tudor period drew attention to the fact that the vernacular word 'burglary', which was becoming increasingly popular among lawyers to describe the breaking of houses with intent to commit a felony, must have derived from the rather rare Latin verb *burgulare*, which he believed excusably but quite wrongly was not to be found in fifteenth-century indictments alongside the adverb *nocte/noctanter*. Reading or hearing of this those who subsequently drafted burglary indictments using what was by then the standard *domum fregit*, concluded they must rightly, should the offence have been committed by night, supplement these words with *nocte/noctanter*. Later on, perhaps through a lack of comprehension amongst lesser court officials, these adverbs were held to be essential whatever the hour of the offence. Hence came Staunford's dictum, which no doubt accurately described contemporary practice.

The history of burglary in the sixteenth century was periodically intertwined with that of benefit of clergy as the statute book clearly shows. The reason for this was a design on the part of those behind the relevant legislation to punish offenders more severely when the house broken into was inhabited at the time. Thus the first statute of this type, 4 Henry VIII c.2, forbade the clerical privilege (unless the miscreant was in holy orders) if 'the owner or dweller of the house, his wife and child and servant being therein were put in dread'. It was the first time there had been in statutes, *Year Books*, or treatises such clear concern for the intended victims, a fact which displays a new sensitivity to the dangers of serious crime, which was probably supported in this instance by recognition that increasing literacy was saving too many felons from the gallows. Another novelty in the statute was the virtual division of a felony into two categories, one more heinous than the other. The statute 4 Henry VIII c.2 lapsed in 1515 and was not revived until the passing of 23 Henry VIII c.1. Both of these acts described the offence they dealt with as 'robbery in houses' for the English word 'burglary' had not yet appeared in legislation. In 1533 there was promulgated an act, 24 Henry VIII c.5, designed to protect from forfeiture the goods of persons who killed thieves, which referred to those who broke into, or tried to break into, dwellings 'burgularly' by night to rob or murder. The next session of the Reformation Parliament gave birth to a statute (25 Henry VIII c.3), which, in closing a procedural loop-hole in the act 23 Henry VIII c.1, referred to the latter as dealing with 'robbers, murderers, burglaries, and felons', 'burglaries' meaning burglars: only the verb form of the latter word was still lacking from the legal lexicon.

Burglary of houses, although the actual word 'burglary' was not used, next featured in legislation in 1552 and once more benefit of clergy was involved. The act 5/6 Edward VI c.9 was passed to resolve doubts as to whether the privilege should be allowed to miscreants when there had been no fear or dread instilled into the victim of the burglary because, although they were within the house broken into, they were either asleep or located in another section away from where the entry was made. It looks rather as if some sharp-witted burglar at his trial had caused concern by protesting he had put no one in dread. In future, so the statute decreed, clergy was to be denied even in such circumstances. The word 'burglary' or its derivatives appeared in a statute for the third time in the Tudor period in 1576. The act, 18 Elizabeth c.7, was yet another concerned with the future restriction of benefit of clergy. It stated that the privilege was no longer to be permitted to those found guilty of felonious rape or burglary. At last, we may say, the term 'burglary' had become legally respectable for there was no reference to 'robbery in houses' in apposition or by way of clarification. There was, however, no clear indication at this point in time of what the crime amounted to in law and whether there had to be persons in the house broken into, and who were put in dread, for the offence to be truly burglary. The evidence of the plea rolls suggests that the persons and the fear were an ancillary rather than an integral part of burglary in Elizabeth's reign. The records of the justices on the south-eastern gaol delivery circuit for the later years of Elizabeth's reign show a number of cases where included in the indictment was a statement to the effect that when the accused broke into the house the owner or members of his family or household were present. This addition was not an essential part of the indictment but rather a phrase of afforcement intended to increase the gravity of the crime and thus the chances of a conviction. From the crown's viewpoint it had the right effect.[52] In such cases petty jurors seem to have been eager to find the accused guilty. However, by James I's reign what had been at first a provision in regard to the claiming of benefit of clergy and later an afforcement had apparently been incorporated into the definition of burglary. Dalton, writing in 1619, stated quite unequivocally that when a house had been broken into 'commonly it is no Burglarie unlesse some person be at that time within the house'.[53]

The statistical picture of the three types of felony under review, as it was in the later Tudor period, is interesting but not dramatic. On the home circuit in the reign of Elizabeth I cases of robbery, burglary, and felonious larceny provided about 80 per cent of the verdicts given. Of these the vast majority, about four-fifths, were cases of felonious larceny, with burglary providing slightly more than robbery of the remainder. In the earlier fourteenth century these crimes had, as we have seen, provided about 70 per cent of the gaol delivery calendar and in the mid-fifteenth century between 75 and 80 per cent. In each of these periods the crimes in their degree of incidence followed the same order, which was felonious larceny well ahead of burglary with robbery a poor third. In the later medieval period the conviction rates of those accused of burglary or robbery were similar: they were in the mid-twenties per cent in the reign of Edward I, about thirty per cent in the earlier fourteenth century, and in the low twenties per cent in the middle of the fifteenth century. In the Elizabethan period, in cases where verdicts were returned, the conviction rate varied considerably for burglary and robbery. In Essex the robbery conviction rate was about 55 per cent, in Kent about 60 per cent, and in Sussex about 65 per cent. Burglary provided a rate of just under 60 per cent in Essex and Sussex but in Kent a very high 71.3 per cent. Felonious larceny, on the other hand, had a conviction rate of about 65 per cent in each of the three counties, a high level because petty juries knew many of those found guilty would escape the gallows through their literacy.[54]

These then, the murders, manslaughters, robberies, burglaries and larcenies, were the offences which provided over 90 per cent of the felonies which came to trial in the later medieval period; they were the staple diet of the criminal courts. As we have seen their scope and nature did not take shape at that time for it had already crystallized in earlier centuries, probably as early as the Anglo-Saxon period, although there were refinements of varying importance in the period under review. These developments, several of which have proved vexing to modern historians largely because of the lack of legal treatises on the criminal law compiled in the later medieval period, have had to be traced from court and administrative records. Other categories of felony, which provided only a very small percentage of cases which came to trial, are outlined in the appendix.

From this necessary excursus we must now turn to details of the actual trial.

Notes

Murder and Manslaughter

1 *Die Gesetze der Angelsachsen*, ed. F. Liebermann (Halle, 1903–16), i, 486.

2 *Leges Henrici Primi*, ed. L.J. Downer (Oxford, 1972), pp. 205, 290–1.

3 *Glanvill*, p. 174. The author makes no suggestion that murder might also be killing a person taken off guard, as had been the case in Anglo-Saxon times.

4 *History of English Law*, ii, 486. Maitland does not state exactly when this occurred.

5 See for example *Select Coroners' Rolls, A.D. 1265–1413*, ed. C. Gross (Selden Society, 9, 1895), pp. 4, 6, 18,19, 26, 29 *et passim*; PRO JUST 1/1043 mm. 1, 1d, 2, 2d, 3, 4, 4d, 5, 5d, 6, 7; PRO JUST 3/71 mm. 3, 11, 14.

6 C. Bonnier, 'A List of English Towns in the Fourteenth Century', *English Historical Review*, xvi (1901), 501.

7 *Bracton*, ii, 298, 340–1, 379.

8 Hurnard, p. 77.

9 J.M. Kaye, 'The Early History of Murder and Manslaughter', *Law Quarterly Review* 83 (1967), 371–3. Maitland, on the other hand, thought 'with malice aforethought' was a reasonable translation; he implied *assultus excogitatus* or *assultus premeditatus* had its origin in the Anglo-Saxon *forsteal*: *History of English Law*, ii, 455.

10 *Bracton*, ii, 340.

11 Kaye, *Law Quarterly Rev.*, 369, 371, 377.

12 *Britton*, i, 50.

13 See *The Chronicle of Walter of Guisborough*, ed. H. Rothwell (Camden Society, 3rd Ser., 89, 1957), pp. 361–2.

14 *Cal. Pat. Rolls, 1334–38*, p. 218; *ibid., 1340–43*, pp. 108, 202, 204, 328.

15 J.B. Post, 'Some Limitations of the Medieval Peace Rolls', *Journal of the Society of Archivists*, 4 (1973), 639 referring to PRO KB 29/9/4.

16 *Cal. Pat. Rolls, 1340–43*, pp. 539, 543; *Calendar of Inquisitions Miscellaneous*, ii, no. 1325; *Cal. Pat. Rolls, 1338–40*, pp. 217–36. A commission to the justiciary of Ireland of May 1346 referred to 'murder, homicide, robbery, and other felony': *Cal. Pat. Rolls, 1345–48*, p. 88.

17 See for example PRO C 260/41/33 and 38, and C 260/39/13.

18 Kaye, *Law Quarterly Rev.*, 378; *Rot. Parl.*, ii, 171–2.

19 J.B. Post, 'Some Limitations', 639.

20 *Cal. Inquis. Misc.*, iii, no. 531; *Cal. Pat. Rolls, 1374–77*, p. 435.

21 *Sessions of the Peace in Lincs., 1360–75*, pp. lxx, lxxiv, 142.

22 For example see *Cal. Pat. Rolls, 1377–81*, pp. 219, 444; *ibid., 1381–85*, pp. 13, 312, 339, 406, 464, 482, 536, 584; *ibid., 1385–89*, p. 71.

23 *Ibid., 1381–85*, pp. 173, 182, 187.

24 *Ibid., 1377–81*, p. 335; *ibid., 1385–89*, p. 136; *ibid., 1388–92*, p. 170.

25 *Ibid., 1381–85*, p. 514; *ibid., 1385–89*, p. 317 and *ibid., 1388–92*, pp. 81, 132.

26 *Ibid., 1377–81*, p. 8; *Cal. Inquis. Misc.* iv, nos. 103, 307; *Select Coroners' Rolls*, p. 123.

27 *Stat. Realm*, ii, 10.

28 *Rot. Parl.*, iii, 83b.

29 *Ibid.*, iii, 84b.

30 For example *Cal. Pat. Rolls, 1385–89*, p. 317; *ibid., 1388–92*, p. 132.

31 Compare Kaye, *Law Quarterly Rev.*, 384.

32 Kaye, *Law Quarterly Rev.*, 369, 393, 569 and T.A. Green, 'The Jury and the English Law of Homicide, 1200–1600', *Michigan Law Review*, 74 (1976), 457. Green, however, argues that the effect was not long-lasting.

33 PRO C 66/254 mm. 14, 23, 27, C 66/260 m. 14, C 66/265 m 8, C 66/266 mm. 28, 30, C 66/276 m. 9, C 66/284 m. 18.

34 The *murdrum* fine was abolished in 1340 (14 Edward III st.1 c.4) but the memory doubtless lingered. Those who drafted indictments may have thought that by this statute the validity of the words *murdrare* and *murdre* was impugned.

35 See for example *William Salt Archaeological Society*, x (1889), 66–9.

36   The lack of a suitable punishment mid-way between hanging and a mere fine contributed to the problem.

37   On pardons see below, chapter four.

38   See chapter four, p. 139.

39   See *Year Books of the reign of Edward I, III*, p. 504, for a case where the wording of a felony pardon was closely examined in court (in this instance by counsel for the victim).

40   T.A. Green, 'A Retrospective on the Criminal Trial Jury' in *Twelve Good Men*, pp. 367, 374; T.A. Green, *Verdict according to Conscience* (Chicago, 1985), pp. 27–64, 67–8; Green, *Mich. Law Rev.*, 424–34, 452–4. Green also argues that the long-term result of the jurors' monopoly of the evidence was to preclude the king's justices from refining the law through consideration of difficult cases: *ibid.*, 414.

41   See the following chapter, pp. 110–11.

42   See Kaye, *Law Quarterly Rev.*, 391–3 and Green, *Mich. Law Rev.*, 462–5. Green takes the words 'ex malitia precogitata' or 'malice purpense' to mean, in the fourteenth century, either 'with malice aforethought' or simply (as Kaye believed) 'deliberately' depending on the context: Green, 'Societal Concepts', 691. This modification of Kaye's interpretation, the latter being quite erroneous as I see it, is forced on Green by the wording of the 1390 statute; for it is clear that there 'malice purpense' means malice aforethought.

43   Also the original petition which requested the legislation was clearly aimed at murder (i.e. 'murdre'), which it distinguished from 'mort de homme': *Rot. Parl.*, iii, 268.

44   British Library, Harleian MS. 773 f. 50. The meaning is surely '. . . all types of homicides, those who lie in wait by malice aforethought in countryside, houses, and other places so as to murder people; and those who kill men in hot blood'; *cf.* Green, *Mich. Law Rev.*, 467.

45   J. Gower, *Confessio Amantis*, in *The Complete Works of John Gower*, ed. G.C. Macaulay (Oxford, 1899), i, 364.

46   *The Boke of Justyces of Peas* (1506), f. A vi.

47   B.L. Lansdowne MS. 1072 f. 43; A. Fitzherbert, *The Newe Boke of Justices of the Peas* (London, 1538), f. xix.

48   B.L. Additional MS. 48047 f. 64v.

49   Green is surely in error in holding (*Mich. Law Rev.*, 473) that 'by the later decades of the fifteenth century all homicide indictments carried the form . . . "murdravit"': see for example PRO JUST 3/213 mm. 1d, 3d, 6d, 7d and PRO Durham 13/229 (where the verb is merely 'interfecit' despite the crime being poisoning); the date of the gaol delivery was December 1500. Both Kaye and Green fail to recognize the emergence of manslaughter, observedly in the form of chance medley, before 1390 and this is a major cause of their difficulties in interpreting developments in the law of homicide in the fifteenth and early sixteenth centuries.

50   See P.L. Hughes and J.F. Larkin, *Tudor Royal Proclamations* (New Haven, 1964–9), i, nos. 2, 15, 17, 30, 63, 128, 204.

51   Fifteen under Henry VIII, four under Edward VI and three under Mary.

52   Baker argues for an increase of interest in the criminal law among lawyers during the reigns of Henry VII and Henry VIII (as shown by readings given at the Inns of Court) and gives part of the credit to cases moved by writ of *certiorari* into the king's bench, or by adjournment into the exchequer

chamber, or debated at Serjeants' Inn: *Spelman*, ed. Baker, ii, 301–4. Baker notes that in this period the element of malice prepense in murder was never defined: *ibid.*, ii, 309.

53 English Reports, Dyer 128b; *ibid.*, Moore 87; B.L. Harleian MS. 5141 fos. 40–1. Raising a weapon in anger versus X and slaying Y inadvertently was felonious homicide according to Marowe: *Spelman*, ed. Baker, ii, 310 noting *Early Treatises*, p. 378.

54 Kaye, *Law Quarterly Rev.*, 581–4.

55 Eng. Reports, Plowden 101. We do not have the exact circumstances of John Vane Salisbury's intervention. He may have happened to come along as the others fought and been drawn in by threat to his person or desire to assist his master and friends.

56 This is the first unambiguous statement of definition.

57 Another case (from 1557) showing chance medley could be deliberate killing is to be found in *Calendar of Nottinghamshire coroners' inquests, 1485–1558*, ed. R.F. Hunnisett (Thoroton Society, Record Series, 25, 1969), no. 323.

58 See *ibid.*, nos. 299, 301, 323, 334.

59 See Kaye, *Law Quarterly Rev.*, 591; also Eng. Reports, 9 Coke 61b. Early in the sixteenth century, argues Baker, if a drunken man slew somebody, the offence was rated felonious homicide because his incapacity was a result of his own excess: *Spelman*, ed. Baker, ii, 301.

60 Eng. Reports, Plowden 474a.

61 Hanawalt, *Crime and Conflict*, p. 66; L. Tunstall, *Gaol Delivery in Yorkshire, 1359–1363* (Carleton University, M.A. thesis, 1990), p. 82.

62 Garay, pp. 205–6; Elder, pp. 68; PRO JUST 3/211 and 213.

63 J. Samaha, *Law and Order in Historical Perspective. The Case of Elizabethan Essex* (New York, 1974), pp. 20, 125–6; *Cal. Sussex Indictments*, pp. 1–431; PRO Chester 21/1 fos. 43–199.

64 PRO ASSI 35/1–44; PRO CHES 21/1 fos. 43–199.

65 Pugh, *Proc. British Academy*, 86; Hanawalt, *Crime and Conflict*, p. 59; Garay, p. 344.

66 PRO JUST 3/211 and 213.

67 PRO ASSI 35/1–44; *Cal. Sussex Indictments*, pp. 1–431; PRO Chester 21/1 fos. 43–199; *Cal. Kent Indictments*, pp. 1–504.

Larceny, Robbery, and Burglary

1 *The Laws of the Earliest English Kings*, ed. F.L. Attenborough (Cambridge, 1922), pp. 4, 41. The Anglo-Saxon laws, like the statutes of the medieval parliaments, failed to provide definitions of the different types of crime; usually they merely added refinements to legal procedures already existing to handle each type of offence.

2 *Laws of the Earliest English Kings*, pp. 70, 127, 157–9; *The Laws of the Kings of England from Edmund to Henry I*, ed. A.J. Robertson (Cambridge, 1925), p. 207.

3 *Laws of the Earliest English Kings*, pp. 49, 127, 157, 169.

4 *Leges Henrici Primi*, pp. 108–9, 114–15, 116–17.

5 *History of English Law*, ii, 495–6.

6 *Glanvill*, pp. 91, 177; *Dialogus de Scaccario*, ed. C. Johnson (London, 1950), p. 102.

7 *The Mirror of Justices*, ed. W.J. Whittaker (Selden Society, 7, 1895), pp. 25–7; *Fleta, II*, ed. H.G. Richardson and G.O. Sayles (Selden Soc., 72, 1955), p. 90.

8 *Bracton*, ii, 425–6, 428–9; *Britton*, i, 59. On bailees see below.

9 *Britton*, i, 61; *Fleta, II*, p. 92.

10 *Bracton*, ii, 412, 425; *Mirror of Justices*, pp. 141, 150.

11 *Mirror of Justices*, pp. 28, 141; *Bracton*, ii, 299.

12 See for example the far from convincing arguments by Plucknett in *Proceedings*, ed. Putnam, pp. cxlii–cxlvi. See also *Spelman*, ed. Baker, ii, 325–6.

13 *Kent Keepers of the Peace, passim*; *Yorkshire Sessions of the Peace, 1361–1364*, ed. B.H. Putnam (Yorkshire Archaeological Society Record Series, 100, 1939), pp. 29, 82, 89, 104; *Proceedings*, ed. Putnam, pp. 435, 437, 440, 452–3; *Sessions of the Peace in Lincs. 1360–75*, pp. 26–7, 55; *Some Sessions of the Peace in Cambridgeshire in the Fourteenth Century, 1340, 1380–83*, ed. M.M. Taylor (Cambridge Antiquarian Society, 1942), pp. 8, 18.

14 PRO JUST 3/123 mm. 17–23; JUST 3/211 mm. 1–27; JUST 3/213 mm. 1–12.

15 *Proceedings*, ed. Putnam, p. cxlii; *Kent Keepers of the Peace*, pp. xxv, 12–13, 15–16.

16 See H. Cam, *The Hundred and the Hundred Rolls: An Outline of Local Government in Medieval England* (London, 1930), p. 92; *Britton*, i, 179. The use of even older aids to formulation, which existed in certain areas, is suggested by evidence from Suffolk. The peace rolls of this county for 1363 show two instances of presenting jurors using the Anglo-Saxon term *hamsocn*; one took the form *fecit hamsok'*, the other *hampsoknyavit*; neither offence was rated as felony, however: *Proceedings*, ed. Putnam, p. 357. Other examples are to be found in *Rolls of the Warwickshire and Coventry Sessions of the Peace, 1377–1397*, ed. E.G. Kimball (Dugdale Society, 16, 1939), pp. 24, 26, 51, 57, 60.

17 *Proceedings*, ed. Putnam, p. 11.

18 *Year Books, Liber Assisarum*, 22 Edward III pl. 39; *ibid.*, 22 Edward III pl. 95; *ibid.*, 27 Edward III pl. 38.

19 *Year Books*, 13 Henry IV Mich. pl. 20; *Proceedings*, ed. Putnam, p. 219. Plucknett argued that breaking a close 'will only be felonious (if at all), if there is intent to commit a felony'. There seems little doubt that in the fourteenth century, for the judges of the two benches, breach of a close was never a felony. Plucknett made unnecessary difficulties for himself in regard to the medieval history of burglary; this was largely because he paid too much attention to Tudor definitions: see *ibid.*, p. cxlv.

20 *Early Treatises*, p. 378; B.L., Additional MS 48047 f. 65r; Staunford, *Les Plees del Coron*, f. 30r. Early sixteenth-century readings at the Inns of Court seem to indicate definitions of burglary at that time varied amongst the lawyers particularly in regard to whether the offence was essentially nocturnal: *Spelman*, ed. Baker, ii, 325–6.

21 *Year Books*, 13 Henry IV Mich. pl. 20; *ibid.*, *Liber Assisarum*, 22 Edward III pl. 39; *ibid.*, 27 Edward III pl. 38.

22 Cam, *The Hundred Rolls*, p. 98; *Proceedings*, ed. Putnam, p. 11.

23 *Early Treatises*, p. 393.

24 *Eyre of Kent*, p. 79.

25 *Year Books*, 22 Edward III pl. 39.

26 *Year Books, Liber Assisarum*, 22 Edward III pl. 95.

27 *Ibid.*, 12 Edward III pl. 32.

28 *Ibid.*, 27 Edward III pl. 39.

29 As long as the value was at least 40 shillings.

30 *Year Books*, 13 Edward IV Pasch. pl. 5. Baker argues strongly that the doctrine of breaking bulk was a judicial invention to deal with servants who absconded with their masters' goods; he points out that the root of the matter was the prevailing notion that felonious theft was violation of possession rather than of title: *Spelman*, ed. Baker, ii, 321. One can readily see that the entrusted servant might have been viewed in the same light as a feoffee to uses.

31 *Year Books of Edward IV, 10 Edward IV and 49 Henry VI, A.D. 1470*, ed. N. Neilson (Selden Society, 47, 1931), pp. 124–6. Milsom has argued that the judges held that certain things had no value before the law out of a desire to be merciful to the miscreant: S.F.C. Milsom, *Historical Foundations of the Common Law* (London, 1969), p. 372.

32 *Proceedings*, ed. Putnam, p. cxli.

33 See for example *Wiltshire Gaol Delivery*, pp. 34, 37, 46, 53, 63, 133; *London Trailbaston*, pp. 63, 64, 78, 80, 119.

34 See for example *Northamptonshire Sessions*, pp. 68–72; *A Cambridgeshire Gaol Delivery Roll, 1332–1334*, ed. E.G. Kimball (Cambridge Antiquarian Records Society, 4, 1978), pp. 60, 76, 78.

35 *Year Books, Liber Assisarum*, 27 Edward III pl. 69; *ibid.*, 25 Edward III pl. 2.

36 PRO JUST 3/211 mm. 2, 3.

37 Milsom, *Historical Foundations*, p. 372.

38 These are my calculations from *Wiltshire Gaol Delivery*.

39 Hanawalt, *Crime and Conflict*, p. 67.

40 The totals are derived from *Sessions of the Peace in Lincs., 1360–75, Warwickshire Sessions of the Peace*, and *The Shropshire Peace Roll, 1400–1414*, ed. E.G. Kimball (Shrewsbury, 1959).

41 PRO JUST 3/211 and 213.

42 M.M. Postan, *The Medieval Economy and Society* (London, 1972), pp. 225–6.

43 *Wiltshire Gaol Delivery*, *passim*; Hanawalt, *Crime and Conflict*, pp. 58–60; PRO JUST 3/211, JUST 3/212, and JUST 3/213.

44 For the reasons for this revival and the degree of success met with by appellants see chapter three.

45 *Boke of Justyces of Peas*, f. A vi; *Early Treatises*, p. 377; Fitzherbert, *Newe Boke of Justices of the Peas*, f. 19; B.L. Yelverton MS. 48047 f. 65r; Staunford, *Les Plees del Coron*, f. 27.

46 *Boke of Justyces of Peas*, f. A vi; Staunford, *Les Plees del Coron*, f. 27r.

47 *Boke of Justyces of Peas*, f. A vi; *Spelman*, ed. Baker, ii, 324.

48 B.L. Yelverton MS. 48047 f. 65r; Middleton MS. (in Nottingham University Library) Mi.02/1 f. 11.

49 Staunford, *Les Plees del Coron*, fos. 27–8.

50 *Boke of Justyces of Peas*, f. B i; *Early Treatises*, p. 378; Staunford, *Les Plees del Coron*, f. 30; Middleton MS. Mi. 02/1 f. 11; B.L. Yelverton MS. 48047 f. 65r. In fact the only commentator to lack a reference of any kind to the nocturnal nature of the crime was the author of the *Newe Boke of Justices of the Peas*; the only extant Inns of Court reading which has the same omission is that of Mountford: *Spelman*, ed. Baker, ii, 326.

51 *Spelman*, ed. Baker, ii, 326.

52 For example in Essex between 1576 and 1594 convictions in burglary cases of all sorts (i.e. however described in the plea rolls) amounted by my calculations to 72.9 per cent of those indicted, but in the cases where the afforcement was introduced they reached 93.1 per cent.

53 M. Dalton, *The Countrey Justice* (London, 1619), p. 232. In later Tudor burglary indictments it was not uncommon for the adjective 'mansion' to precede the noun 'house' as a description of the building feloniously entered. Presumably this was to emphasize to the petty jury that no barn, stable, or out-house was involved but rather the private living quarters of the family. I suspect the practice originated in a Tudor judge observing the note on *burglarie* at *Year Books, Liber Assisarum*, 22 Edward III pl. 95 where there is reference to theft 'hors de un meason ou mansion'.

54 *Calendar of Assize Records, Indictments, Elizabeth I*, for Essex, Kent, and Sussex.

3

TRIAL AND THE
VERDICT REVOLUTION

In outlining the nature and dimensions of the most common felonies some attention has been given to their incidence and the outcome of cases before the courts. We must now examine more closely the fluctuations in the rates of conviction and acquittal for felony in general in a greater number of geographical areas and periods of time. Then we may be able to address the dual problem of why it was these rates prevailed and the nature and mechanics of the trial process in the courts.

For the reign of Edward I, the time when the gaol delivery system became firmly established, there are figures to be obtained from the rolls and files for Wiltshire and London-Middlesex. The prisoners in the latter instance were in the gaol of Newgate and although the capital and its region may have provided the bulk there were a substantial number from the counties immediately surrounding London, namely Essex, Surrey, Kent, and Hertfordshire. As we have seen, the Wiltshire delivery records of 1275–1306 show a conviction rate of 26.3 per cent when it was robbery, and 25.4 per cent when it was burglary. Of those who committed homicide (murder or felonious slaying) 19.8 per cent were found guilty. These rates are not at all dissimilar to those for the Newgate prisoners, of whom 21 per cent were convicted of homicide, 27 per cent of burglary, and 31 per cent of what Pugh called 'theft', a category combining grand larceny and robbery.[1] From her investigation of crime between 1300 and 1348 in eight scattered English counties Hanawalt calculated a conviction rate of 22 per cent in regard to felonious larceny, 30.6 per cent where the offence was robbery and 31 per cent when it was burglary. Only where the crime was homicide was the percentage of those found guilty (12.4) significantly different from the figures Pugh drew from Edward I's reign. It is the homicide figures which are largely responsible for lowering slightly the overall conviction rate from 30 per cent for Pugh's Newgate cases and 25.8 per cent for his Wiltshire cases, to the 22.9 per cent which Hanawalt discovered for her counties. If we eliminate the figures she drew from three counties to the north and west of the Fosse Way then the overall conviction rate of the five counties remaining lay between 25 and 30 per cent. For the counties of England as a whole in the year 1348 Pike found a gaol delivery conviction rate of 24.6 per cent.[2]

The visitation of bubonic plague in 1348–9 brought not only changes in English economic life but also equally arresting alterations in conviction rates for felony. The percentage of accused who were convicted at a number of Essex peace sessions held between 1377 and 1380 was only 18.7 per cent yet the offences dealt with, of course, included a good number of trespasses, which always produced a higher number of convictions than the felonies. By the second half of Richard II's reign the rate had declined further. The research of K. Garay shows the percentage of accused in the English counties as a whole who were convicted at gaol delivery of felony between 1388 and 1399 was just over 13. Were we to include, as Garay does not, those of the accused who claimed their clergy the conviction rate was still a mere 15.2 per cent. Of the six assize circuits the home counties had the highest rate at 20.4 per cent, the Oxford circuit was second at 18.3 per cent, and the south-western third at 17.2. The first decade of the reign of Henry IV seems to have produced a similar level of convictions: Garay discovered an overall rate of just over 14 per cent but she did not examine the records of the northern circuit for this period and we may fairly surmise a conviction rate for the whole of England at about 15 or 16 per cent. This would be very similar in fact to the level in the later years of Richard II's reign. One notable difference between conviction rates in Richard's reign and those of his successor lay in the number of persons found guilty of homicide. In Richard's last decade these amounted to 22 per cent but in 1399–1409 to only just over 12 per cent.[3]

The decline in convictions for felony apparently continued into the two succeeding reigns and it may have even accelerated in pace. Investigations into the gaol delivery records of the south-western circuit (the counties of Cornwall, Devon, Somerset, Dorset, Wiltshire, and Hampshire) of the period 1416–30 reveal an overall conviction rate of only 10 per cent. In the last six years of Henry V's reign those suspected felons who were found guilty amounted to 13 per cent of the total who were arraigned before the justices, and in the first eight years of his son's reign they totalled a mere 9 per cent. This, we may note, was in the region which in the last decade of Richard II's reign had had the third highest rate among the circuits. Examination of the conviction rates for different categories of felony in the period 1416–30 shows homicides found guilty most frequently (18 per cent) and then, in descending order, burglars (12 per cent), robbers (10 per cent), and those who indulged in felonious theft (8 per cent).[4]

The early years of Henry VI's reign may have been the low point for felony convictions in the later middle ages. The eastern circuit, which in the period 1399–1409 had ranked third highest of six for the percentage of convictions recorded (at a mere 9.56 per cent of persons arraigned) increased this rate threefold in the gaol delivery records of 1437–9. These provided in the case of the most prevalent types of felony (i.e. homicide, burglary, robbery, and grand larceny) 'guilty' verdicts in 33.2 per cent of instances. The rolls of the same circuit for 1440–1 show this was no temporary aberration: in the later years those found guilty amounted to 35.4 per cent. We notice that in these records felonies which involved violence or threat of violence were much more likely to bring conviction than other crimes. Indeed those found guilty of homicide equalled in number those found not guilty. In regard to robbery the rolls for 1440–1 show no fewer than 13 of the 22 persons who were arraigned for that crime found guilty (59.1 per cent) and only 8 acquitted.[5] The northern circuit in the last decade of Richard II's reign had had the highest acquittal rate for felony in England and the exceedingly low level of convictions (4.98 per cent) in Northumberland, Westmorland and Cumberland in the period 1439–60 has recently been emphasized.[6] There are indications that the attitudes of petty juries in these border counties were somewhat different from those in other parts of the country. The conviction rate in Yorkshire in these years was certainly very different from that in the extreme north. For homicide, burglary, robbery, and grand larceny taken together the rate was as high as 36.9 per cent, a remarkable figure considering that in the earlier fourteenth century the rate had been a lowly 13.7 per cent, and that in the 1420s and early 1430s it seems to have been just over 22 per cent. Those found guilty of homicide amounted to 32.6 per cent of those arraigned for that offence.[7] It seems undeniable that from perhaps about the middle of the 1430s English petty juries began to lose their erstwhile strong reluctance to convict.

For the historian who relies on evidence from late medieval gaol delivery records the year 1460 is really the terminating point. Apart from palatinate records and, for the earlier sixteenth century, those of certain Welsh counties, there is no substantial body of similar evidence to turn to until the gaol delivery records of Middlesex and the home counties' circuit recommence in the second half of the sixteenth century. It is true that gaol delivery files from the late fifteenth and early sixteenth centuries have survived for a number of towns but the total of cases contained therein are probably too few to enable us to reach any firm conclusions about conviction rates in general. The extant gaol delivery records of Elizabeth's reign are from an area of England, the south-east, in regard to which historians have been wont to argue that the prevailing rate of conviction even in the fourteenth century was considerably higher than that in counties remote from London.[8] Even when we allow for this particular peculiarity the degree of increase over late medieval levels seems remarkable. There appears to have occurred between the middle years of the fifteenth century and the later years of the sixteenth a rise in the number of those found guilty of felony of between 50 and 80 per cent. Thus the Kent gaol delivery records for the period 1559–72 in regard to crimes of grand larceny, robbery, burglary, rape, and felonious homicide provide a conviction rate of 56.5 per cent. Of those persons indicted for the various types of theft and felonious homicide during the same years in Sussex and on whom petty juries returned a verdict 54.2 per cent were found guilty, while in Essex the rate was as high as 63.6 per cent.[9] This change from a conviction rate of say just over one in three of persons accused to, in the case of Essex at least, nearly two out of three, must surely have amounted to a virtual revolution in criminal law administration. In the later middle ages the person arraigned for felony could reckon on having a good chance of acquittal; in the later sixteenth century he probably knew he was likely to be convicted. It can be argued that this is one of the very few features which truly distinguished life in early modern England from that in the late medieval period.

Contributing greatly to the vagaries of the felony conviction rate, especially in the late medieval period, were appeals. Their role in regard to accusation we have already noticed: appellees still amounted to about 10 per cent of persons arraigned in the fourteenth century and the first half of the fifteenth, only to virtually disappear before the reign of Elizabeth. In regard to verdicts of guilty, however, they played a much bigger part, whose significance grew steadily. In the thirteenth century appeals appear to have resulted in no more convictions, measured proportionately, than did indictments. The extant Wiltshire gaol delivery records of Edward I's reign show a mere 24 persons appealed where the verdict is known. Of these a mere five were convicted, a percentage of 20.8 and 5 per cent less than the rate of convictions overall. The surviving Norfolk gaol delivery rolls of the period 1308–16 show that of the 48 persons who were appealed and whose cases proceeded as far as a verdict, 15 were set free and 14 were found guilty; the conviction rate thus being 29 per cent.[10] The extant records of the Yorkshire gaol delivery sessions between 1399 and 1407 contain references to 43 persons on whom verdicts were returned on private appeals. Of these 29 were convicted (67.4 per cent) and 14 were found not guilty (32.6 per cent). In the south-western circuit rolls of the period 1416–30 only 11 of the 47 appellees (23.4 per cent) were found guilty by the juries but this was a much higher proportion than among those indicted (9 per cent).[11] This period appears to have seen the lowest level of conviction in three centuries. In the files and rolls of the eastern circuit for 1437–9, in contrast, as many as 27 out of 29 persons appealed were found guilty while in those of 1440–1, in the 17 cases where the verdicts are known to us, 15 persons were convicted, a total overall of 91.3 per cent. For the years 1439–60 Yorkshire provides a larger sample and the rate is lower although still very high. Out of 92 persons concerning whom the verdict is known who were appealed in private suits no fewer than 68 were found guilty (73.9 per cent).[12]

To discover conviction rates of this magnitude in the middle ages is quite startling, yet there is a greater shock. Since those who were appealed were so frequently convicted the percentage of persons found guilty on indictment was necessarily less, sometimes substantially less, than the rates for convictions on both types of accusation combined as have been given above. Thus if we deduct the convictions on appeals from the overall number of persons found guilty in the gaol delivery records of the Willoughby roll of 1329–35, the rate drops from

15.2 per cent to 10.1 per cent; those found guilty on the south-western circuit in 1416–30 drops similarly from 10 per cent to 7.6 per cent; those in the eastern circuit records of 1437–9 decline more dramatically from 31 to 18.5 per cent, and those who appear in the same records of 1440–1 diminish from 29 to 20.8 per cent. If the convictions of appellees are deducted from the overall total of convictions in the Yorkshire gaol delivery records of 1439–60 the percentage of accused found guilty decreases from 41 to 23.[13] Such arithmetic brings out much more clearly the revolution in the verdicts returned by juries which occurred between about 1460 and 1560, for in fact the rate of convictions against those indicted increased in that period not by 50 to 80 per cent but by something in the order of an enormous 150 per cent. To all appearances the conviction rate of those indicted in England between the Black Death and the reign of Edward IV never surpassed 25 per cent and indeed this level was only achieved after a hundred years of fluctuation at levels considerably lower. Yet, while indictments largely failed to produce convictions for felony, appeals by private parties, as distinct from appeals by approvers, were in the fourteenth and fifteenth centuries highly and increasingly successful in achieving them. Furthermore the success was not limited to one or two particular types of felony: appeals of homicide, murder, grand larceny, burglary, and robbery were equally likely to result in convictions. How are we to account for the vagaries of medieval conviction rates and the startling alteration which occurred in the sixteenth century? Some contributing factors have already been mentioned in the previous chapter, yet before we can turn to evaluating the relative weight of these and others we need to try to understand the essential nature of the English criminal trial as it was between 1300 and the mid-sixteenth century.

Recent research on the criminal trial in the period under discussion has tended to focus on the composition of the jury which provided the verdicts, the 'petit' jury as it was coming to be called by the mid-fourteenth century.[14] Contemporary commentators on the nature and functioning of the English criminal law had little to say about the jury and even less about the verdicts and the general rate of acquittal and conviction. We have noticed above the high incidence of acquittal verdicts yet not a single legal commentator, nor even indeed any traveller or chronicler of the period, thought fit to say the conviction rate was low or that men and women were being acquitted who should not have been.[15] Not until the reign of Elizabeth I did a writer suggest the system of criminal law was failing to punish miscreants, and even then he did not put the blame on the petty jury.[16] However, those in political office were likely to have been concerned that a good number of felony suspects should be convicted, as the correspondence of Thomas Cromwell clearly shows.[17] Yet they too were careful to refrain from criticizing openly the prevailing generosity of petty jurors. Individual juries might be admonished for a particular acquittal (returning a 'not guilty' verdict contrary to the evidence, acquitting against their 'consciences'), but those in authority who must have known of sessions where a very high ratio of acquittals to convictions had resulted never thought fit to comment in writing. Thomas More's asperities were directed against the accusatory part of the trial process not the arraignment. He appears to have accepted, and he pointed out so did the judges, that it should never be enquired how a petty jury came to its verdict.[18]

Modern historians, naturally enough, have been less inclined to allow the decision-making process of the trial jurors to remain a mystery. They have chiefly attempted to throw light on the matter by analysing the membership of the juries, concentrating on the social status and place of domicile of the individual jurors. It has been argued that while it was rare for most of the jurors to be inhabitants of the accused's hundred very few felons were tried by juries which did not contain one juror from there. Two-thirds of the time, in fact, there were at least two such, this arrangement being standard when there was more than a single accused from the hundred in question. Jurors therefore, so the argument goes, must have placed a great deal of reliance on the information provided to them by those of their fellows who had some knowledge of the circumstances of the offences at issue through their familiarity with the 'common fame' in the locality where the misdeeds had been perpetrated: the garnering of local gossip in fact.[19] Such information was, apparently, the more readily available because quite often the jurors were local petty officeholders and similar.[20]

Parallel research has produced the argument that, on the contrary, the jurors were drawn from the relevant hundred not in ones and twos but as the major part of any trial jury although, admittedly, there seem to have been occasions when the jury as finally sworn, because of rampant absenteeism, might have to be composed of 'talesman' (substitutes) chosen from lesser officials who happened to be present at the sessions.[21] These men, it seems reasonable to assume, would only rarely be inhabitants of the hundred where the offence had been committed. Now it is quite possible that these two views of jury composition are complementary rather than contradictory, since the second was formulated from a study of late fourteenth-century jurors while the first was based on an examination of jurors of the earlier fifteenth century. The difference in the findings could have been caused by the time-frame of each study, men from the neighbourhood of the crime becoming increasingly reluctant to fulfil their obligations as jurors, which compelled the crown to select local officials for the task more and more. Providing we accept the premise that jurors who did not live in the locality of the crime, because they were less certain of the circumstances, were less likely to find suspects guilty, then there is support for this argument in the fact that felony conviction rates appear to have declined quite considerably in the period between about 1380 and 1430.[22]

Commissions of gaol delivery of the fourteenth and fifteenth centuries usually contained a section wherein the sheriff was instructed to produce at the sessions not only the prisoners in his charge but also, as petty jurors, twenty-four knights or other proven and law-worthy men from each hundred, who were not related to the suspects.[23] The emphasis was on proximity of residence and substantial possessions, as commentators confirm. Fortescue held that petty jurors were to be drawn from the neighbourhood of the vill where the misdeed was committed, while Coke said the jurors should be dwellers in the town or parish involved, and Lambard referred to them as the accused's 'owne Countreymen, Neighbours and Peeres'. According to Sir Thomas Smith the jurors should be substantial yeomen living around the place, or at least the hundred, of the crime.[24] That in the later fifteenth and the sixteenth centuries the crown was not ready either in theory or practice to waive the requirements concerning the trial jurors' place of residence seems likely, even if there were individual sheriffs who ignored the rules. However, concessions may have been made in practice in regard to the wealth of jurors since the records of the later sixteenth century assure us that by then the juror of substance was becoming a rarity. Many petty jurors, it appears, were poor men serving for payment in one form or another, or men who had been dragooned into the job by sheriffs and their officers.[25]

So far we have been considering trial juries in cases where the accused was indicted, but we must not omit to give attention to the jurors whose job it was to decide appeals. Historians of medieval English criminal law have tended to assume that the rules and practices concerning the status of petty jurors applied equally whether the accusation was made by indictment or by appeal yet, in fact, the matter is in some doubt. There are grounds for suspecting that in the later middle ages appeal cases were tried separately from indictment cases. A *Year Book* case of Easter term 1464 shows the justices trying appeals before lunch and the 'gaol delivery' cases after.[26] If appeals were tried apart then it is quite possible that the juries were of a different composition. There is evidence from the mid-thirteenth century of appellees having the opportunity to obtain a specially chosen trial jury. This they were allowed to return for a usual payment of half a mark. There are also in the same records, we should note, examples of persons, who had been indicted, similarly paying the crown in order to have inquests of a particular type.[27] From these indictment cases, which appear to have been peculiar to the thirteenth century, we learn something about the nature of such special juries. In one instance the indictee paid for one to be drawn from two hundreds, while in another he paid 'in order to have a good inquest', which presumably meant containing jurors of substance. In a third case a woman charged with larceny paid the big sum of twenty shillings for an extra large jury comprising two groups of twelve men plus the representatives of the four neighbouring vills. Similar instances of special juries paid for by indictees, appellees, or even appellors have not been reported by scholars working in fourteenth- or fifteenth-century records, but the matter is by no means closed. There is no evidence of indictees being able to obtain special juries, but the revival, or at least the continuing popularity, of appeals of felony in the later middle ages may well have owed something to the fact that the selection of the members of the trial juries was influenced in some way by the appellor, who by that period must usually have been a fairly wealthy person. There is a case of particular significance in the *Year Books* of Edward II's reign. An appellor non-suited and the appellee was then arraigned at the king's suit. Presumably because it was a point of law the accused was able to obtain counsel (a 'clerk'), who argued that the original panel of jurors had been summoned for a suit of party and that therefore his client should now be tried by a new jury since he was being arraigned at the suit of the king.[28] The plea was allowed and the accused was tried by a new jury. From this we may conclude that in the early fourteenth century juries in appeal cases, in contrast with those which tried indictees, were expected to favour the party suing rather than the accused.

The report of the case does not make it clear if the appellor had made a payment to obtain this favourable jury or if it was normal for special jurors, possibly of higher status, to be empanelled in appeal cases. It may have been the case that the cost of bringing an appeal included a fee for the provision of such a jury. If appellors were able, in some periods at least, to obtain juries different from those used at the arraignment of persons who had been indicted, it would help to explain one of the most noticeable trends in late medieval felony verdict statistics, the high conviction rate in appeal cases. With the employment of a 'special' jury and with the victim/accuser being of necessity present in court at the arraignment it is no wonder that petty juries inclined towards conviction. The number of appeals which came before the late medieval courts were, of course, never more than a fraction of the total of indictments heard there and we must attribute this largely to the expenses involved and the penalties for failure to secure a conviction for appellors.

The law allowed those who were arraigned for felony to challenge the jurors chosen to try them. The accused might base his challenge on the fact that the jurors were not drawn from the hundred where the crime had been committed, or that they had been members of the indicting jury, or that they were related to the victim, or that their wealth was insufficient.[29] However, there was no need for the person indicted of felony, nor an appellee, to state the reason for his challenge. He was allowed to make it against thirty-five potential trial jurors without saying why. The rule was that such a peremptory challenge was permissible when a person was on trial for his life. An oddity of the law was that the accused might challenge some of those selected for the jury peremptorily but others by giving cause.[30] Richard Littleton in his reading on the criminal law, given perhaps in 1493, implied that the peremptory challenge was the normal one. The accused, he said, did not have sufficient courage to show a particular cause because their lives were at stake.[31] Thomas Smith does not mention the peremptory challenge. He merely states that the accused can say nothing against the jurors because he does not know them. In the gaol delivery records instances of juror challenge are rare, as they are elsewhere. This may have been because they only secured a place in legal records if they were made by appellees. One of these, instructively, shows a challenge by an appellee against a jury of the hundred of Diss (Norfolk) on the grounds that several jurors did not come from or possess anything in the hundred where the crime had been committed.[32] This is the only instance of a challenge to be found in some 300 Norfolk cases recorded in the gaol delivery rolls of 1433–41; there are no examples at all in the records of over 400 Yorkshire felony cases of 1439–60.[33]

If the composition of the late medieval jury has not yet been explained totally satisfactorily by historians neither has the use made in criminal cases of witnesses and evidence. That witnesses were allowed to testify in criminal cases in the late middle ages is a thesis which has not yet gained general acceptance.[34] Until relatively recently it was widely held that witnesses only appeared at criminal trials after the middle of the sixteenth century, a view which derived from the absence of references to witnesses in medieval criminal court records. Yet for Thomas More, writing around 1530, witnesses and their testimony were a common feature of treason and murder cases, and also figured in instances of 'more single' (i.e. noteworthy) felony. He pointed out that they frequently appeared before justices of the peace (presumably when the latter examined victim and suspect) and that their depositions were given in evidence to the trial jurors, who would ask the witnesses at the bar to inform them. More went as far as to say that the jurors would ignore strong testimony by witnesses at their peril, since the king's council was ready to investigate obvious cases of such neglect.[35]

There can be little doubt as to the accuracy of More's comments. A collection of documents relating to the trial of a band of Devonshire robbers sent to Thomas Cromwell in 1538 demonstrates the use of two confessions, four reported statements and five depositions taken at examination as evidence. No fewer than seventeen witnesses gave testimony against a suspected murderer in London early in 1533.[36] A Star Chamber case of 1516 refers to evidence about a homicide being given by five witnesses to, in turn, a coroner's jury, a petty jury at gaol delivery sessions, and then a similar jury in the king's bench. The conciliar record of a trial for perjury of jurors who had falsely acquitted a robber at a delivery of Oxford castle gaol in July 1498 noted that the jurors had done so despite proof by several trustworthy witnesses that the accused was guilty; and there is extant a reference to a similar acquittal at Bury St Edmunds (the witnesses being described as giving plain and manifest evidence) at about the same date.[37] Some indication that the use of witnesses was frequent rather than occasional in common law criminal procedure in the reign of Henry VII is offered by the statute 19 Henry VII c.4. This act stipulated that any person who gave 'open evidence' at sessions in regard to someone he had seen using a crossbow for the purpose of killing the king's deer, evidence which resulted in a conviction, should have ten shillings as a reward. 'Open evidence' we may take as meaning testimony in court before the petty jury, and the manner in which the word 'evidence' figures in the statute seems to indicate a well-established association with prosecution at the king's suit.[38] Fortescue, writing no doubt of the period when he was chief justice of the king's bench, tells us somewhat obscurely that witnesses were permitted to give testimony in criminal cases 'in the presence of twelve trustworthy men of the neighbourhood in which the fact in question occurred'. Although we cannot be certain it seems likely Fortescue was referring here to the petty jury rather than that of indictment.[39]

References to the giving of evidence at arraignment in reports of particular cases are few before the reign of Henry VII, but happily they are clear in their meaning and illuminate the matter greatly. The record of a case in the king's bench in 1461 shows the victim of a robbery intending to appear in court to give evidence against the miscreant; a common enough situation, we may suppose, but one which court rolls universally omit. We know of this instance only because the victim was threatened with recriminations by a third party while on his way to court.[40] A case from 1407 is even more revealing. The bailiff of the liberty of the Savoy, apparently in attendance at the court of the steward and marshal of the household as part of his official duties, was instructed by the court to tell the jurors on oath what he knew about an offence for which a man was being arraigned on an indictment.[41] The case provides a clear example of a third party, not the victim, giving evidence, but it was someone who happened to be in court as part of his official duties. Furthermore, so it seems, he did not offer testimony on his own initiative but on the court's orders. For the historian what is lacking before the later fifteenth century is an unequivocal reference to a non-victim, an observer of the crime who was not a law officer, giving testimony to a petty jury. That they in fact frequently did so, however, seems very likely.

Persons who, intent on securing the indictment of a suspect, informed the justices about the crime or told their tale to indicting jurors, might, if it could be shown they had discussed their information informally before indictment with either the former or the latter, be subject to actions of conspiracy. Whether such suits could be brought (for example on the grounds that the witness was in cahoots with the victim) with reasonable prospects of success by the person acquitted against an observer of a crime, who gave testimony at the actual arraignment, is not clear but there do not seem to be any such cases in the *Year Books*. Very likely those who testified at a criminal trial were protected from actions of conspiracy. As we have noticed above in regard to such actions against those responsible for persuading juries to indict, the judges were ready to argue that if a man had taken an oath to inform the court truthfully, or if he was liable to amercement if he did not come to inform, or if the felon was accused by common fame, or if proclamation had been made that anyone who wished to 'show anything for the king' should be listened to, or even if he happened to be in court for some reason and the judges told him to give evidence, he was protected from such a suit.[42] Only the third of these 'protections' (common fame) appears to have been connected solely with those who informed juries of indictment. The other four seem to have had a more direct application to the trial witness than the latter.

Proclamations inviting those wanting to 'show anything for the king' to participate in the prosecution of the accused are worthy of closer study not only in regard to accusation but particularly in regard to trial. It was common form in late medieval commissions of gaol delivery, and in subsequent royal commands pertaining to them, for an order to be given to the sheriff of the relevant bailiwick to proclaim that all who wanted to sue, complain about, or prosecute the prisoners soon to be arraigned should be in attendance at the sessions.[43] Even where there was no specific royal invitation to prosecute, the justices of gaol delivery in the course of the arraignment might have proclamation made (presumably in the court precincts) summoning such persons to come forward.[44] Who were these 'prosecutors' and what did they intend? If there was held simultaneously with the gaol delivery trials an indictment sessions, which fed in indictments and suspects to the former, then the 'prosecutors' in question might, perhaps, be offering bills of indictment.[45] Despite the use of the verb *conqueri* (to complain) in the commissions it is not likely these 'prosecutors' were being invited to offer *querelae* since the sessions were of gaol delivery not oyer and terminer. Nor is it probable that the commissions were inviting victims of felony to bring appeals at such a late stage, at least not for determination at the current sessions. Rather the precept to the sheriff must have been intended mainly to ensure warning was given to those who had already begun appeals to be there to pursue them, and to tell those whose suffering and loss were already the subject of indictments that they should attend. The presence of appellors was essential if they were to win their suits and those indicted of felony were unlikely in the middle ages to be convicted unless the victim (or in homicide cases his kinfolk) were in court, as has been noted above. Victims of felony in cases where the miscreants were accused by indictment, if they obeyed the proclamation, must have been in court to testify about the offence and to identify the felon. They would be motivated by a desire for revenge, to see the miscreant got his deserts, for they would certainly have known there was scant chance of having the stolen goods restored to them by the court.

In addition to those indicted and appellees there was also present at gaol delivery sessions, as we have seen, a third type of felony suspect: the person who had been arrested but was not formally accused. When a suspect appeared before them and he had not been indicted or appealed the justices of gaol delivery in the mid-fourteenth century would order the sheriff to enquire about him in order to discover, as a roll of 1336 succinctly put it, 'if anyone wished to indict him'. In the 1330s this was apparently done at the sheriff's next tourn but by the early 1350s it was done immediately.[46] In the 1370s the job of conducting an inquest (*inquisicio de fama et gestu*) into the suspect was shared between the sheriff and the justices of the peace, but by the 1390s it had become the task of the latter alone.[47] The intention in holding such an inquest was still, late in the reign of Edward III, to see if anyone wished to indict the suspect, but by the early fifteenth century specific reference to this line of enquiry had disappeared. The records of that time simply state the justices of the peace have enquired and found nothing bad concerning the suspect. Whereupon, so we are told, the court has ordered a proclamation to be made that if anyone wished to prosecute the suspect he should come and be heard. When, as was nearly always the case, no suer or 'prosecutor' appeared the suspect was freed on finding surety or was freed after his good fame had been attested.[48] There were, of course, occasions when the suspect was in some way found to be of bad fame; in that case he was remitted to gaol.[49] By the middle of the fifteenth century references to enquiries were no longer inserted in the records – only the proclamation and the lack of a would-be prosecutor.[50] Perhaps this truncation was only in the verbal formula used by the clerk and not in the process itself, but we cannot be certain.

The importance of these clues to the handling of unappealed and unindicted suspects at gaol delivery in the current context is that they reveal a number of stages in the trial process where the giving of testimony by witnesses, although never featuring in the records, seems to have been very likely. The fifteenth-century records tell us that the good fame of the *captus* was 'testified' to. Until that time the verb only appears in court records very infrequently. It is to be found on occasion in the crown pleas of the thirteenth-century eyres. Those testifying seem to have been officials and they were reporting that, for one reason or another, a suspect could not be brought before the court.[51] In the fourteenth century the verb again appears to have been connected with law officers reporting back to the court. But by the fifteenth century, when it appears in court records, the word 'testify' seems rather to have links with the use of witnesses: persons who knew the facts about a crime stating those facts, and most likely in answer to questions put by justices.[52]

Among the witnesses who testified must frequently have been the reeve and four men of the township where the felony had been committed. Usually at the end of a commission of gaol delivery instructions were given for the sheriff to ensure that these men should attend the sessions. Such precepts can be found in commissions from Edward II's reign onwards and are present in nearly all those surviving from the fifteenth century.[53] The references in other parts of the records to the reeve and the four men of the vill are sited in such a way as to suggest they played an important, if not vital, role in the process of delivery by proclamation. Once the appearance in court of the suspects and whether, at the time of arrest, they were carrying mainour have been noted, there is frequently a comment to the effect that no reeve and men are present from this or that vill, which is therefore amerced (usually half a mark). Then comes reference to the making of proclamation, the asking for prosecution, a comment that no one has brought charges against the suspect, testimony he is of good or bad fame, and finally dismissal *sine die* or remittal to gaol. Reference to the fining of those vills, whose representatives were absent, in the middle of these procedural notes surely implies that the reeve and the four men were expected to play a vital part in the process.

Very likely they would be able to provide testimony concerning the arrest of any suspect in the vill (the suspiciousness of the person's behaviour, whether he carried mainour), testimony which they could offer in support of any bill of indictment put in in response to the proclamation, although we should not expect them to put in such a bill themselves. They would be very well suited for service on a *de fama* inquest, or for testifying before it, since they would know the suspect's (their own neighbour) background better by the fifteenth century, perhaps, than the petty juror did.[54] Their duties, as the crown saw it in 1417, were to 'testify and inform the court what suspicion of felony there is against the person taken', which fits in very well with what we have surmized from the general nature of *captus* cases.[55] The king's instructions to sheriffs also occasionally make reference to the duties of the reeve and the four men but much more obliquely. Thus we are told the reason they should attend the gaol delivery sessions was 'in order to do those things on behalf of the king, which will be told to them'.[56] This too rather supports the interpretation of their duties just suggested, although it is also possible they were expected to be available to give evidence at the trial itself, if such materialized. Thus in the fifteenth century their role was clearly an active one and the way the references to their duties were phrased hints at a growing interference by the crown in the prosecuting of criminals.

In the sixteenth century evidence came before the trial jurors not only from witnesses appearing at the bar in person but often in the form of written depositions, which were the answers made by suspects to justices of the peace who had examined them soon after arrest.[57] Thomas Smith tells us that the examining justice, as was required by statutes of Mary's reign, bound over the victim of the felony, the peace officer who had made the arrest (if there was one), and anyone who could give evidence about the crime, to be present at the arraignment. Although there was no binding-over rule in his time, Thomas More, writing in 1533, tells us similarly that the depositions of witnesses who had appeared before justices of the peace together with 'such contrary othes and all the cyrcumstaunces therwith' were given in evidence to the jury at the bar of the gaol delivery court.[58] We may add that examinations (i.e. depositions) of witnesses might be offered as evidence even if no witnesses were present in person. Witnesses, who no doubt had to pay their own expenses, must have been reluctant to appear before both the indicting and the trial jury. How many years previous to More's time in public life examinations were being taken by justices of the peace and used in evidence is unclear, for references in records and in the writings of legal commentators are virtually non-existent. Indeed the only mention of examination in regard to felony in the *Year Books* of the fifteenth century appears to be some comments made in discussion of an action of conspiracy in 1481. Catesby, a king's serjeant, is reported as saying that when a man, before the quarter sessions, tells a justice of the peace how he has been robbed by a particular person and informs him about the circumstances, the justices can put questions to him and he will answer on oath.[59] This would be how a deposition originated. The case, unfortunately, tells us nothing about examination of the suspect or of witnesses.

Should examination of felony suspects have originated considerably earlier, as surely it must have, its origins are probably as likely to be found in a statute, royal ordinance, or administrative order by the crown as in what might be termed the slow and natural development of the criminal law, or in 'construction' of the law by the professional judges. The very nature of examination, questioning by justices outside the arraignment, and therefore not in public view, was hardly in keeping with the spirit of the common law and may well have been introduced through a policy decision by the government. In fact it seems likely a critical decision was made by those responsible for the statute 34 Edward III c.1. This act commanded the newly titled justices of the peace to enquire concerning pillagers and robbers, and to arrest and imprison those they discovered. Such discovery was to be achieved either by indictment or by suspicion, the latter being a new piece of terminology in the statute book. The act does not disclose what were the mechanics of discovery by suspicion but receiving reports from local officials or information from ordinary citizens, which deduction suggests was very likely the method, must have led to a vetting of the information through their questioning of the suspects, the arresting officials, and any witnesses.[60] The intention, most likely, would be to provide evidence, which, in the first place, would persuade a presenting jury to find a true bill, and secondly, probably in a somewhat later period, to help secure a conviction at arraignment. Although there were no other statutes of that period which stipulated or openly sanctioned the use of examination in regard to felony, there were such for trespass. The Statute of Labourers of 1351 ordered officials, when labourers were thought to be receiving excessive wages 'to enquire diligently by all good means', which strongly suggests examination. The findings were apparently to be used as evidence with which to obtain an indictment and a conviction. The act 2 Henry V st.1 c.4, designed similarly to deal with the problem of labourers' wages, gave authority to justices of the peace to examine employees and their masters on oath. Should a suspect admit the offence the justices of the peace would punish him forthwith.[61] Should he deny it he was probably arraigned in the normal manner, with, perhaps, the examination being offered by the crown in evidence. With examination being used as an actual method of trial in fifteenth-century England for certain types of trespass it had clearly taken root in the criminal law;[62] and if, because of English prejudice, constitutional bias, and particular statutes it would never be acceptable as a method of trial for offences which carried a sentence of death, its value as a simple instrument of prosecution must surely have been recognized and accepted by the professional judiciary.

Those who popularized the use of examinations as evidence may well have been the justices of the peace. Their power and opportunities to determine felonies waxed and waned in the later middle ages and so, necessarily, did their weight in medieval society, since he who sat in judgment in court was a valued ally in the upper class feuds of the time. Almost as important in maintaining or increasing their social prestige must have been the ability, through the taking of examinations, to increase the likelihood of achieving indictment and even conviction. Furthermore the certifying of the examinations to the justices of gaol delivery must have made their role in felony procedure more visible.[63] Examinations did not, of course, grow on bushes. Suspects had first to be discovered either by local law officers or by justices of the peace themselves, which sometimes must have necessitated detective work. Before 1555 there was no procedural rule enjoining the examination of felony suspects, and there was never any law limiting which justices might do so and on how many occasions. A case in Elizabeth's reign shows the justices of gaol delivery examining a suspect themselves subsequent to reading the deposition he had made at an earlier examination before justices of the peace.[64]

Thomas More, when writing about examinations of witnesses before justices of the peace being offered in evidence to the jury at the bar, added, as we have seen, the suggestive words 'with such contrary othes and all the cyrcumstaunces therwith'.[65] Presumably he meant that the justices of the peace examined the victim and those whom, through him, the arresting officers or common fame, they knew were knowledgeable about the offence; then they certified to the justices of gaol delivery all the examinations, that is to say every one, not merely those which tended to prove the accusation but those which threw doubt on it as well.[66] More's tribute to judicial fairness needs qualification. The appearance at arraignment of witnesses whose testimony favoured the accused must have been largely by chance, that is to say because the crown erroneously believed the testimony would help to secure a conviction.[67] There is little to suggest that before the mid-sixteenth century suspects were allowed at their trials to have witnesses named by themselves come and give testimony, and there was no likelihood that examinations tending to disprove the charge would be offered as evidence. At his trial for treason in 1554 Sir Nicholas Throckmorton made great play with these practices of the law, pointing out that the queen had recently commanded that in crown cases witnesses for the accused should be allowed to testify: that 'whatsoever could be brought in favour of the subject should be admitted to be heard'.[68] Despite bombastic denials by the bench on that occasion

Throckmorton may well have been correct for we know the queen said the same a short time later when the case of Dionysius Thimbleby was reported to her. The case is instructive. Thimbleby had been convicted of highway robbery 'contrary to common justice'. He had asked for his own witnesses to be sworn and permitted to give evidence, but was refused. The justices stated categorically that no witness was to be sworn and examined against the queen in cases of treason or felony 'the same being first duly proved for the queen by diver witnesses'. They were not saying witnesses should never be allowed in support of the accused but rather that they should not be where witnesses could be found whose testimony strongly supported the indictment. Yet the judges admitted that in the past such defence witnesses had, in fact, been heard, although they were never allowed to testify on oath. They admitted further that despite this limitation it had not been uncommon for the accused in such cases 'to unjustly escape their condign punishment'.[69]

Under Elizabeth defence witnesses continued to be permitted at times. John Udall, on trial for seditious words (a felony) in 1590, offered to produce witnesses to testify on his behalf. The judges forbade it on that occasion but a man indicted of murder in 1596 was reported as having been convicted because none of his witnesses was at hand, the sense being that they would have been heard if they had been.[70] In a gaol delivery case in Kent in 1580 two gentlemen accused of robbery were allowed to have witnesses to their innocence giving testimony, but only viva voce and probably on account of direct intervention by the privy council. An answer given to the duke of Norfolk at his trial for treason in 1572 appears to indicate that if the accused made request for particular witnesses or proofs (examinations, depositions) to be heard in court the crown would consider it.[71] All that we can safely conclude about defence witnesses in regard to felony cases is that they were not categorically forbidden; they might occasionally be allowed to testify because the crown approved or because it was slack in safeguarding its own interests.

The question of whether there was direct crown involvement in the prosecution of felons at arraignment in the medieval period is difficult to answer. In the thirteenth and fourteenth centuries the bench seems to have acted as prosecutor. In treason cases there is clear evidence from the early fifteenth century onwards of law officers of the king, king's serjeants, the king's attorney and similar, undertaking the task.[72] References to their presence and activity at felony cases are few and do not illuminate their role very much. There is a mention in a report of a homicide case heard in the king's bench early in Henry VI's reign of the king's attorney (attorney general) being present in court. The accused turned approver but then confessed his appeal to be false. Whereupon the king's attorney demanded of the justices he should not be hanged, but arraigned again. Despite some judicial opposition that was what happened. The king's attorney is also recorded as having been in court, indeed at the bar, in a case involving appeal of homicide in 1481.[73] Whether in either instance he acted in a prosecutorial capacity is not revealed. There are brief references in the 1440s to clerks of the crown at quarter sessions acting as king's attorney and prosecuting indictments and appeals.

Only in the later years of Elizabeth's reign do we find a clear example of a crown attorney prosecuting in a felony case and even then the crime was one falling within More's category of 'single' (singular) felony although it was tried at a Surrey gaol delivery sessions. The case in point was one of seditious libel, brought under the statute 23 Elizabeth I c.2, and the accused was the puritan John Udall (1590).[74] The attorney for the crown in this instance was a Mr Daulton, who in businesslike fashion explained what law had been broken and how he intended to make his proof. Then the clerk of the court was instructed by the justices to read out the depositions as and when Daulton requested. Daulton's forensic manner was in no way tentative but rather practised and assured and with a clear strategic plan. He had obviously had much experience. He began with an account of puritanism and of puritan versions of the book of common prayer before proceeding 'to the proof of the points in the indictment'. He addressed his remarks directly to the jury: 'You of the jury consider this', he said several times. At several points in the trial he introduced evidence against the accused which was no more than hearsay. The role of the two justices, who throughout treated Daulton with deference, appears to have been firstly to insist Udall should answer each of the points which Daulton made against him, secondly to explain the statute, and thirdly to put an occasional question to the accused themselves. One of these was a simple demand to say if he had indeed committed the offence.[75] Overall the impression given by the Udall trial is that the crown attorney was in complete control of the prosecution with the judges merely acting as masters of ceremonies, an image which probably owes something to the political bearing of the case. We know from the records that also in attendance at the trial were a number of Surrey justices of the peace, but the contemporary account fails to give them mention.[76] The presence of these local magistrates at assize arraignments seems to have been largely ornamental (i.e. for prestige and propaganda purposes) although they may have been of occasional use in explaining features of examinations which they had taken.

It has been argued that the key phase of the medieval and Tudor criminal trial, the part which was responsible for the conviction of many felons, was the altercation, which often occurred when the victim or witnesses came face to face with the accused in court.[77] In some trials this confrontation was delayed because depositions of the witnesses were introduced as evidence initially rather than the witnesses themselves. The latter were produced later on, perhaps in response to the accused's demand. The argument of the crown was that to prove guilt the appearance in person of a witness was not essential for 'the testimony of a man absent was sufficient, if it were proved to be his upon the oaths of others'.[78] Yet it must have been aware that should the witnesses not be present in person the accused might be able to make capital out of their absence by asking why this was so. Thomas Smith tells us that normally, when facing the accused, the victims would say something like 'I know thee well ynough, thou robbedst me in such a place, thou beatest mee, thou tookest my horse from mee, and my purse, thou had then such a coate and such a man in thy companie'. The suspect would then deny he was the miscreant and so the victim, much incensed, 'telleth al that he can say'.[79] With his emotions aroused the victim was perhaps able to recount details of the circumstances of the crime in a way which had a big impact on the trial jury. Those who had been present when the offence was committed, or when the suspect was captured, then gave their evidence, apparently *in extenso*.

This confrontational free-for-all, so graphically described by Smith, and indeed the forensic style of crown prosecutors, provoke the question of how dominant in their courts were the justices who tried felonies. In the thirteenth century, it seems, justices who heard and determined felonies conducted a trial, even where the suit was a private one (an appeal) as if they were subjecting the accused to what became known later as an examination. Their behaviour was a mixture of bullying, contempt, and wheedling. They sneered at the accused's explanations, and they tried to elicit an admission of felonious deeds and information about accomplices. They would advise the suspect to think of God and tell the truth so he might the more easily have mercy, although whether this was to be obtained from the court or the deity was not specified. As in the sixteenth century they might use rhetoric to emphasize the heinousness of a particular type of crime, such as petty treason.[80] The time available for the hearing of each case was just as brief in the thirteenth century as in the sixteenth, if we judge by the frequent admonitions by the bench to the accused not to waste the court's time and by recent calculations in regard to the number of prisoners arraigned per day. For trials of felony in the fourteenth and fifteenth centuries we have even less information to draw on, although there survive lawyers' collections of exemplary cases which demonstrate procedural options and knotty points of law, and which provide in places the supposed comments of the justices. The latter declare what the law was, approve or deny claims by the accused for particular procedural benefits, and correct errors by bailiffs, sheriffs and other officers.[81] There is, however, no hint of the accused being questioned by the bench. In such illustrations of court process, written no doubt to instruct aspirant lawyers (and in one case, perhaps, to show the wisdom of a particular judge), the justices appear as virtual court moderators rather than petty tyrants: but this could be because the writers were not interested in what might be called the style of justice's questions or the nature of the accused's responses but rather in the niceties and their outcome. Because of this absence of emotional overtones it is hard, therefore, to discern if the heavy exercise of judicial power did not exist or was the reverse, the merest common form and therefore unworthy of comment.

To try to establish the role of the justices at arraignment is important since it has been argued that in the later middle ages, because the petty jurors had personal knowledge of the circumstances of the crimes and criminals they tried, the justices, who did not, had to treat them with circumspection. In later Tudor times, in contrast, so the argument runs, petty jurors rarely possessed knowledge of the facts of the case themselves; they received their knowledge primarily from the evidence presented before them in court. Therefore the jurors' importance was lessened while that of the justices, who in the later sixteenth century were able to acquire knowledge of the circumstances of the crimes from witnesses who appeared there and particularly from the examinations of suspects, which were forwarded to the court, was enhanced.[82] To this thesis there are several objections to be raised. The first is that, as we have seen, those who tried felons must have been wont to receive examinations of the same from justices of the peace from the mid or even the early fifteenth century onwards, not merely from after 1555. Secondly, probably from as early as the later fourteenth century, the judges were able to acquire for themselves knowledge of the felons and felonies they were to try through the bills of indictment. The receiving of the latter, en route to the indicting jurors, was the task in the late medieval period of the justices of the peace (and occasionally of justices of oyer and terminer) rather than of the justices of gaol delivery. However, since the gaol delivery justices were appointed to the peace commissions of each county in their circuit, even if they did not themselves attend quarter sessions or the indicting sessions held simultaneously with the gaol delivery, they certainly had access by right to such bills.[83] They would also have probably heard how strongly each bill was 'followed', that is to say whether there was good testimony to support it. In regard to evidence presented by witnesses in court there is little doubt that it was being given before petty jurors from the early fifteenth century onwards and was not a novelty of the later Tudor period. However, it needs to be emphasized that one particular event of the Tudor age, but the earlier not the later part, the passing of the statute 21 Henry VIII c.11, must have greatly increased the number of victims appearing in court and thereby provided not only testimony but also opportunities for questioning and comment by the bench, which enabled it to demonstrate its authority more openly.[84] Having knowledge about the crime and the criminal before the trial progressed very far may have allowed the justices, by taking a more active role in the proceedings, to help achieve a higher rate of convictions. Yet the same factors (bills of indictment, examinations, witnesses, victim's presence) which provided them with the knowledge also influenced the petty jurors' decisions more directly. The justices' behaviour simply supplemented the procedural factors here and the latter were surely much more important in achieving convictions. However, to the lay public of the later sixteenth century and to those who commented on criminal trials the justices, who appeared more active at arraignment than hitherto, may have seemed the key factor in producing verdicts of 'guilty'.

Even if we set aside any knowledge of the felony and the felon which came to the petty jurors through the procedural improvements just noted, it is likely these men in the fifteenth and sixteenth centuries knew more about the offence and offender they were to try than has recently been allowed. The thesis has been offered that by that time most petty jurors, because they did not live in the neighbourhood where the offence occurred, knew little about the crime or the miscreant themselves but had access to the knowledge of one or two of their fellows who lived in the locality of the crime and were therefore cognizant.[85] Yet it seems not unlikely these 'less knowledgeable' jurors may have been selected, not just because they were local officeholders or worthies as has been suggested, but because they were on the contrary knowledgeable. Their knowledge might have derived from commercial dealings with the suspect, or being involved in his pursuit and arrest, or living near his home. Such men were certainly to be found serving on trial juries in the later thirteenth century. In that period it seems there were sometimes several juries giving a verdict on a suspect and it was the justices who decided from where the jurors should be drawn.[86] Quite possibly in the fourteenth and fifteenth centuries the justices still made decisions, either personally or more likely through the sheriff, about who should serve on the petty juries; and the fifteenth and sixteenth centuries jurors, whom historians have tended to regard as being for the most part ignorant of the circumstances of the crime in question, may have had some connection with it along the lines just suggested, a connection which has not yet been noticed. What is often forgotten in the study of late medieval and Tudor juries is how many of those arraigned for felony committed their offence outside their own township. One investigation of the problem has found that as many as 44 per cent of the accused in the records of the gaol delivery sessions of the south-western circuit, 1416–30, were in this category, and that three-quarters of them committed their felonies six or more miles from their homes; and half of these more than twenty-one miles away.[87] Until the homes, places of offence and arrest of the suspects have been plotted against the jurors' residences, movement patterns, commercial connections, and the area where they exercised any non-legal office, it is too early to come to firm conclusions about their knowledge of the crimes and the suspect felons who appeared before them.

The situation of the accused in a felony trial is also worthy of our attention. There are very few reports of arraignees' comments on the trial process before the sixteenth century and these are largely from persons accused of treason. What these men said, however, could in many cases have been said by suspect felons for much in their situations must have been common to both. They usually complained that their sojourn in gaol had worn them out, mentally as well as physically, a belief which may have been reinforced by their recognition that they were not being able to make the apposite response or objection when they might have. They complained also of not having been given any accurate information about the charge against them, which was true, for the prisoner was not shown his indictment unless he had a royal warrant for that purpose. Nor would he be told who was expected to testify against him, or be allowed, necessarily, to answer the accusations which witnesses made immediately after their utterance. This might well cause him, through forgetfulness occasioned by the stress of the situation, to omit to make any answer to crucial points. He was, of course, permitted no legal counsel to provide him with advice or prompting.[88] Yet we may suspect that until 1530 the prosecution was often inconclusive at best because of the absence of the victim, which deprived the court of any altercation as well as the most crucial part of the testimony.

The trial of the accused came to a close, so we are told by an early seventeenth-century source, when the judge had heard enough. He would ask 'Is there any more evidences?', or more tersely issue the command 'No more!', meaning he would allow no more additional witnesses. In the early sixteenth century the justices, if the trial was of importance to the crown, might repeat the evidence for the jurors' benefit before they gave their charge.[89] Evidence from later in the century shows that at times the justices might have the clerk at this point read out their commission so as to impress the jury with the majesty of the law.[90] In the majority of cases there was probably no judicial summing-up at all or it was in the most perfunctory form. The early seventeenth-century source implies that the judge simply said a few dry words to show he expected a verdict of 'guilty': 'These be witnesses enow . . . to condemne' and 'Here is an Harlottrie indeed!'[91] Some sixteenth-century treason trial reports suggest the accused was allowed to have the final word, though a very brief one, to the jury. This seems to have taken the form of a declaration of innocence, perhaps with an insistence that the evidence against him was untrue, coupled with an adjuration to the jurors that they should follow their consciences.[92]

The commentator, who shows the justice hinting to the jury what type of verdict he expects, provides us with a valuable piece of information in regard to the jurors' ruminations. His words *in extenso* are 'Here is an Harlottrie indeed . . . (saith the Iudge), Iurie, if you be agreed give in your verdict'.[93] There is in this sentence, we should note, no suggestion of the jury being allowed to withdraw from the courtroom in order to come to a conclusion on the accused's guilt or innocence. Rather it seems to have been expected to give a verdict forthwith. Recently the argument has been advanced that jury retirement in criminal cases was a rarity before approximately the middle of the seventeenth century, and that in most instances juries produced a verdict without withdrawing to another room or building. They were not, in fact, allowed an opportunity for proper deliberation.[94] This was certainly not the practice in sixteenth-century treason trials, nor, apparently, at the arraignment of a batch of suspected felons if among them was one in whom the crown had an especial interest. A report of John Udall's first trial (July 1590) says that 'the Jury after they had heard the Evidences of the other Felons at the Bar departed to consult about them'.[95] If we look for earlier proof of withdrawal by petty jurors in felony cases we find it in the statute 26 Henry VIII c.4, which ordered an officer to be deputed to 'keep' the jurors. He was not to allow them food, drink, or like comfort, or to talk to other persons – even himself. The act was in regard to jurors in the marches of Wales but the tenor is that withdrawal was standard practice. The novelty was in the keeper appointed. Thomas Smith on the matter of jurors withdrawing to consider their verdict does not appear to prevaricate. He emphasizes their physical departure from the courtroom to 'a chamber' by informing the reader about the rules which govern their comfort and their legal duties while in retirement. He also tells us that frequently a jury has only 'one or two' accused to deliver verdicts on although 'sometime' it is charged with 'two or three'. If there are more, he adds, the jurors are likely to protest that their memories of the evidence will be overtaxed.[96] Lately Smith's accuracy on this matter has been challenged, and it has been shown that on the home circuit from the beginning of the reign of Elizabeth I to the death of James I the average number of persons arraigned before each petty jury was 6.7, although sometimes there were twelve or more. A jury could not possibly, the argument goes, conduct meaningful deliberations on as many as six different suspects at one time; nor, if the jurors were able to keep the several pieces of evidence separate in their minds, was there time to embark on extended discussions.[97] Yet Smith is so clear on what he says about jury withdrawal and multiple arraignment that we ought, perhaps, to give these matters further thought. It may have been that a jury withdrew to consider verdicts after it had heard two or three cases and then returned to hear several more before it retired again. While it was in retirement cases could be heard before one of the other two juries, for there were often three such at work at each sessions in this period.[98]

The hearing of more than a single case by a jury before it retired may have been a late medieval practice or it may not, the evidence is not clear. Medieval gaol delivery records, although they provide the membership of some juries, rarely associate such with particular cases.[99] Nor does the general format of gaol delivery rolls help us even if at first sight it may appear to. Some fifteenth-century rolls contain a good number of felony cases in batches (i.e. grouped together). Thus there might be provided the details of five or six cases, one case at a time, but with no verdicts appended until the end of the batch. Then it would be recorded that the jury found A and B guilty but C, D, E, and F not guilty, or similar. At first sight it appears to be a multiple arraignment of the type referred to by Smith, but the incidence of these entries in the rolls may cause us to have second thoughts. The batch method is the usual one utilized in the extant fifteenth-century gaol delivery rolls of the midland and northern circuits, but not in those of the eastern or south-western circuits.[100] It was the usual form of enrolment on the northern circuit even in the mid-fourteenth century. It also appears occasionally in eastern circuit rolls of the 1350s (Cambridgeshire and Suffolk) but it was not standard practice and was later jettisoned.[101] These variations in enrolment make us ask if they reflect different methods of arraignment or merely different methods of record keeping. If it was the latter then we have no direct evidence that the arraigning of several suspects at one time for different crimes, with verdicts being given only after the last of the batch had been tried, was a medieval practice at all, even if a good argument can be made from schedules of the sessions and the work-load of the justices that some such speedier method of processing was likely.[102]

When the petty jurors retired, says Thomas Smith, they took with them the indictment, the clerk of the assize having verbally summarized it for them first. Should they wish to interrogate any person who had given evidence at the trial, or question a witness lately arrived, they might do so. We know little about how the jurors reached their verdict. Hales, writing in about 1520, tells us that in reality it was usually decided by a mere two or three of the jurors, the rest simply concurring in their decision.[103] In the fifteenth century there seem occasionally to have been justices of the peace chosen as petty jurors, and possibly as foremen. There were also coroners who served, as well as subsidy collectors, commissioners of array, and even close relatives of the gaol delivery justices.[104] It was, perhaps, men such as these who assumed the dominant role in the reaching of verdicts. Reports of arraignments of the early sixteenth century suggest that jurors were sensitive to interest shown in the fate of the accused by the crown, which was infrequent, and by the magnates, which must have occurred fairly often. Magnates were quite eager at times to protect clients, servants and tenants from deserved conviction, driven on, we may suspect, by county feuds and rivalries and a need to prove they had the power to intervene successfully.[105] Jurors appear to have also been nervous about the intentions of relatives of homicide victims, even in late Tudor times. The jurors felt safest at felony trials when there was a good attendance of county gentry, the presence of such apparently persuading aggrieved magnates and relatives of victims to conceal their hostility and postpone direct action. Such a well-attended sessions, it was said, allowed the jurors to follow their consciences without trammel in finding verdicts.[106] The distance in time from the commission of the offence to the date of the trial seems to have had considerable impact on jurors' attitudes. When there was a long delay, one of more than three years, conviction was only just over half as likely as it was on average; whereas if the crime had been committed between one and six months before arraignment a verdict of guilty was two and a half times as likely as the average.[107] Presumably the more extended lapse of time blunted the impact of the testimony of victims and witnesses or made their appearance in court less likely. Great desire for revenge was certainly likely to wane in the interim. An early arrest after the committing of the crime was thus important if a substantial rate of conviction was to be achieved.

In deciding their verdict the petty jurors may also have been affected by the stature of the justices on the bench, that is to say their importance in the legal hierarchy and their personal influence with the king. An examiner of Yorkshire gaol delivery records of the first eight years of Henry IV's reign has reached the conclusion that the relatively high conviction rate of suspects to be found therein may be attributable to the presence on the bench of William Gascoign, the chief justice of the king's bench. Writing about gaol delivery in the earlier fourteenth century Hanawalt has noted that in Yorkshire convictions rose from 13.7 to 20 per cent when the sessions were held by justices of the king's bench.[108] However, there appears to be no contemporary reference in either the medieval period or the sixteenth century to a judge with a notable ability to wrest convictions from juries which served at his sessions. Should the justices consider a case before them to be important, that is to say one where an acquittal would upset the king or his ministers, and thus reflect badly on themselves, they might make considerable efforts to monitor the jury's ruminations. The justices might send a messenger to talk with the jurors, or summon the foreman back before them, perhaps on the pretence they needed to explain the scope of the law further. On the other hand he might go at the behest of the other jurors. It was also not unknown for a section of the jury to be called back.[109] The intention of the justices in these instances was almost invariably to ensure convictions would be forthcoming in regard to particular suspects. Jurors, for their part, were known to send out messages to the accused urging him to submit, that is to say to put himself on the king's mercy. This was tantamount to an admission of guilt but without a formal confession. It offered some hope of a penalty lesser than the one a person convicted in the normal manner would incur.[110]

After a period of rumination, short or longer, the trial jury was asked to give its verdict or verdicts. The varying percentages of suspect felons found guilty and of those acquitted over a period of three and a half centuries have been shown early in this chapter but it is necessary now to demonstrate the connections between these statistics and what has been said above about the nature of the trial process. Firstly we must try to account on the juridical plane for the high level of acquittals which lasted from the thirteenth century until at least the later years of the fifteenth. Here our initial consideration must be the intention of those who sought to have a felon indicted. A good number of indictments, it has been argued, were brought forward by juries of presentment intending merely to give the indictee a lesson and a fright and there was no intention to pursue the matter further by giving evidence at the trial. This argument is not particularly convincing as it stands; it needs to be elaborated. It seems not unlikely that magnates engaged in a land war might promote the indictment of their opponents' followers, but this move does not appear to have been intended simply to give a fright: it was aimed to harass or embarrass.[111] The indictments would not be supported at the trial, however, if the two factions before that time had arrived at a settlement of their differences. It was this absence of support at trial, it should be emphasized, which must have been a major reason (perhaps the greatest) for the high level of acquittals in the later medieval period. Furthermore the most crucial aspect of this support was the appearance or failure to appear of the victim, or (in homicide cases) of his relatives.[112] The petty jurors' attitude to their task is clear: it was 'no visible sufferer, no conviction'. Victims, other than appellors, probably failed to appear in court because there was little satisfaction for them even in a verdict of guilty unless they were seeking primarily revenge. During the medieval period and until half-way through the reign of Henry VIII, even if the suspect was convicted on his evidence, the victim could not obtain restitution of property stolen from him since it went to the king. His most profitable line of action, therefore, must frequently have been to strike a bargain with the suspect whereby he, the victim, in return for compensation for his losses or repossession of the mainour, agreed to absent himself from the arraignment and thereby virtually guarantee the accused person's acquittal.[113] The absence from the trial of victim and witnesses must have been a major reason for the brevity of the proceedings on many occasions, a feature which may also have contributed to the high rate of acquittals; for surely jurors even in that age would not be willing, unless there was some admission of guilt, to send to the gallows an accused whose arraignment had not been allowed to last for more than two or three minutes.

The argument is sometimes offered that the late medieval rate of acquittal of felony was high because petty juries considered the penalty for those convicted, which was hanging, to be too severe. While it is true there was not available the mid-Elizabethan option of the 'partial' verdict (whereby, it has been argued, the accused was persuaded to change his plea of not guilty in regard to felony to guilty to a lesser charge of trespass/misdemeanour) the medieval trial jury might decide to find stolen property to be of a value of less than twelve pence and therefore the crime was not felonious.[114] Yet this could only be done within reason. In these cases the articles taken do not appear ever to have been of a true value much in excess of a shilling, showing that the jurors' room for manoeuvre was limited. They were also known to reduce crimes not connected with illegal asportation. An offence called murder in an indictment might be found manslaughter by a trial jury, or even self-defence, while rape might be held to be only abduction. Such lessening of the heinousness of the offence was, however, only an infrequent occurrence. Generally medieval juries preferred, where the value of the goods stolen was only a shilling or two, to acquit, and this was probably true of crimes of doubtful legal classification. The only type of felony suspects jurors seem to have been eager to convict were not perpetrators of a particular class of felony but members of a particular social group, the clerics. Even so their enthusiasm for this did not endure through the whole of the later medieval period. Investigation has revealed some remarkably high levels of convictions of clerics in fourteenth-century records, but there was a sharp decline in incidence, almost as soon as the fifteenth century began, to only just over the rate for those in other occupations.[115] Very few suspects who claimed the clerical privilege, which they did in the fifteenth century almost invariably *after* they had been found guilty, seem to have been refused, and this rather than the overall total of 'benefit' cases may have been the cause of continuing popular and governmental concern.[116] The obvious unfairness of a system where a large group of convicted felons escaped the gallows and lay punishment so easily may, perhaps, have inhibited petty jurors from finding verdicts of guilty in general.

One of the most likely causes of the high ratio of acquittals to convictions in the later medieval period was probably the county society in which the jurors lived. In a period of clientage, retaining, and service, few men were without formal social and economic obligations and these carried with them concern and protection on the part of the beneficiary for the obligated which we should be foolish to imagine counted for naught when a person was arraigned for felony. Even if a patron should think his servant, tenant, affinity member, or relative of the same, well deserved to hang for his felony, he must often have felt the need to try to intervene in the trial process, not only to protect his own dependants but also to preserve the reputation of his personal potency in local politics. This he would do by pressuring the sheriff to empanel a sympathetic jury or by making sure that the jurors knew of his interest in the particular case and its outcome.[117] Of course, victims and their relatives also had patrons and these, contrarywise, would be trying to ensure the jurors were inclined towards a conviction; but only, one suspects, so the likelihood of a verdict of guilty would allow their clients to obtain compensation through an out of court agreement with the suspect. Both sides, both interests here, and the large number like them in the country at large must have been a potent factor against a high incidence of convictions. Such off-stage manoeuvrings and labouring can hardly have failed to come to the notice of the jurors, who must have realized they had much to gain from returning an acquittal but only danger, personal harassment, or economic hardship if they convicted. So they usually acquitted.[118] This state of affairs probably continued until magnatial power was substantially reduced in the later fifteenth and early sixteenth centuries and when a number of procedural factors which we have met above began to have a substantial impact on the verdicts of criminal juries.[119]

On the other side of the coin, the reasons for the arrival of a much higher rate of conviction in the sixteenth century reveal themselves a little more clearly than do the causes for the frequency of acquittals. The stimulation of prosecuting zeal among individuals must rank highly here. Bills, or at least information, offered by private persons to the presenting jury in order to gain an indictment seems to have been acceptable procedure from the thirteenth century but only became common practice in the fourteenth and fifteenth.[120] By the later fifteenth century bills of indictment rather than charges originating from the hearsay gleanings of the presentment jurors must have been the commonest origin of indictments. The bringer of the bill, usually the victim, was more likely to 'follow the charge' (i.e. give evidence to the indicting jury and later appear at the arraignment for the same purpose) than a person who had suffered from a felony but whose misfortune was reported and made into a charge on his behalf by a jury of presentment. The bill bringer, who often handed in his bill to a justice of the peace before it went to the jury of indictment, was surely likely to be asked about the felony by the justice so that the miscreants could be located and arrested. The justices 'can have him sworn and ask questions of him' a *Year Book* case of Edward IV's reign tells us.[121] Presumably when the suspect was taken he was treated in a similar way. Bill bringers must have frequently been accompanied before the jury of indictment by their witnesses. When the victim, as he must have done more regularly as the sixteenth century progressed, appeared at the arraignment he would have his witnesses with him, or at least the court would have their examinations/depositions; all of which made the trial jurors less dependent on their own knowledge of the suspect's behaviour, or even on those of their members who came from the locality of the crime or the suspect's home.[122]

Prosecuting zeal among felony victims must have been raised to new heights by a statute of 1529, 21 Henry VIII c.11. This act, sadly neglected by historians of English crime, was surely crucial in producing a higher rate of convictions. Most felonies involved illegal asportation of property and by offering restitution to a victim who appeared at the arraignment and gave evidence leading to the suspect's conviction, it must have made his appearance in court much more probable and greatly reduced the likelihood of a furtive deal between him and the felon.[123] Should the injured party and his witnesses not appear at the trial to give their account of the crime the accused, says Sir Thomas Smith unequivocally, 'is without difficultie acquited'.[124] A quarter of a century later, under the statute 2/3 Philip and Mary c.10 (1555), justices of the peace were given the power to bind over witnesses to the felony so they might give evidence against the suspect at the trial, thereby making the appearance of the victim even more likely. Another section of the same statute and an act of a few months earlier (1/2 Philip and Mary c.13), which it slightly amended, formally linked the trial of felony suspects with their prior examination by justices. There can be little doubt, as we have already seen, that such suspects were being examined over a century earlier, although proof in the form of actual examinations and depositions does not appear to survive from before the second decade of the sixteenth century. The papers of Thomas Cromwell display very clearly that by the 1530s examination of suspect felons by justices of the peace, mayors, and bailiffs was a well-established and sophisticated practice. Its widespread use must have had a big impact on verdicts. Thomas More opined that 'such examinacions hath caused yet many mischevous to be brought to their punishment' and that they were crucial to the successful operation of the criminal law.[125]

It is from the reign of Henry VIII that we learn a great deal about another factor which contributed towards the rising rate of felony convictions. This was the monitoring of criminal law verdicts by conciliar bodies, especially by the council of the marches of Wales and the council of the north. Correspondence between those two bodies and the ascendant ministers, Wolsey then Cromwell, shows clearly the interest the former were expected to take in the fate of suspect felons arraigned at gaol deliveries in their areas. The councils frequently provided for their masters a breakdown of the outcome: those convicted and hanged, those convicted and reprieved, those acquitted by verdict, those delivered by proclamation, and they described cases or circumstances which had caused them particular trouble.[126] The general tone of these missives is usually that the region has benefited from a good number of executions of criminals and that the total of 'guilty' verdicts has been satisfactorily high; the implication is that this has occurred because of conciliar supervision. This supervision, it appears, was exercised in two ways: there was the threat of arraignment before council for jurors who returned an unwarranted acquittal (which was usually one which went against the evidence), and there were occasions when members of a regional council sat on the bench at common law criminal sessions alongside common law justices. Evidence that the regional councils tried felonies on their own is lacking, although their members were certainly given the power to do so by commission on at least one occasion. Thus the original regulations governing the council of the north of 1484 restricted its jurisdiction to hearing bills about riots, forcible entries, and feuds, that is to say the various manifestations of the dark side of bastard feudalism. However, the order for its re-establishment, 'the devices for a council to be established in the north' of June 1537, quite differently, gave the councillors additionally a commission to hear and determine felonies.[127] The intention here seems to have been to have the councillors sit alongside the justices of assize at their gaol delivery sessions, where suspect felons were tried, but to sit separately for cases dealt with by 'bill, witness, and examination' (i.e. misdemeanours and private suits). Proof that the members of the councils did in fact determine felonies is hard to find. The council of the north appears to have held sessions only for misdemeanours and private (bill) suits, which it tried in the normal conciliar manner. This, furthermore, was at the same time as the justices of assize undertook the arraignment of felons from local gaols.[128] Where the members of a council can be shown actually to have sat with common law justices was at quarter sessions, both when the business in hand was indictment and when it was arraignment.[129] However, the records suggest that this involvement in doing justice through the courts of common law was an occasional rather than a frequent occurrence. It took place when, for example, those arraigned for felony were from the upper classes, or when the felony and its punishment were considered to threaten the peace of the region.

The other supervisory function exercised by conciliar bodies in regard to felony verdicts was in the disciplining of petty jurors held to have acquitted, or very occasionally convicted, against the evidence. It has been argued that jurors were immune to such disciplining in the medieval period and certainly there is little evidence of the practice to be found;[130] but this may be because of the failure of most medieval conciliar records to survive. The king's council, we know, was much involved with criminal justice in the late fifteenth century, but largely in regard to the types of misdemeanour perpetrated by participants in the 'gentlemen's wars' such as riot, maintenance, embracery, forcible entry, and illegal retaining and livery giving. The notorious act of 1487, 3 Henry VII c.1, established a conciliar-type court of notables to deal with failure to empanel jurors in the proper manner because of these offences. The result of this malpractice, the act stated, was that perjury was so common 'nothing may be found by enquiry', though whether such inquests were of indictment or trial, or both, was not explained. In practice the court founded in 1487 entertained prosecutions brought against petty jurors. There survives a record of a case where petty jurors in Norfolk had convicted for felony because of embracery, and of two others where suspect felons were acquitted despite strong evidence of their guilt being given by several witnesses.[131] The charges (informations) against these juries were brought on the king's behalf by the attorney general and the practice of using this officer continued into the next reign when the court employed was the Star Chamber. A statute, which was operative from 1495 to 1504 (11 Henry VII c.25), was more clearly concerned with the petty jury. It allowed any person grieved by perjury on the part of the trial jurors to put in a bill to the justices of the same sessions, who would forward it to a court of notables (like that envisaged in 3 Henry VII c.1), who would try the matter by examination. However, it seems doubtful if this statute would benefit those convicted of felony unless they had the influence or wealth to get a reprieve while they employed a lawyer to draft and present such a bill. Nor, we may conclude, was there more than a small number of official informations/bills going into the conciliar courts between 1487 and 1530.[132] Why the crown should concern itself with these particular cases is not clear. It cannot have been that they were the only corrupt verdicts on felony, nor even the most flagrantly corrupt ones, of that time. Most likely they were cases which interested the crown because the person who suffered from the corrupt verdict had the wealth or the sponsorship (by a magnate) to induce the attorney general to prosecute, or because the verdict had somehow damaged the king's authority or his financial interests.

From the 1530s there is evidence of new procedures being used to deal with errant petty jurors. The papers of Thomas Cromwell show a minister of the king well informed about such cases. Cromwell appears to have obtained his knowledge sometimes from the justices of assize/gaol delivery but more often from the council of the marches and the council of the north.[133] Their reports, which provided details of the cases, assumed that the further ordering of the matter lay with the minister. Cromwell's habit was to make the miscreant jurors appear before the council in the Star Chamber with himself as a member. There, so it seems, the matter was treated less as an abuse of legal process, a transgression of the law, and therefore to be decided by expert legal opinion, than as an administrative matter the decision on which rested mainly with the minister. Indeed errant behaviour of particular juries in felony cases might well be perceived as a political threat. A minister might fear that the corrupt verdict would inflame factional rivalries in the county, or that his rivals for the king's favour would make political capital out of it. Thirty years later Thomas Smith, the lawyer, viewed the disciplining of juries which had acquitted felons unreasonably with considerably more detachment than had Thomas Cromwell, the politician. He tells us that such jurors were likely to be rebuked by the justices and probably ordered to appear in the Star Chamber or before the privy council. However, should they answer there 'with most gentle wordes' that 'they did it according to their consciences and pray the Judges to be good unto them' the matter would likely be dropped. Smith could remember, so he said, only two juries being fined and both before the reign of Elizabeth. Such treatment he considered a necessity, but he admitted many considered it tyrannical.[134] William Hudson, in his treatise on the court of Star Chamber, to whose records he had ready access, gives a different impression. He notes that in that court from Henry VII to the beginning of the reign of Elizabeth 'there was scarce one term pretermitted but some grand inquest or jury was fined for acquitting felons or murderers'.[135] These two commentators certainly do not give the impression of there being a great number of such cases, although what Smith tells us is only in regard to the middle years of the sixteenth century and what Hudson says concerns the Star Chamber alone. Cromwell's monitoring, on the other hand, seems to have been both extensive and thorough. It was sufficiently so, one suspects, for word to travel around the country that a juror ignored manifest evidence at his peril, a message which may well have had lasting effect.[136]

In addition to disciplining petty juries and monitoring the activities of some common law courts, we should notice that the king's council and conciliar bodies were instrumental in reducing felony acquittals in another, more general way. Conciliar courts were part of the wide-ranging attack from the early fifteenth century onwards on the evils of bastard feudalism such as maintenance, embracery, illegal livery giving and taking, illegal retaining, forcible entry, and riot. What made them so useful to the crown in this respect was that, together with the new, truncated, common law procedures that were another crucial element in the campaign, they were much less amenable than jury-based systems to outside pressures. In essence the great men of the shires lost much of their power to interfere in the trial process, and since this interference was usually directed towards obtaining acquittals the outcome was a rise in convictions.[137]

If we look closely at the numerical evidence in regard to felony cases at the end of the period under review, the later sixteenth century, it becomes very clear that while there was a great increase in convictions over the rate for the earlier fifteenth century it was not a continuing increase. Each Elizabethan decade did not necessarily produce a greater percentage of convictions than the last. Indeed, in the majority of the counties for which we have statistical evidence, while the rate for the 1570s was an increase over that for the 1560s, the curve of improvement, so to speak, then flattened out and declined a little in the 1590s.[138] The rate in one county differed quite noticeably from this general trend: Middlesex statistics reveal a consistent and evenly paced decline in convictions from the 1560s to the end of the century; from nearly 74 to just under 60 per cent.[139] One of the most notable features of the numerical evidence is the lack of sudden increase or sudden decline. A normal change in the rate over a period of ten years would not be more than five percentage points. Where the changes are greater they are never so in more than a single county at any particular time. There is no evidence of direct governmental interference in the handling of serious crime. The 5 to 10 per cent increase in the conviction rate between the 1560s and the 1570s which we notice in the statistics for Essex, Kent, and Surrey it is tempting to attribute to the putting into practice of the rules about examinations (taking and certifying) and bail, which were the subject of statutes in 1554–5, but such a thesis is weakened by the statistical evidence of Middlesex gaol deliveries immediately prior to Elizabeth's reign. The most striking felony conviction rate known to us in the whole century was that for Middlesex for the period 1549–53. It was no less than 80.7 per cent, a peak from which it declined at an even pace, Mary's reign apart, during the rest of the century.[140] In the 1580s the Middlesex rate was the same as that in four out of five counties on the home circuit while in the 1590s it was slightly lower than theirs. The very high Edwardian rate seems to demonstrate what has already been argued above, namely that examination of suspect felons and witnesses to their offences was common practice, in some areas at least, before the Marian statutes. Most importantly the Middlesex statistics suggest that the great increase in the felony conviction rate referred to at the outset of this chapter may have occurred before the reign of Elizabeth I, and that all the other factors which have been mentioned above as contributing, such as the statute of 1529, the war against the evils of bastard feudalism, conciliar monitoring of petty jurors, greater use of witnesses, and improved indictment procedure, had already had a big effect by the 1540s. It is also difficult to dismiss the thought that the high Edwardian conviction rate may have owed something to an increased zeal for performing their duties among the justices of the peace, a number of whom, after the bench was remodelled for the new reign, must have been of a radical persuasion in their religious beliefs.[141]

In addition to the procedural factors which affected the trial process and conviction rates, there were others, perhaps best called operational, which also had a considerable impact. Whereas procedure affected all, or a large segment, of those arraigned, these touched only certain groups. There were, for example, the instances of multiple charges. These were cases where a felony suspect was put to answer for more than a single offence. A study of Hertfordshire trial juries and their verdicts in the period 1573–1624 discovered a conviction rate of 62 per cent where two or more offences were involved but only 46 per cent where the count was a single one. The records of the south-western circuit, 1416–30, provide a conviction rate of 15 per cent for multiple offenders in contrast with one of only 9 per cent for single ones. The extant Yorkshire gaol delivery records for the years 1439–60 show those indicted of more than a single felony were convicted in almost 40 per cent of instances, while those found guilty on indictment overall (i.e. of single or multiple offences) totalled only 23 per cent.[142] The numerical evidence, we may conclude, seems to support the argument that putting a felony suspect to answer more than a single charge increased the likelihood of his conviction considerably, probably by about 50 per cent.

Committing a felony with the assistance of another person or several persons, that is to say with confederates, also made it more likely the accused would be found guilty. Hertfordshire assize records of 1573–1624 show a conviction rate of 59 per cent, as against one of 47 per cent when a felon committed his misdeed without associates. The gaol delivery records of the south-western circuit, 1416–30, reveal that the accompanied felon was convicted twice as often as the unaccompanied, 14 per cent against 7 per cent. On the other hand the Yorkshire conviction rate for associates in felony at gaol delivery sessions between 1439 and 1460 was only about the same as that for all felons who had been indicted, 24 per cent against 23 per cent, although here the totals are probably distorted by two indictments which involved no fewer than 45 men (who were all acquitted) and a more representative conviction rate for group felony would be just over 30 per cent.[143]

In contrast with gang membership and the committing of multiple felonies the fact that the accused was female generally lessened the chances of being convicted. At the Hertfordshire assizes for the half century subsequent to 1573 only 30 per cent of the women arraigned were found guilty, whereas the rate for men was about 52 per cent. Gaol delivery records from the end of the fourteenth century and the beginning of the fifteenth tell a similar story. The rate of female conviction, assessed from six circuits, was 10.4 per cent in Richard II's reign, and in the first eight years of his successor's (assessed from five circuits) a virtually identical 10.2 per cent. In these two periods the conviction rates for men and women accused combined were 13.0 and 14.4 per cent respectively, while the rate for all thirty years for men alone was about 15 per cent.[144] If, however, we go back in our investigations to the early years of Edward III's reign we find there was very little difference between the conviction rates at gaol delivery for the two sexes. Newgate records for 1329–35 provide us with a rate for both of about 12.5 per cent.[145] The picture which emerges, therefore, is one which reveals English petty jurors becoming increasingly sympathetic to the females arraigned before them over the three centuries or so under review which contrasts markedly with the rise in the felony conviction rate overall.

Another factor to be considered for its possible effect on acquittal and conviction rates is the impact of inflation. The Phelps Brown and Hopkins index, which sets the price of a unit of consumable goods against the wage rate of building craftsmen, shows a one to one ratio for the year 1510, a three to one ratio for 1548, a six to one ratio for 1580, and a ten to one ratio for 1600.[146] The wage rate, in fact, halved between 1510 and 1600 while the consumables increased in price by nearly 500 per cent; the sixteenth century was hard times indeed for the lower class wage earner. The value of goods stolen for which a man might be hanged in 1600, twelve pence worth, would have been worth a mere three pence or less in 1510 or in the mid-fifteenth century. In theory men and women were being hanged in the last years of Elizabeth's reign for stealing goods to only a quarter of the value that felons at the end of Henry VII's reign or in the middle of Henry VI's were executed for. The criminal law, it might be argued, where the offence was grand larceny, had become four times more severe. To this it might be said in mitigation that when we examine the value of the goods feloniously stolen in the south-east in Elizabeth's reign we notice few persons found guilty of theft of goods worth less than ten shillings. Where the asported goods were worth between twelve pence and ten shillings the suspect felon was only likely to be found guilty in cases where he was able to successfully claim benefit of clergy, or where he had assaulted or burgled his victim (i.e. put him in fear) in addition to stealing from him.[147] Thus Elizabethan records, on the face of it, give the impression that Tudor juries were taking a relatively generous attitude towards felonious theft, and demanding a value in goods stolen of well over the twelve pence mark before they would convict.

Fifteenth-century gaol delivery records, however, show even fewer convictions for felonious larceny where the value of the objects stolen was under ten shillings, than do their Elizabethan counterparts. The Yorkshire records for 1439–60 provide only a single example among the 202 persons indicted for that offence, and the record of the south-western circuit for 1416–30 yield none at all among 114. The average value of goods stolen (in the same Yorkshire records) where a suspect felon was found guilty, appears to have been not far short of sixty shillings.[148] We are therefore led to the conclusion that Elizabethan trial juries were indeed ready to find a person guilty of the theft of goods of only about one quarter of the value, in real terms, that their fifteenth-century predecessors had found appropriate. Now it may be argued that when, in the later sixteenth century, a suspect was indicted of the theft of goods worth a mere two or three shillings there was a chance of a 'partial' verdict. By this the jurors found the goods stolen to be of a value under a shilling and the offence, therefore, only trespass, in exchange for a plea of guilty by the accused. Yet against this we must set the fact that in the fifteenth century an indictment for a theft of such small value would almost automatically produce an acquittal. Late Elizabethan 'partial' verdicts apart, there seems to have been little recognition among the professional judiciary, the crown's legal advisers, or even lawyers in general, that inflation had increased the severity of the criminal law dramatically. There was certainly no noticeable desire for reform.

Notes

1   *Wiltshire Gaol Delivery*, pp. 44–165; Pugh, *Proc. British Academy*, 86–7. The calculation of conviction rates for Wiltshire is my own.

2   Pugh, *Proc. British Academy*, 89; Hanawalt, *Crime and Conflict*, p. 59; L.O. Pike, *A History of Crime in England* (London, 1873), i, 480.

3   *Essex Sessions of the Peace, 1351, 1377–1379*, ed. E.C. Furber (Essex Archaeological Society Occasional Papers 3, Colchester, 1953), pp. 59–60; Garay, pp. 338–9, 344, 364–5.

4   Elder, pp. 111, 119, 305–19. Those indicted or appealed of felony who were acquitted amounted to 68 per cent.

5   I have calculated these figures from PRO JUST 3/210 and 212.

6   The low level of felony convictions has been demonstrated by C.J. Neville, *Gaol Delivery in the Lancastrian North, 1439–1459* (Carleton University, M.A. thesis, 1980), pp. 264–5.

7   I have calculated the fifteenth-century figures for Yorkshire from PRO JUST 3/199, 208, 211, and 213.

8   Hanawalt, *Crime and Conflict*, p. 56.

9   The Kent and Sussex statistics I have calculated from *Calendar of Assize Records, Indictments, Elizabeth I.* The statistics for Essex are my own computation from PRO ASSI 35.

It has been observed that in regard to crime in the early modern period Essex was a more typical county than, for example, Sussex or Hertfordshire: *Crime in England, 1550–1800*, ed. J.S. Cockburn (London, 1977), p. 66.

10   *Wiltshire Gaol Delivery; Crime in East Anglia.* The calculations are my own.

11   Ellis, p. 94; Elder, pp. 305–29.

12   PRO JUST 3/210–13.

13   The figures are compiled from PRO JUST 3/123, 198, 202, 205, 210–13.

14   *Year Books, Liber Assisarum*, 43 Edward III pl. 25.

15   In regard to Fortescue's and Smith's failure to comment on conviction rates we should remember that both had lived abroad and had apparently been so appalled by the emphasis in continental criminal law on the extracting of confessions by means of torture that they were ready to sing the praises of English criminal process regardless of any weaknesses.

16   J. Strype, *Annals of the Reformation* (Oxford, 1824), pp. 405–12.

17   Thus for one year, 1538, see *Letters and Papers, Henry VIII*, xviii (i), nos. 311, 519, 1411; *ibid.*, xviii (ii), no. 21.

18   More, *Works*, pp. 970–90.

19   B.W. McLane, 'Judicial Attitudes toward Local Disorder: The Evidence of the 1328 Lincolnshire Trailbaston Proceedings', in *Twelve Good Men*, p. 57; Powell, 'Jury Trial', pp. 85–7; T.A. Green, 'A Retrospective on the Criminal Trial Jury, 1200–1800', in *Twelve Good Men*, pp. 368–9.

20 Fortescue implied that men might live a good distance away from where any crime occurred yet still, if they were attuned to the county 'grapevine', acquire good knowledge of the circumstances: Fortescue, p. 67. The crux, although Fortescue does not say so, seems to have been for the person to want to know and be known to want to know. Such a person would probably be one holding local office.

21 Post, 'Jury Lists', pp. 69–71.

22 Contrarywise it could be argued that those who held local or court offices, being 'establishment' figures, were more likely to be in general favour of a high rate of convictions than the normal juryman.

23 See for example PRO JUST 3/126 m. 2, JUST 3/213 m. 18.

24 Fortescue, p. 65; J.B. Thayer, *A Preliminary Treatise on the Law of Evidence* (Boston, 1898), p. 91; Lambard, *Éirenarcha*, p. 436; Smith, ed. Alston, p. 98.

25 Cockburn, *Assize Introduction*, pp. 60–1.

26 *Year Books*, 4 Edward IV Pasch. pl. 18.

27 *Placita Corone*, p. xxvii; Clanchy, *Berkshire Eyre*, pp. 312, 346, 380, 387.

28 *Year Books*, 16 Edward II Trin. p. 493. In certain fourteenth- and fifteenth-century appeals in gaol delivery records the jurors are said to have been elected with the consent of the parties and not simply 'electi et triati': PRO JUST 3/145 mm. 7d, 8d and JUST 3/ 83/3 mm. 2, 3, 4, 7, 9, 10, 13.

29 *Year Books*, 11 Henry IV Mich. pl. 5; *ibid.*, 8 Henry IV Mich. pl. 4; *ibid.*, *Liber Assisarum*, 38 Edward III pl. 19.

30 Fortescue, p. 71; *Year Books*, 9 Edward IV Trin. pl. 40; *ibid.*, 32 Henry VI Hil. pl. 14. Appellees were also allowed to challenge peremptorily: *Year Books*, 3 Henry VI Hil. pl. 5. After 1530 only twenty petty jurors could be challenged peremptorily: 22 Henry VIII c.14.

31 Cambridge University Library MS Hh.3.6, ff.8–8v. Littleton's comment means, presumably, either that the victims were nervously perplexed by their situation or that they feared a challenge might increase the likelihood of their being found guilty. See also *Readings and Moots at the Inns of Court in the Fifteenth Century, II*, ed. S.E. Thorne and J.H. Baker (Selden Society, 105, 1990), p. 276.

32 PRO JUST 3/209 m. 7. The Diss challenge was at the Thetford gaol delivery sessions in February 1433.

33 PRO JUST 3/209–13.

34 See, however, Bellamy, *Criminal Law*, pp. 33–5 and particularly Powell, 'Jury Trial', pp. 105–11.

35 T. More, *The Complete Works of St. Thomas More, X*, ed. J. Guy, R. Keen, C.H. Miller and R. McGugan (New Haven and London, 1987), pp. 147–55.

36 *Letters and Papers, Henry VIII*, xiii (ii), no. 21. In 1537 the foreman of a petty jury was examined before the council because he and his fellow jurors had convicted merely on the 'noise of the country' and without actual evidence: *Letters and Papers, Henry VIII*, cii (ii), no. 303.

37 *William Salt Arch. Soc.*, New series, x (i), 5; *Select Cases in the council of Henry VII*, ed. C.G. Bayne and W.H. Dunham (Selden Society, 75, 1958), pp. 69, 74–5. Unlike the clerks who kept common law records, those who were concerned with conciliar justice were in no way inhibited about referring to witnesses used in common law criminal procedure.

38 The crime was, however, only rated a trespass/misdemeanour. A *Year Book* case (4 Henry VII, Pasch. pl. 1) notes that persons of one county might not give evidence in regard to a felony in that county at a sessions in another county.

39 Fortescue, p. 67.

40 The victim's intent as described in this record was 'to prosecute on the king's behalf' the suspect: see Powell, 'Jury Trial', p. 109.

41 *Year Books*, 9 Henry IV Mich. pl. 24.

42 *Year Books*, 30 Henry VI Mich. pl. 24; *ibid.*, 20 Henry VII Mich. pl. 21; *ibid.*, 27 Henry VIII Pasch. pl. 6.

43 For example PRO JUST 3/145 m. 1, PRO JUST 3/163 m. 1, PRO JUST 3/164 m. 1, PRO JUST 3/204 m. 1, PRO JUST 3/206 m. 1.

44 PRO KB 9/269/21 shows a 'de gestu' inquest, as they have been called, taken 'at the suggestion' of five persons who had been robbed of £40.

45 See above pp. 45–6. Palatinate records of Henry VII's reign, however, show proclamations by the sheriff asking any justice of the peace, serjeant at law, or attorney of the king, who knew of any crime to come forward: PRO Durham 13/229 mm. 1, 2.

46 PRO JUST 3/126 m. 24d; JUST 3/136 m. 19. See also chapter one.

47 PRO JUST 3/163 m. 5; JUST 3/180 mm. 8, 25d, 38d.

48 PRO JUST 3/163 m. 1; JUST 3/180 m. 9; JUST 3/209 m. 9. Presumably a 'suer' was an appellor and a 'prosecutor' was a person who offered a bill of indictment. These inquests are usually referred to as being 'concerning reputation and behaviour'.

49 The wording might be that the justices 'were given to understand' that the suspect was of bad fame: PRO JUST 3/212 m. 5d.

50 Occasionally there is a comment such as 'no one (prosecutor) offered himself' (PRO JUST 3/211 m. 14d) or 'no one offers to say anything' (JUST 3/211 m. 19d) or 'no one comes' (JUST 3/211 m. 18), or 'no one comes to be heard' (JUST 3/211 m. 22). Justices of the peace were not allowed to deliver *capti* at the peace sessions although the commons in parliament asked for that privilege in July 1455: *Rot. Parl.*, v, 332.

51 See *Shropshire Eyre*, pp. 225, 278, 290, 292.

52 Thus when a coroner's inquest's verdict of homicide by a husband of his wife was brought (as an indictment) to a gaol delivery sessions it was testified 'by several oathworthy persons' that at the time of the crime the man was 'non compos mentis': PRO JUST 3/212 m. 5d.

53 For example PRO JUST 3/76 m. 4, JUST 3/126 m. 2, JUST 3/136 m. 6, JUST 3/189 m. 3d, JUST 3/199 m. 7, JUST 3/204 m. 1. The reeve and four men of vills where felonies had been committed were summoned to eyres as a matter of course in the thirteenth century.

54 Thus the reeve and the four men would probably be the 'several worthy men' referred to as testifying X was a 'common wandering thief': PRO JUST 3/163 m. 3, JUST 3/164 m. 50. The reeve and the four men appear more frequently in the gaol delivery records of the earlier fifteenth century than in those of the fourteenth century.

55 PRO JUST 3/198 m. 18.

56 PRO JUST 3/204 m. 1.

57 See *Letters and Papers, Henry VIII*, xiii (ii), no. 21.

58 Smith, ed. Alston, p. 90; More, *Complete Works, X*, p. 151.

59 *Year Books*, 21 Edward IV Mich. pl. 49.

60 See Bellamy, *Criminal Law*, p. 94 for the delating of information under this statute. In theory

the criminals whom the statute was directed against had first practised their misdeeds overseas and were now returned to England. Did the army of Edward III bring back to England elements of continental criminal process? The only earlier reference to examination by the crown is in *Glanvill* and concerns treason where the offence was notorious but there was no accuser. In such cases the truth was to be established by enquiries and interrogations before the justices: *Glanvill*, p. 171.

61 Bellamy, *Criminal Law*, pp. 8–9, 12, 28, 34, 45.

62 Two statutes of 1423 and one of 1432, also based on the Statute of Labourers, allowed examination to serve as the actual trial. Should the suspect being examined by the justices be considered by them to be guilty, he could be punished. The statute 8 Henry VI c.4 permitted similar procedure in regard to livery offences, the sentence in this case being only a fine. In Edward IV's reign there were promulgated five other statutes stipulating investigation and conviction by examination: the offences were to do with illegal livery giving, manufacturing trade practices and the wearing of apparel, all trespass/misdemeanour: see *ibid.*, p. 14.

63 Edward Hext, in the late sixteenth century, stated that a justice of the peace should be present in person at the trial of any suspect he had examined so as to inform the court what he had discovered thereby (i.e. explain any obscure point in the examination itself), and also to see that the victim gave what evidence he could: Strype, *Annals*, iv, 405–12.

64 *Unpublished Documents relating to the English Martyrs, 1584–1603*, ed. J.H. Pollen (Catholic Record Society, 5, 1908), p. 352. The case was one of treason, but treason procedure was very similar to that used in felony except the crown was more thorough in the former in its management of the accusation and the arraignment.

65 More, *Complete Works, X*, p. 151.

66 More notes that witnesses on behalf of the suspect were examined as well as those for the victim: *ibid.*, p. 148.

67 More also refers to witnesses being sworn and clearing the accused 'in a temporal court' (presumably a gaol delivery sessions): *ibid.*, p. 150.

68 See Bellamy, *Tudor Law of Treason*, p. 161.

69 PRO SP 11/13/47. An additional excuse which the justices offered for refusing to allow defence witnesses was that the crime in the Thimbleby case was especially heinous in that it was perpetrated on the highway and against the queen's revenues, and that it was 'presumptuous'.

70 *State Trials*, ed. W. Cobbett and T.B. Howell (London, 1809), i, 1281; PRO SP 12/254/55.

71 *Acts of the Privy Council*, xii, 88; *State Trials*, i, 993.

72 *Year Books*, 1 Henry V Pasch. pl. 8; *Letters and Papers, Henry VIII*, iv (ii), no. 4331; *Cal. Pat. Rolls, 1485–94*, p. 149.

73 *Year Books*, 3 Henry VI Trin. pl. 16; *ibid.*, 21 Edward IV Pasch. pl. 17; *Cal. Pat. Rolls, 1446–52*, p. 84.

74 An account of the case is to be found in *State Trials*, i, 1277–1318. As might be expected the official record of the trial at the Croydon assizes (PRO ASSI 35/32/7) contains no mention of a crown prosecutor.

75 *State Trials*, i, 1280–3.

76 PRO ASSI 35/32/7.

77 Powell, 'Jury Trial', p. 107.

78 See *State Trials*, i, 1282.

79 Smith, ed. Alston, pp. 99–100.

80 *Placita Corone*, pp. 16–21.

81 *Year Books of the reign of Edward I, III*, pp. 496–527, 528–45.

82 Green, 'Retrospective', pp. 359–60; Cockburn, *Assize Introduction*, pp. 111–12.

83 See Powell, 'Jury Trial', p. 82.

84 The act only concerned felonies of asportation but these were, of course, the substantial majority of the felonies tried.

85 Powell, 'Jury Trial', pp. 85–8; see also P.G. Lawson, 'Lawless Juries? The Composition and Behavior of Hertfordshire Juries, 1573–1624', in *Twelve Good Men*, p. 123.

86 Pugh, 'Reflections', 93–5.

87 Elder, pp. 206–8.

88 Bellamy, *Tudor Law of Treason*, pp. 142–5. For all offences the indictment was read out in court but the accused never had an opportunity then, earlier or later, to read it unless he obtained a warrant from the crown: *Les Reportes del Cases in Camera Stellata, 1593 to 1609*, ed. W.P. Baildon (1894), p. 100. Those arraigned for felony on indictment could not receive counsel in court from any lawyer they had hired, but they might have been advised on their defence by the same while in gaol: see R.C. Palmer, 'The Origins of the Legal Profession in England', *Irish Jurist* (New Series, 11, 1976), 130–1.

89 R. Bernard, *Isle of Man or the Legall Proceeding in Man-shire against Sinne* (1626), pp. 130–2; *Spelman*, ed. Baker, i, 48–9.

90 *The Rambler*, New series, iii (1860), 369, 371; *Unpublished Documents*, ed. Pollen, p. 356.

91 *Isle of Man*, pp. 131–2. Such hints are probably what Thomas Smith meant by judges' 'watchwords': Smith, ed. Alston, p. 109. In John Udall's trial at Croydon a justice said bluntly in summation that the evidences against the accused were manifest on the crucial issue: *State Trials*, i, 1289.

92 *Ibid.*, i, 898; Bellamy, *Tudor Law of Treason*, pp. 165–6.

93 *Isle of Man*, p. 132.

94 J.S. Cockburn, 'Twelve Silly Men? The Trial Jury at Assizes, 1560–1670', in *Twelve Good Men*, p. 177; Cockburn, *Assize Introduction*, pp. 110–11.

95 *State Trials*, i, 1289.

96 Smith, ed. Alston, pp. 100–1,

97 Cockburn, 'Twelve Silly Men?', pp. 178–9; Cockburn, *Assize Introduction*, p. 110.

98 Thus, for example, there were three trial juries sworn at East Grinstead (Sussex) assizes in February 1573 for a total of fifteen prisoners indicted of felony: *Cal. Sussex Indictments*, pp. 90–2.

99 There is a reference in a law report of 1469 to situations when a delivery jury 'was asked' to give a verdict on 'two or three' men. We must balance this hint that such a demand was not usual against the fact that the accused might all have been indicted of the same crime: *Year Books*, 9 Edward IV Trin., no. 40.

100 PRO JUST 3/195, JUST 3/198–9, JUST 3/203, JUST 3/209–13.

101 PRO JUST 3/145 *passim*. Occasional appearances of the practice in Cambridgeshire and Suffolk are in JUST 3/136 m. 12d, JUST 3/139 mm. 11, 15d, 19d, 24. There is an isolated fifteenth-century Suffolk example in JUST 3/204 m. 3d.

102 See Powell, 'Jury Trial', pp. 82, 98–9.

103 Smith, ed. Alston, pp. 100–1; J. Hales, *Oration in Commendation of the Laws*, f. 38v. The verdict, supposedly, had to be unanimous although *Britton* states that where the jurors could not resolve their differences the greater part should prevail: *Britton*, i, 31.

104 *Proceedings*, ed. Putnam, p. 274 (see *Letters and Papers, Henry VIII*, xiv (ii), no. 530 for a sixteenth-century example); PRO JUST 3/84/5; Powell, 'Jury Trial', pp. 89–92.

105 *Letters and Papers, Henry VIII*, iv (ii), no. 2402; *ibid.*, xii (i), no. 731; Bellamy, *Bastard Feudalism*, pp. 96–100.

106 Historical Manuscripts Commission, *Calendar of Manuscripts of the Marquess of Salisbury* (London 1883–1976), vi, 148; *Letters and Papers, Henry VIII*, iv (ii), no. 2402.

107 Elder, pp. 176–7.

108 Ellis, p. 168; Hanawalt, *Crime and Conflict*, p. 56. The Yorkshire felony conviction rate was certainly higher in 1399–1407 than it was in the fourteenth century or in the reign of Henry VI, and it was also higher than the contemporaneous rate on any other circuit. However, political disaffection may have played a role.

109 *Letters and Papers, Henry VIII*, xii (i), no. 731; *ibid.*, xviii (ii), no. 74; *State Trials*, i, 1289–90; *The Rambler*, New Ser., iii, 371.

110 A famous case of such submission, although in that instance the offence was only malversation, was that of Richard Willoughby III, C.J.K.B. in 1341: *Year Books of Edward III, V*, p. 260.

111 For indictment as sufficient punishment in itself see Hanawalt, *Crime and Conflict*, p. 53; for indictment intended to delay a private action see Powell, *Kingship*, p. 70. It has been suggested that only about 30 to 50 per cent of those indicted in the thirteenth and fourteenth centuries ever went to trial: *ibid.*, p. 77.

112 The appearance of the victim or his relatives would prove to the jurors that the indictment was not simply a tactical move in a feud.

113 See above pp. 31–2. Such deals were not always originated by the victim of the felony. They were illegal; strictly speaking a royal licence was necessary to treat with thieves: see *Cal. Pat. Rolls, 1381–85*, p. 322. For the additional indictment of a thief because he tried to bribe the victim to conceal the felony see PRO JUST 3/135 m. 29.

114 On 'partial' verdicts see Cockburn, 'Twelve Silly Men?', pp. 171–3, 176 and Cockburn, *Assize Introduction*, pp. 115–16. We have no knowledge of the actual mechanics of this procedure. Perhaps the justices suggested it as soon as the suspect was arraigned; or maybe the jurors, when in retirement, sent a message back to the court advising a change of plea, rather as in private suits they were wont sometimes to suggest to a party, who was likely to lose the verdict, he should non-suit.

115 Clerics/clerks were those in holy or minor ecclesiastical orders and, for the purposes of the judicial system, literate laity also. Hanawalt found a conviction rate for clerics of 60 per cent for the period 1300–19 and one of over 75 per cent for 1320–48: *Crime and Conflict*, p. 55. Garay found 43 per cent of clerics were convicted in 1388–99, but only 23 per cent in 1399–1407: Garay, pp. 352–3. Elder found a clerical conviction rate of 19 per cent on the south-western circuit, 1416–30: Elder, p. 245.

116 Bellamy, *Criminal Law*, p. 130.

117 Bellamy, *Bastard Feudalism*, especially chapters one, two and four.

118 There may well have been still other reasons for the high rate of acquittals for felony in medieval times but their relative weight is hard to assess. It has been implied (Powell, 'Jury Trial', p. 112) that in felonies involving the theft of livestock acquittals were probably frequent because of a genuine difficulty at that time in deciding ownership of the asported animals. Another possible but unproven factor may have been the composition of the petty jury. If, indeed, there was an absence or minimal presence of jurors from the hundred of the crime might it not have depressed the rates of conviction?

119 See Bellamy, *Bastard Feudalism*, chapter six, for the erosion of the power of the upper classes through governmental measures against the pernicious side of bastard feudalism.

120 See chapter one.

121 *Year Books*, 21 Edward IV Mich. pl. 49.

122 In the late fifteenth century petty jurors still wanted to know about a suspect's reputation in his home locality. In a case heard at Michaelmas term 1489 one judge argued it had always been the practice, when a person was arraigned, for the jurors to enquire what the common fame and the voice of his home neighbourhood said about him: *Year Books*, 5 Henry VII Mich. pl. 10. Presumably the reeve and the four men of the vill assisted here.

123 Restitution had hitherto only been allowed in regard to land into which there had been forcible entry: 8 Henry VI c.9.

124 Smith, ed. Alston, p. 95.

125 More, *Works*, p. 990.

126 For example *Letters and Papers, Henry VIII*, iv (i), no. 1223; *ibid.*, viii, no. 457; *ibid.*, xiii, no. 1042.

127 R.R. Reid, *The King's Council in the North* (London, 1921), pp. 504–6.

128 *Letters and Papers, Henry VIII*, xviii (i), no. 372; *ibid.*, xx (ii), no. 109. An instance where councillors sat with justices of assize to determine felonies at gaol delivery sessions (1586) is in *Calendar of State Papers, Domestic, Edward VI, Mary, Elizabeth I and James I, Addenda 1580–1625*, p. 196.

129 *Letters and Papers, Henry VIII*, iv (ii), no. 3383; *ibid.*, xiii (i), no. 152.

130 Green, *Verdict according to Conscience*, p. 27.

131 Bayne, pp. 63, 68–70, 74a, 75a. In one case (p. 69) witnesses had given plain and manifest evidence, the mainour had been recovered, and the accused had confessed his guilt (outside the court) to several persons. In another case there were several witnesses who deposed in court against the suspect (74a).

132 Guy has noted five corrupt verdict cases in the Star Chamber in Wolsey's period in power (plus five of embracery or perjury) out of 473 cases where the extant documentation is sufficient to show the nature of the case: J.A. Guy, *The Cardinal's Court* (Hassocks, 1977), pp. 52–3; but these totals must include instances of private informers/suers against the jurors as well as prosecutions by the attorney general.

133 Cromwell's interest in cases which might in some way be damaging to the crown if they were not handled correctly is also demonstrated by his keeping of jury lists: *Letters and Papers, Henry VIII*, vii, supp. no. 123, *ibid.*, xii (i), no. 777. For examples of Cromwell's communication with regional councils concerning jurors see *ibid.*, viii, no. 457, *ibid.*, xiii (i), nos. 371, 824, *ibid.*, xv, no. 681. For reports from justices of assize see *ibid.*, iv (i), no. 1223.

134 Smith, ed. Alston, pp. 109–10.

135 W. Hudson, *A Treatise on the Court of Star Chamber in Collectanea Juridica*, ed. F. Hargrave (London, 1791–2), ii, 72.

136 Cromwell's relationship with the criminal law in general I hope to deal with in a forthcoming work.

137 Bellamy, *Bastard Feudalism*, particularly chapters one and six; also Bellamy, *Criminal Law*, chapters one to five.

138 The statistics for the Home Circuit in this paragraph are from Cockburn, *Assize Introduction*, pp. 175–81.

139 *Middlesex County Records*, Middlesex County Record Society, ed. J.C. Jeaffreson 1886–92, ii, 245–87.

140 *Ibid.*, ii, 245.

141 However, it has been argued in regard to Suffolk that there was no great influx of radicals on to the peace commission there during Somerset's ascendancy: D. MacCulloch, *Suffolk and the Tudors* (Oxford, 1986), p. 167.

142 Lawson, p. 152; Elder, p. 278; PRO JUST 3/211, 213. The Yorkshire gaol delivery records for 1399–1407 provide a conviction rate for multiple-count offenders of 54.2 per cent compared with an overall one (i.e. single plus multiple) of 23 per cent: Ellis, p. 147.

143 Lawson, p. 153; Elder, p. 274; PRO JUST 3/211, 213.

144 Lawson, p. 151; Garay, p. 349.

145 Gadbois, p. 76.

146 *The Price Revolution in Sixteenth Century England*, ed. P.H. Ramsey (London, 1971), pp. 38–41.

147 *Calendar of Assize Records, Indictments, Elizabeth I*, for Essex, Hertfordshire, Kent, Surrey, and Sussex. The observations are mine.

148 PRO JUST 3/211, 213; Elder, pp. 305–29.

4

AFTERMATH

Those acquitted were released from prison when they had paid their prison charges. We do not know if their indictment and trial was in any way prejudicial to their status in the community (other than giving them a reputation), but it is possible that holders of office under the crown might have been debarred from the same for the future. Immediately on the pronouncement of guilt the clerk of the court asked the jurors what lands, tenements and goods the prisoner possessed at the time of the misdeed, a question to which they could rarely give an answer and which was therefore left to the sheriff to determine. The verdict of the person accused of felony could not be altered or refined in any way by the justices, although in a judgment (i.e. sentence) on the convicted person it was necessary for them to ask him what he could say in arrest of judgment, to say why he should not be sentenced to death.[1] It was at this point, says Smith, that those who could read demanded benefit of clergy.[2]

There is no reason to doubt Smith's veracity here: in the mid-sixteenth century claims for benefit of clergy were doubtless made immediately before the justices gave judgment. This had not always been the case. Until approximately the middle of the fourteenth century it had been more common for those accused of felony to plead their clergy at the outset of the trial; sometimes, indeed, they claimed it before they had offered a plea. In the late twelfth and the early thirteenth centuries *clerici* (i.e. clerks: those in higher and lower ecclesiastical orders) accused of felony might well refuse to answer in lay court and deny its jurisdiction, basing their refusal on church policy and the concession by Henry II in 1176.[3] Even in the later thirteenth century this practice of refusing even to enter a plea to the charge against them and demanding to be handed over to the jurisdiction of the bishop cannot have been uncommon. The response of the secular authorities was not to proceed to try them in a normal trial but to hold a so-called *ex officio* inquest into their guilt. This inquest provided the secular authorities with a verdict, but since its findings were not an integral part of the lay trial process the justices could not use it to pronounce a judgment. Rather it was used to give the crown title (usually temporarily, but possibly permanently) to the goods of the *clericus*. Such an inquest, where it found the suspect principal guilty, cleared the way for any accessories to be indicted or appealed.[4]

From the end of the thirteenth century the majority of those who believed they might claim the privilege successfully seem to have inclined to the offering of what has been called a 'lay plea'. That is to say they accepted the jurisdiction of the secular court and answered 'not guilty' when the charge was put to them.

They were then tried in the manner of other suspect felons and there was no need for an *ex officio* inquest. Only if the trial resulted in their conviction would they demand the benefit of their clergy.[5] The accused were prompted to adopt this strategy because they knew a refusal to plead coupled with a demand to be handed over to the jurisdiction of the bishop might result in a lengthy period in an ecclesiastical gaol, or even put them in danger of *peine forte et dure*. If, on the other hand, the accused on arraignment gave no indication he might seek the clerical privilege but allowed his trial to take the normal course he had a chance of escaping punishment entirely. If, however, he was convicted, he might still escape the gallows by claiming the benefit providing he could pass a test to determine he was indeed *clericus*. In the thirteenth century one way to prove this status was for the accused to provide evidence of having been clerically tonsured, or to offer a certificate of his orders; but by the early fourteenth century the successful completion of a reading test had become the dominant element in the process. This examination of literacy did not apparently necessitate the prisoner reading aloud from a book before the middle of the fourteenth century. Before that time the clerical test was not solely one for literacy and therefore probably not open to the criticism that it saved from the gallows lay felons who happened to be literate.[6]

In the late thirteenth century the judges of the two benches appear to have made a number of procedural rules about benefit of clergy, rules which the ecclesiastical authorities seem to have been forced to accept, although under protest. Thus should the ordinary claim as a clerk a man who later proved not to be so his prelate would lose his temporalities. However obnoxious or of criminal background the clerk was known to be, should the lay justices themselves be of the opinion he was indeed *clericus* the ordinary was obligated to claim him. Nor would the justices concede that when the ordinary had claimed a prisoner as *clericus* he should be delivered to the ecclesiastical arm immediately. They held he should be remanded back to gaol if there were believed to be other charges pending against him. The justices also forced the church to accept that in certain cases a prisoner might be handed over to the ordinary with the obligation that he should be held in the episcopal gaol 'absque purgatione', that is to say without being able to compurgate and therefore gain his freedom at some future date.[7]

The number of successful claims for benefit of clergy was not great in the later middle ages. The extant Wiltshire gaol delivery records of the period 1275 to 1304 provide a figure of only 3.5 per cent of those arraigned, a gaol delivery roll covering the years 1329–35 yields a total of about 5 per cent, while Yorkshire gaol delivery records for the period 1359–63 offer a low rate of about 1.5 per cent. The records of the same county for the period 1399–1407 show a level of 4.27 per cent. The extant rolls of the south-western gaol delivery circuit for the years 1416–30 reveal only 1.39 per cent of persons arraigned were allowed their clergy (all at the outset of their arraignment and thus there was not a single mention of a 'clericus convictus'). However, the gaol delivery records of the eastern circuit for the period 1437–41 provide a rate of just over 5 per cent and the Yorkshire records for the years 1439–60 yield a not dissimilar incidence of 4.32 per cent. The eastern circuit roll for the years 1440–1, it is worth noting, contains reference to what is a rarity in the later medieval period: accused who claimed but were refused the privilege.[8]

If we place the successful claims for benefit of clergy alongside the numbers of felons found guilty in the periods and areas just mentioned, an exercise we ought not to undertake for the period before the mid-fourteenth century when clerics were frequently claimed before trial, we notice that the percentage of those convicted who obtained the privilege was usually in the 13 to 17 per cent range. The figure for all six circuits between 1388 and 1399 was 16.9 per cent,[9] for the eastern circuit from 1437 to 1441 about 17.5 per cent, for Yorkshire 1439–60 just over 13 per cent, which was no different from that county's rate for 1359–63 although lower than that for the years 1399–1407 (26 per cent).[10]

In the last two-thirds of the sixteenth century benefit of clergy was allowed for virtually only those men who had been arraigned for manslaughter or felonious larceny. The key statute here was 1 Edward VI c.12, which in essence reaffirmed the rules made by 23 Henry VIII c.1; this statute had restored the act 4 Henry VIII c.2.[11] These statutes denied the privilege for those accused of murder, highway robbery, burglary (i.e. breaking houses by day or night with the inhabitants put in fear), and the stealing of horses, all crimes considered particularly obnoxious. Until 1566 the cut-purse could claim his benefit if he was literate, but by the statute 8 Elizabeth c.4 the privilege was taken away. The most notable feature of the history of the clerical privilege in the sixteenth century was the very high incidence of such cases in the reign of Elizabeth, at least on the circuit whose records have survived. Four home circuit counties in the 1560s show percentages of between 41 and 47 of those convicted, although for Surrey the figure was almost 58 per cent, a level it was to sustain throughout the remainder of Elizabeth's reign. The Essex rate for the 1580s was 58 per cent also, but it declined to 52.5 per cent in the last decade of the century. Kent maintained its level of the 1570s throughout the 1580s but this then rose for the 1590s to over 54 per cent. In Sussex there was a large leap in the rate from the 1570s to the 1580s, from 41.4 to nearly 59 per cent, but as with Essex there was a decline in the 1590s (to 36.5 per cent).[12] The Middlesex sessions records show a rate which rose steadily: it was about 23 per cent in the 1560s, 33.5 per cent in the 1570s, 36.4 per cent in the 1580s and 39 per cent in the 1590s. Rather remarkably the rate for the Edwardian years 1549–53 was only 8.5 per cent and that for the reign of Mary 8.75 per cent.[13] Occasional references to gaol delivery sessions in the official correspondence of Henry VIII's reign suggest a fifteenth century rather than an Elizabethan rate.[14] The gaol delivery records of the palatinate of Chester provide a rate, up to 1580 at least, which is also much more akin to those we have noted in regard to the fifteenth century: it was about 18 per cent of those convicted in the 1560s and 17 per cent in the 1570s. Yet by the end of the century the Chester rate had risen markedly and was approaching that of the south-east: in the 1580s it was about 28 per cent and in the 1590s just over 40 per cent of those convicted.[15] Whether Chester was typical of the midlands or of the north is impossible to ascertain. Very similar to the Chester rates for the 1560s and 1590s were those of the Middlesex sessions, although they were about 7 per cent higher in the two intervening decades. The Middlesex rate for the 1590s, it is worth noting, was not very different from that of the home circuit counties in the 1560s.

The Middlesex incidence of successful claims for the clerical privilege increased two and a half times over between the 1550s and the 1560s. It seems unlikely that literacy increased at the same rate, but such a social phenomenon cannot be entirely ruled out. It is just possible that a protestant regime, with the accompanying emphasis on the study of the written word of the scriptures, did tend to foster rudimentary reading skills. There is also the possibility that the literacy test was being administered with a new degree of generosity early in the reign of Elizabeth. How this might have occurred we can only conjecture. Perhaps the gaol delivery justices had achieved a dominance in this part of court procedure whereby they, rather than the bishop's officer, usually decided which criminals could read satisfactorily. No administrative order to this effect has yet been discovered and indeed Thomas Smith implies the decision lay totally with the ecclesiastical officer; but then we are not certain when Smith wrote his piece.[16] His comments may have been about the Marian legal system.

In 1576 the system of benefit of clergy was drastically altered. The statute 18 Elizabeth c.7 stipulated that those who were allowed the privilege in future, rather than being delivered to the ordinary, should be branded on the hand and then put in a secular gaol for a year or set at liberty. This must have meant not only the end of imprisonment in the bishop's gaol and of purgation but also the elimination of the bishop's officer from his watching brief at the arraignment. Thus the lay justices were established in total control of the reading test. At a time when the conviction rate for felony had risen to notable heights the justices may have been tempted to use the awarding of the clerical privilege as a way of differentiating the felony or felon of no great moment from those which were truly heinous. How far such notions of equity persuaded them to manipulate the reading test is still unclear.[17]

In this period the person convicted could not get his case moved by way of appeal (in the modern sense) to a superior court, nor could the jury be attainted as in a private action. If benefit of clergy was not obtainable then the most likely way for the felon to escape the gallows was by means of a king's pardon. A royal pardon relevant to the felonies he had committed might be pleaded by the suspect on his arraignment or at any subsequent moment up to the giving of judgment, and even, although infrequently, up to the execution of the judgment. It might be granted by the king himself, by the king and parliament, by those given the power to do so by royal commission, or by the holder of one of the great franchises of Durham, Lancaster, and Chester.[18] The granting of royal pardons in substantial numbers has been traced back to Edmund II in the tenth century. The increase in the categories of crimes which were unemendable and the parallel extension of the king's suit, it has been argued, made necessary the 'possibility of mitigation of punishment in approved cases'. The Saxon, Norman, and Angevin antecedents of the later medieval pardoning system show themselves very clearly.[19] Indeed it seems fair to say that of all the different procedural parts of the English criminal law in the centuries under review the conventions governing the royal pardon were the longest lasting and least subject to change. Thus if the culprit was seeking an individual pardon (i.e. peculiar to that person) there had to be a petition to the king, and nearly always there was the employment of an important man or woman as an interceder; there had also to be payments by the supplicant. It was not uncommon for a pardon, when issued, to contain reasons why clemency was in this instance deserved. Whether these justifications were given in order to soften the hostility of injured parties, or because the community at large was generally antagonistic to pardons is not clear. Medieval kings on occasion granted pardons, so they said, because of a religious festival or a holy person, or because of the poverty of the felon.[20] The last reason was still given periodically in the sixteenth century. Possibly it meant the felon was being awarded the king's grace because he stole to provide himself or his family with the necessities of life.

There were also pardons which were granted because of some fault or peculiarity in the legal process which prevented the doing of proper justice. Thus these were given because a person had killed another but not with malicious (i.e. felonious) intent, the deed being done accidentally or in self-defence; or the killer was insane; or the crime was some other type of felony but the accused was insane. In these cases the justices had the power to recommend mercy and they did so almost universally. Furthermore, as far as we can detect, pardons were forthcoming with equal regularity. In these instances the person pardoned probably did not need anyone to intercede on his behalf with the king apart from the justices and therefore was spared all but administrative expenses. The justices were also expected to recommend a pardon when they believed a person arraigned before them had been wrongly convicted by the jury.[21] This was because there was no other way to right the wrong in this period. As we have seen the judgment given by the justices had to follow the verdict of the jury. Death was the only possible sentence when a person was convicted of felony. There was no alternative punishment available as there was when the offence was a misdemeanour. As might be imagined it was the death penalty which enhanced the value of pardons and benefit of clergy.

With these aspects of the system of pardoning, contemporaries found little fault. They were less happy about the many pardons which allowed the accused to go free for misdeeds which were not excusable. Periodically there were complaints in parliament. In 1309 Edward II promised he would only permit pardons for killing in self-defence, by misadventure, or from insanity, but it was said he was giving his peace lightly in 1312. Nor was the promise being honoured in the early years of the subsequent reign. In 1328 and 1330 the king was compelled to make the same pledge once more.[22] Parliament's intention in the middle years of the fourteenth century was to see that those receiving pardons, if they wanted them to remain valid, should find mainpernors to their future good conduct; and also to ensure that felons, if they were pardoned, were pardoned 'in parliament', that is to say with the approval of the lords and commons or the king's council.[23] The parliamentary commons' demands in 1390, however, were in another direction. Parliament had given up its attempts to limit pardoning to the time of its own sessions and its efforts in this session to stop pardons altogether were rejected by the king. Yet it did manage to secure that to be excused treason, murder, or rape, the pardon must specifically mention these crimes, and that those persons who interceded for the accused should have their names recorded on the pardon so that if the miscreant repeated his offence the intercessor might be fined. In 1404 the act of 1390 was extended by statute to stipulate the endorsing of any pardon granted to an approver with the name of he who had been instrumental in its procurement; he was to be fined £100 if the culprit offended again.[24]

The statutes of 1390 and 1404 have additional significance for the historian. The Ricardian act demonstrates some of the administrative stages in the felony pardoning process. The petition for pardon, having been acceded to by the king and the name of any interceder endorsed on it by the chamberlain, was sent normally to the keeper of the privy seal whose warrant took it to the chancery where, if it was an individual pardon, it was engrossed by one of the two crown clerks there.[25] These rules were not immutable. On occasion the king gave instructions for the drafting of a pardon to the chancellor by word of mouth. The grantee paid a standard fee into the hanaper, pleaded the pardon before the justices and gave the clerk of the court a pair of gloves or the value thereof as payment for its enrolment in the record. The pardon was then proclaimed.[26]

The statute of 1404 (5 Henry IV c.2) also tells us something about the pardoning system from the viewpoint of the accused felon. It mentioned those who on arraignment became approvers. They did so, apparently, in order to gain the time to find allies in the world outside: they would seek pardons by means of 'brokerage, grants, and gifts to divers persons'. Here we have the reality of the felony pardon system laid bare. For all those arraigned of felony it must have been obvious that self-help and friends' help and intercession with the king was the most certain way out of their present difficulties. Crucial, therefore, to the person accused of felony was the period between being taken into custody and arraignment, and also the time immediately subsequent to the giving of the verdict. At these times he had to have his family or friends vigorously seeking to achieve his pardon. It may well have helped him to make his interest in gaining a pardon known to the officers of the law, that is to say the gaoler, the sheriff and his servants, and the court officials including the justices' clerks, at the earliest opportunity. There is, we might expect, no reference to such manoeuvres in court records and little in other sources but there can be no doubt that such was the way the system operated. In 1302 it was argued successfully that when a man commits a felony and is taken he seeks to purchase a pardon from the king while he is in gaol, and that this was commonplace.[27]

To provide the time for his friends to arrange intercession with the king the accused felon usually needed to have the justices remand him back to gaol without arraignment or, if convicted, to have him reprieved.[28] We may suspect pressure from magnates, douceurs to the justices' clerks, with perhaps the financial ability of the accused to employ an attorney, played a part in achieving these delays.[29] If the accused was remitted to gaol without arraignment the justices did not need to give a reason for their actions. If found guilty there were, as the records show, several official reasons why he might be remanded. The justices might consider the verdict unjustified as the evidence was weak; or the law might be 'doubtful' in regard to the particular circumstances of the crime; the justices might consider the jury's verdict had been unduly influenced by the accused's place of origin.

It was the task of the friends of the accused to interest in the suit for pardon to the king some minister or courtier of influence who had regular access to the monarch. There was no shortage of candidates here, be it the thirteenth or the sixteenth century, for the profits were good. James I was moved to comment on one occasion that if Judas were alive and had been condemned for betraying Christ some courtier for sure would be found to beg his pardon.[30] The mechanics of intercession are well displayed in the case of Adrian Skell, who was accused of manslaughter in 1535. The interceder was Lord Lisle, the lieutenant of Calais. First of all, Lisle sent his agent John Hussey to solicit the king's chief minister Thomas Cromwell for the pardon. Cromwell does not seem to have taken any part in its obtaining; very possibly he simply made it known he would not object to it. Perhaps it was Cromwell who referred Lisle and Hussey to John Norris, gentleman usher of the king's privy chamber, for it was the latter who appears to have been largely instrumental in obtaining the king's assent; later on Hussey advised his master to write to Norris to thank him for the pardon.

It seems as though Norris's request to the king did not bring instant royal assent but rather some careful negotiation between king and supplicant. This was undertaken by Hussey, who thought it best to circumvent any scruples the king may have had by explaining that the death had occurred in a drunken affray.

King Henry suggested the pardon would be worth £100 to Lord Lisle since many others had sought it but had been refused. Presumably the king was estimating that Lisle could charge £100 for his services and thinking that the royal coffers should benefit by a proportionate amount. Hussey reported to his master that the pardon (and a writ of allowance) had cost him an hundred shillings, which seems to have been the administrative charges. These were larger than usual because of the elaborate manner in which the indictment had been drafted and which demanded the aid of 'the best practitioners in chancery' to annul in drawing up the pardon. Individual or 'special' pardons, as this was, must usually have necessitated the services of a lawyer for their drafting so that every term of the accusation in the indictment was countered and the places of residence of the person pardoned and the 'additions' to his name correctly given. This pardon, we notice, was to be for the preservation of Skell's life only. He was to receive back none of his forfeited goods since the king had already given them to Lord Howard. Because of the danger of a suit Skell might bring against Howard at some future date the king required the latter's approval for the pardon to be gained in advance, presumably by means of another payment or an agreement.[31]

Of particular interest is the king's comment that the securing of this pardon was being sought by a number of notables (a 'bidding' war?) and the information by Hussey that Lisle was a front-runner in this competition because he was in royal favour at that moment.[32] The correspondence dealing with the case is also of particular value in demonstrating that the king, even in the sixteenth century, took a personal interest in felony pardons, at least where the supplicant and his friends had the wherewithal to pay a substantial amount. The employment of, or at least the utilization of, the advice of an ally in the royal household should not surprise us; it had been common for centuries. The case also reminds us that felony pardons might or might not restore forfeited (i.e. where the accused had been convicted) or sequestrated (i.e. where he had been indicted only) possessions. Furthermore, quite often they did not provide for the release of the accused felon from prison; he would also have to pay prison charges.[33]

Having obtained his remand a not uncommon recourse in the later medieval centuries for the felon of means was to have his case certified by the justices into the king's bench. For this a writ of *certiorari* from chancery was necessary. Whether this was obtainable by mere payment or whether the king's justice either at Westminster or at the gaol delivery had their say on the matter is not clear. In the early sixteenth century the chancellor might need a royal warrant before he issued a writ of *certiorari*.[34] The sending up of the case was not achieved, we may suspect, simply because of a point of law; for example because of the insufficiency of the indictment. There were so many cases of such insufficiency that the errors of the clerks who drafted the indictments, or unalloyed judicial reflection on the case seem inadequate explanations.[35] Moving his case into the king's bench almost always resulted in the accused being acquitted. However, in strictly legal charges alone the expense must have been substantial and few can have been able to afford this recourse. A good number of lesser persons guilty of felony seem to have benefited in the sixteenth century from judicial sponsorship of their petitions to the king for pardon. Whether the justices' 'subscriptions' to these petitions were induced by gifts from the prisoner or his friends, or pressure from notables, is not clear. What is striking is that the justifications for the pardons were only partly of a legal nature. Several felons were pardoned because many of those they had robbed had had restitution of their goods. One murderer obtained his pardon at the instance of several magnates who were moved by the man's penitence; two others because their victims had provoked them. A man was pardoned for being an accessory to felony because it was believed by his neighbours he did it out of ignorance and against his will. Twenty-five convicted felons from one circuit were pardoned on a single occasion apparently because of their financial state ('poor prisoners').[36]

In sixteenth-century records are to be found references to pardons and to recommendations for pardons given on the grounds that the accused, having confessed to or been convicted of a felony, had 'appeached' (or was ready to) particular felons. These were persons who were probably earlier or recent associates in crime of the accused. Thus the 'appeacher' appears to have been very similar to the medieval approver, the confessed felon who, to extend his life, appealed his confederates.[37] By the sixteenth century the motivating factor for this strategy had changed from temporary escape from the gallows, coupled with the possibility of trial by battle and no certainty he would not be executed later anyway, to secure pardon of life and limb. In these 'appeachers' we seem to have found the origins of the practice of turning king's evidence. We may even be able to identify the first such case: in 1522 Henry VIII in person promised a pardon (for theft) to Robert Holforde of Cheshire if he named his two confederates. The king was apparently moved to make this offer because Holforde had not himself received anything from the sale of the articles stolen, because he had a wife and four small children, and more particularly no doubt because Holforde had been responsible for the recovery of one of the royal falcons.[38] A few years later the draft of an intended treason act (c. 1530) proposed that when there was a conspiracy against the king the conspirator who revealed it so that the rest were convicted was to have a free pardon and one quarter of the inheritance and goods of those who forfeited as a result of his zeal.[39] In January 1535 the under-sheriff of Cheshire and two associates tried to induce a prisoner in Chester castle to 'appeach' one Piers Bryen by means of a promise of a pardon. In 1560 the leader of a gang of burglars, after conviction, was remanded to the Marshalsea prison where he confessed to other felonies and as a result his accomplices in these were arrested. In consequence he was granted a pardon. The practice was still continuing at the end of the century. In 1597 a William Harris, after his conviction for horse stealing, 'appeached' several unknown felons, as it was said, and as a result many victims of crime had restitution of their goods; Harris was pardoned.[40] In the later sixteenth century the form of 'appeachment' was still inchoate yet one crucial element is very noticeable. This was that the approver only benefited if his accusation brought about the conviction of the person he had charged yet the 'appeacher' seems to have been pardoned merely for making the accusation of his confederates, not because his charge resulted in their conviction. Only in the 1590s does it appear that pardons were offered to these felons at the suggestion of the justices who tried the cases. It rather looks as if, earlier, some agent of a minister or of the council was instrumental in arranging matters.

Those seeking a pardon for felony and their friends, even when they were persons of wealth, might on occasion find the king and his ministers unresponsive to their supplications. In 1510 Henry VIII commanded that a pardon, already sealed and in the hanaper, should not be handed over to the would-be beneficiary. In 1535 a supplicant asked Thomas Cromwell to prevent the lord chancellor from procuring a pardon for a particular person, telling him that if the law proceeded the crown could make a much greater profit from a later one.[41] Bishop Rowland Lee, president of the council of the marches of Wales, reported in March 1540 to Cromwell that suits were likely to be made for the pardon of a particular murderer and asked the minister should see they were unsuccessful because of the need to make an example. A year earlier Lee had made a similar request but in regard to a servant of Lord Ferrers. He asked Cromwell that if any suit for the man's pardon came into his hands he should stop it 'for the hanging of such a one, being a gentleman' would save lives and do more good than the hanging of an hundred 'petty wretches'. The tone of these letters from Lee is that he was sure Cromwell was very ready to intervene to prevent suits to the king achieving success when they clashed with his policies on public order.[42] In June 1541 Lord Dacres of the South pleaded guilty before the lord high steward to killing a park keeper. Chapuys tells us that his judges, when they sentenced him, wept and in a body asked for his pardon from the king. Henry, however, refused and Dacres was hanged. The king's refusal to pardon evoked a lot of comment not simply because Dacres was a peer but also because Dacres had changed his plea to guilty and thrown himself on the king's mercy. In this instance, in refusing a pardon, the king was probably indulging his own prejudice as well as making an example of an errant nobleman, for the Dacres family had been an object of royal hostility since the 1520s.[43] Also idiosyncratic in regard to pardons was Queen Elizabeth. She would refuse to grant them where the beneficiary had a reputation for adultery or vicious living, and she is also on record as going against a commission's recommendation of pardon for a pirate and insisting on his execution.[44]

Most pardons were absolute but a fair number were granted with conditions attached. A recurring example of felony pardon in the fourteenth century was where the recipient was pardoned his offence on condition he went with the army to fight in the wars. This particular arrangement was still practised in Elizabethan times. For example in 1563 a list was made of prisoners in Newgate, a central gaol for felons, who were 'fit to be pardoned' because they were 'able to serve' (i.e. in a military capacity).[45] In the later fourteenth century pardons were granted for felony on several occasions with a proviso that they were invalid for murder, rape, if the recipient was a common thief or taken with mainour, or had broken gaol, or had killed a named royal official.[46] Amongst felons at large it seems to have been thought that a pardon could sometimes be won by serving the king in a police capacity. In 1535 several murderers made submission to the council of the marches and offered to capture thieves in order to earn their pardon.[47] What may well have been the impact of strong protestantism on legal thinking appears to have affected the granting of pardons in Elizabeth's reign. Pardons for felony were sometimes given conditionally on the recipient making improvement in his moral conduct or at least in hope of the same. Thus one of 1593 was granted in the expectation of amendment of life and of good service, and one of 1599 was awarded with the comment it was the beneficiary's first offence and given because he had promised to be good in the future.[48] Moral improvement was of concern to the queen herself. In 1560 she ordered the release of a pirate in order to judge his conduct before his pardon was delivered to him.[49] We should not forget that in one sense all medieval pardons for felony had been conditional: the recipient was pardoned the king's suit but accepted he must answer any appeal brought against him for the same offence.[50]

The pardons mentioned so far were individual or special pardons, granted in answer to separate petitions. There were also granted by the king from the late fourteenth century onwards general pardons. These were issued, usually at the request of parliament, theoretically to celebrate a notable royal event such as a coronation, or a jubilee, or a coming of age. Such pardons commonly covered treason and trespass as well as felony. There were also general pardons which were not nationwide but limited to the inhabitants of a particular area.[51] General pardons, when on offer, were available to anyone who came to collect them and paid a small fee (eighteen shillings and four pence) into chancery. In Henry VI's reign they were sought by between two and three thousand persons on each of five occasions. A similar number appear to have been awarded on the occasion of the general pardon at the outset of Henry VIII's reign.[52] This pardon was accompanied two days later by a ratification of the pardons granted by Henry VII and the pardoning of all those being sued by the crown at that moment. The burden on the chancery was great enough for the chancellor, early in May 1509, to be allowed to amend the pardons, which were being produced, by inserting or excluding causes as was suitable. This general pardon listed a number of persons who were to be excepted from the king's grace and there were also government instructions within a few months barring others from benefiting. This was followed in October 1509 by the issue of warrants awarding the general pardon to persons who had been excepted. The final modification of this pardon came in 1510 when the king's council recommended it should not be allowed where the offender was a common murderer.[53]

In the sixteenth century general pardons were usually promulgated by parliament and indeed the majority of parliaments were responsible for one.[54] Often they were acceded to by the monarch, so it appears, in return for the granting of a subsidy. The statute might well refer to the financial loss the pardon would cause the king and emphasize his love for his people and his desire to lead them to better ways by an example of kindliness and forgiveness.[55] It was common for a sixteenth-century general pardon to contain a proviso to the effect that the recipient need only pay a token sum to the crown; this was for the sealing and other administrative costs in chancery.[56] The general pardons of the fifteenth century extended to all types of offences and the general pardons of he earliest years of Henry VIII's reign (1509 and 1514) were just as extensive, but thereafter the statutes which announced them contained lists of exceptions. Thus the act 7 Henry VIII c.11, while it affirmed that those who committed any offence which was felony by statute should be pardoned, excluded those accused of common law felonies such as homicide, burglary, robbery, and felonious theft.[57]

The general pardon of 1523 (14/15 Henry VIII c.17) extended to felonies 'made by statute' and also to manslaughter, theft of objects worth less than 20 shillings and escapes from custody. Excluded, therefore, were murder, robbery, burglary, and the theft of valuable objects, crimes which comprised over half of a typical gaol delivery calendar. In the general pardon statute of 1529 (21 Henry VIII c.1) there was an extensive list of excepted crimes. In the felony category appeared murder, robbery, felonious theft of over 20 shillings value, arson of houses, and rape. These, with the addition of escape of felons from custody, were to be the standard exceptions later in the century although piracy appeared in the 1540s and witchcraft from 1566. Occasionally prisoners in particular gaols were excluded from general pardons. In the pardon of 1548 it was those in the Tower, the Marshalsea, and the Fleet.[58] The latter exception also appeared in the pardon of 1585. In the general pardon of 1576 (18 Elizabeth c.24) excepted felonies were murder, robbery, rape, escape of those imprisoned for felony, witchcraft and sorcery, and theft of 40 shillings in value from a dwelling house; nor were felons who obtained the pardon to be excused the forfeiture of their lands, goods, chattels, and revenues. The pardon of 1585 added burglary to the list while that of 1597 did the same for arson of barns, the making of seditious and slanderous books, and the theft of horses.[59]

A statute of 1336 stipulated that pardoned felons must find sureties for their future good behaviour within three months of getting their pardons.[60] This was to control recidivism among those who had obtained individual pardons. The earliest evidence we possess of what might be called the vetting of those who pleaded the general pardon comes from the first months of the reign of Elizabeth. The privy council instructed the justices of gaol delivery that they should reprieve all those claiming under the coronation pardon but only, apparently, so long as they were known to be of good behaviour; they were also to make a report on each case to the lord great seal.[61] References to this practice operating when other general pardons were granted later in Elizabeth's reign are lacking. However, in 1592 the privy council instructed that in Ireland no pardons should be granted before 'the causes for the graunting thereof' and 'the quallyties of the offences' to be pardoned had been considered by the deputy and his council. In addition the privy council stipulated that no pardons were to allow the return of forfeited lands without a special warrant by the crown.[62] Granting to the felon his life but not his forfeited possessions appears to have been regular practice in the sixteenth century. The privy council, on this occasion, ordered that persons pardoned should pay some reasonable fine, that is to say one graded according to their condition and wealth. There is no suggestion of this in any of the general pardons for England.

Because felony as covered by general pardons was so narrowly defined by the late sixteenth century perhaps over half of felons were excluded from benefiting. Nevertheless a good number of felons did profit and until Elizabeth's reign there was no vetting of the applicant's reputation. When a person's offence fell within one of the 'pardonable' categories its heinousness or the obnoxiousness of the perpetrator was irrelevant. This suggests that the same may have been true of individual pardons. Hurnard, viewing homicide in the thirteenth century, was of the opinion that pardons were given for sound legal reasons, although she recognized there was little proof of this.[63] It seems more likely that since individual pardons were procured essentially by means of intercessors of social importance, who were paid for their services, with probably additional, smaller, payments to other persons involved, sound legal reasons were by no means essential. Sometimes the justices had to be persuaded to remand or reprieve the prisoner so that he would have time to arrange for intercession but influence or payment were likely to remove any initial objections.[64] The only manner in which this self-help road to pardon might be blocked was when the king was personally hostile to the petitioner or his particular offence.

How many persons accused of felony were able to secure a pardon either individual or general? Only by obtaining some answer to this question can we gauge if the system of pardoning undermined the keeping of public order or merely moderated the heavy hand of criminal justice in the period under review. The medieval plea rolls seem to indicate that pardons were pleaded in only a few cases. The Wiltshire gaol delivery records of 1275–1305 show that less than one per cent of those accused of felony offered one. Hanawalt's survey of serious crime in eight counties 1300–48 reveal that only 1.5 per cent of those arraigned were pardoned and Garay has shown that for the period 1388–99, for the six main circuits, the rate was only 3 per cent. For the first ten years of Henry IV's reign there was, if we exclude the northern circuit, a rate of 7.5 per cent.[65] During the reign of Henry V and that of his son there seems to have been a reversion to the low rate of a century before. The records for the south-western circuit for 1416–30 provide a pardon rate of a mere one per cent, those of the eastern circuit for the years 1437–41 an even lower one, while the records for Yorkshire (a county of substantially higher levels from 1350–1410) yield for 1439–60 a rate of about 2.3 per cent.[66] If we judge by the records of Essex, Kent, Sussex, and Surrey, the level had risen substantially by the reign of Elizabeth. In the 1560s 6.6 per cent of those arraigned were pardoned, in the 1570s 5.4 per cent, in the 1580s 3.5 per cent, and in the 1590s approximately 6.8 per cent. There were, of course, local variations in the pardon rate, but the only one of note was the low percentage at the Essex and Sussex sessions in the 1590s (3.5 per cent) in comparison with the high level for Kent and Surrey (9.5 per cent).[67]

The proportion of pardons which were obtained under general pardons rather than by individual supplication is at the moment unknown but there are a few pointers from particular periods and regions. The relatively large number of pardons pleaded at gaol delivery sessions in the first decade of Henry IV's reign can probably be explained by the fact that there were at least five general pardons issued in that period. Similarly there were a great many pleaded in the last year of Richard II's reign, which also was the time of a general pardon. In this year the percentage of accused who pleaded pardons was a notable 12.5. In the next reign there were even higher peak years: the sixth year of Henry IV provided a rate of 15.5 per cent, and the fifth year one as great as 17 per cent.[68] These peaks, it will be noticed, were as much as twice as high as the average for the decade. As might be expected those who obtained pardons tended to plead them in court soon after they came into their hands. An investigation of mid-fourteenth century practice has shown that about 70 per cent of recipients presented their pardons within six months of issue and only 10 per cent after more than a year had elapsed.[69] It is difficult to tell if the long delays were because the pardon had been obtained in anticipation of being arraigned, because the recipient could not find sureties for future good behaviour, because he could not pay the administrative fees, or some other reason.

As to the categories of felony which were pardoned most frequently a clear pattern is discernible. Hurnard commented that of the 1,900 pardons to be found in the patent rolls for the period 1226–94 only 140 were not for homicide. Such a preponderance still prevailed in the middle of the fourteenth century but by the first decade of the fifteenth a change had occurred.[70] Out of close to 400 persons arraigned for felony at the Yorkshire gaol delivery sessions 1399–1407 55 were pardoned. This large number was apparently because of the several general pardons promulgated during the period; indeed 35 persons benefited under them. Twenty-five of those felons who pleaded a pardon at these sessions were accused of homicide (45 per cent). Of the remainder nine were charged with grand larceny, seven with receiving felons, five with burglary, and three with felonious escape. Of those accused of homicide who were pardoned three had been charged with murder, four with non-felonious killing (accidental or in self-defence), and the rest with manslaughter.[71] As might be expected the extant Elizabethan assize records reveal a very different pattern. Those for Essex and Sussex, if taken together, show that most pardons pleaded were by that time for grand larceny (about 42 per cent), while approximately 20 per cent were for burglary, and around 13 per cent were for robbery. A mere two per cent were for murder, which was the same rate as for manslaughter.[72]

A pardoned felon was not necessarily able to go free immediately after successfully pleading his pardon. He had first to pay his prison charges which could be substantial. This was because securing the services of an interceder could take a considerable time and prisoners, if they did not wish to spend their incarceration in great discomfort, had to pay a variety of relieving charges (i.e. for food and quarters). Prisoners were remanded and reprieved from execution from session to session, and the gaoler, who provided the comforts at a price, and his normal master, the sheriff, profited greatly thereby.[73] Imprisonment in the later middle ages and the sixteenth century was utilized primarily for the holding of those suspected or accused of crimes prior to trial. Only occasionally was it a mode of punishment. The centuries under review and the reigns within them do not offer a static picture nor even an image of steady evolution in attitudes to imprisonment, although there were several constants. Thus the overriding notion was that the proper penalty for the convicted felon was death, and imprisonment was a punishment for particular misdemeanours where a fine, the normal sentence, was inappropriate or insufficient, or temporarily beyond the means of the accused to pay.[74]

It was in statutes of Edward I's reign that terms of imprisonment were first stipulated as standard punishment. The second Statute of Westminster (13 Edward I c.12) imposed on an unsuccessful appellor not only damages for the acquitted appellee but a sentence of a year in gaol. Under the first Statute of Westminster (3 Edward I st.1 c.13) those found guilty of ravishing or abducting a woman were to suffer two years' imprisonment and pay a fine. If they were unable to pay then the gaol term was to be longer. Abduction also figured in the second Statute of Westminster: those who were convicted of abducting a nun were to serve a prison sentence of three years, and those who abducted a child whose marriage belonged to someone else were to be sentenced to two years. Should the child not be restored they were to suffer imprisonment for life. The only other employment of imprisonment in Edward I's legislation against crime was in regard to the killing of the king's deer.[75] The penalty in future was to be not death but a heavy fine, which, if the guilty party could not pay, would be commuted to a year and a day in gaol. This Edwardian legislation was concerned with procedure and offences which touched, or were close to, felony, which was not true of comparable statutes in the fourteenth century or the fifteenth before 1487.

Imprisonment as a punishment appeared in governmental measures in the fourteenth century for the first time in the Ordinance of Labourers (23 Edward III cc.1–7), which commanded that labourers refusing to work at the pre-plague rate were to be imprisoned until they gave surety to do so. Later, in 1424, masters and servants might by summary conviction be sent to gaol for a month for giving or taking excessive wages. In 1381 forcible entry into land was made an indictable offence to be punished by imprisonment, the prisoner to be ransomed at the king's will.[76] Those committing other crimes typical of bastard feudalism were subjected to similar statutory punishments soon after. By the act 2 Henry IV c.2 yeomen accepting livery were to suffer imprisonment and a fine, and two years later (by 4 Henry IV c.8) any disseisor attainted by private suit was to be put in gaol for a year and pay double damages. There seems to have been only one other statute before the Tudor period which stipulated imprisonment as punishment and this was directed against occupiers of houses who allowed their premises to be used for unlawful games (dice, quoits and similar). A convicted occupier was to suffer three years' imprisonment and pay a fine, the players two years and a lesser fine.[77] Two of the several statutes of Henry VII's reign directed against the feuding upper classes allowed imprisonment at the justices' discretion, but the measure which must have noticeably increased the number of felons, as distinct from misdemeanants, in gaol was 3 Henry VII c.2. By this act the custom whereby the crown did not arraign murder suspects for a year and a day, so as to permit a relative of the victim plenty of time to bring an appeal (in reality often to extract compensation from the misdoer), was terminated. Instead arraignment was to be within the year, and if the accused was acquitted he was to be remitted to gaol until the year and day had expired.[78]

There was no statute concerned with serious crime promulgated in the reign of Henry VIII which specifically penalized those convicted by a prison term. In part this may have been because Thomas Cromwell was in favour of keeping the gaol population at a low level.[79] The reign of Edward VI was quite different in this respect. The assembling together of between two and twelve persons in order to break down enclosures or kill people was made punishable by a year in gaol and a fine; so was refusing to assist justices of the peace to suppress such groups. Another act from the same parliament provided the same penalty for anyone who made 'fantastical and fond' prophecies to the peril of the king.[80] A second conviction for this offence was to carry the punishment of imprisonment for life, the first time this sanction had figured in legislation since the reign of Edward I. It appeared again five years later: printing matter which slandered the king and queen and encouraged insurrection (but was not treason under the statute of 1352) was, when done a second time, to carry a penalty of prison for life.[81] Early in Elizabeth's reign imprisonment was for a time a punishment very popular with legislators. In 1563 the statute 5 Elizabeth c.14, which was directed at those who forged deeds and charters or offered such in evidence in court in cases involving title to land, imposed, as part of the punishment on those convicted, imprisonment for life. Mere perjurers in such cases, so another act of the same parliament commanded, were to suffer six months in gaol. Also in 1563, in the notorious act which created the felony of causing death by witchcraft, it was stipulated that using witchcraft to discover treasure or to 'provoke unlawful love' was to carry a penalty of a year's imprisonment and, if the crime was committed a second time, the miscreant was to suffer imprisonment for life. These Edwardian, Marian and early Elizabethan statutes demonstrate clearly how legislators and lawyers made a sharp distinction between serious offences, which should be punished (and were increasingly) by a gaol sentence, and crimes which should be felony and must therefore be punished by death. There were still no felonies carrying a lesser punishment.[82] However, in 1576 the traditional practice of handing over to the ordinary felons who had successfully claimed the benefit of their clergy was ended. Instead such men were to be burned on the hand and discharged, although the justices were given the authority to put them in gaol for up to a year should they want to.[83] If the justices exercised this option to any substantial degree it would have been an intolerable burden on the prison system and we may take it that in general they were hesitant to do so. We have little information on the number of felons who were incarcerated, under the act of 1576 or otherwise, for the purpose of punishment. A rare insight from before that statute was passed is provided by an enquiry into the population of the main London gaols in July 1561.[84] At that time Newgate, which contained mainly London and Middlesex felons, held 36 prisoners, of whom 23 had been attached for felony and were very probably awaiting trial, and 13 were persons already convicted (including 3 of robbery and 9 of 'felony' i.e. felonious theft). Those awaiting trial had all been attached between March and June 1561 as had seven of the persons convicted. Thus only six prisoners (16.6 per cent) had been in the gaol for more than six months.

By the late sixteenth century many of the statutes which prescribed prolonged imprisonment for those offending against them were no longer applicable. Appeals of felony were almost extinct and the law of rape-abduction had been altered. Furthermore offences like 'fantastical' prophesying, the forging of title deeds, and witchcraft, because of their relatively esoteric nature, cannot have figured in many court cases. If we limit our attention strictly to felony then only those who had committed felonious larceny or manslaughter and gained benefit of clergy were candidates for a prison sentence. However, by the last decades of the sixteenth century the number of those being arraigned each year for serious crime was rising markedly, which, even if a number of additional gaols were constructed, seems to have caused the government to search for an alternative to confining felons in prison. The answer, apparently, was galleys. The privy council intended to man galleys with Scottish prisoners of war as early as 1542, and in 1545 the king planned to utilize vagabonds living from theft and vice in London for the same purpose.[85] The first decision to deal in a similar way with those convicted of felony at gaol delivery was probably taken in the early 1580s. There is extant a command from the queen to the justices of assize asking them to certify the names of those persons convicted at their sessions so they might be committed as prisoners to galleys. Later in the decade priests and recusants were being considered for the same fate.[86] Service in the galleys was for those thought not deserving the gallows nor yet the lesser punishment of banishment. By the early 1590s we notice sentences to a set number of years in the galleys being given. In 1602 the privy council instructed the justices of assize to reprieve all condemned felons, except those guilty of rape or burglary, to the galleys. To obtain this remission the felons had to find friends who would pay £3 a year 'for their maintenance', as it was put. Contemporary correspondence suggests this scheme was indeed put into operation.[87] There was, we may conclude, a definite intent in the sixteenth century on the part of the government to use prisons, or at least some type of confinement, for the punishment of convicted felons as well as those guilty of serious misdemeanours.

The last part of the criminal trial was the giving of judgment on those accused whom the juries had convicted. For this the prisoners were called to the bar to receive sentence of death but they were, in theory, allowed first to speak in arrest of judgment. Such statements, where they made a point of law at all, were usually concerned with the insufficiency (i.e. inaccuracies or omissions) of the indictment. However, John Udall tells us that at the Southwark assizes in February 1591 he was able to advance a number of arguments as to why the verdict on him was unsound. These amounted to misdirection of the jury by the justices, failure on the part of the latter to leave the jurors to their own consciences, and to the fact that his misdeed did not properly fall within the statute under which he was tried; he pointed out further that since there was no malicious intent there could be no felony, that no witness had testified against him face to face, and that the chief deposer against him was of dubious character. The justices took issue with Udall over his exceptions against the witnesses but, if we can believe the report of the trial, they did not make objection to his other arguments. In theory if a prisoner wished to make a point of law he was entitled, from the fifteenth century at least, to the assistance in court of an attorney but not otherwise. However, there was no restriction even in the medieval period on a prisoner, or his friends, hiring a lawyer to advise him outside the courtroom, which may be one reason for many of the successful motions against 'insufficient' indictments.[88]

The sentencing of the prisoners was punctuated, we are told, by their cries that the justices should be good to them. Some of those sentenced might be reprieved at this point on instructions received from the king or his council or one of his ministers. Thomas Cromwell was asked by Rowland Lee before sessions were held whether everyone who had been indicted was to be arraigned and whether any of those found guilty were to be reprieved. The tenor of the question was that this was normal practice. From later in the sixteenth century there is a privy council list of prisoners who are to be executed, and another list of those to be reprieved.[89] Much less clear than how those convicted might be reprieved from the gallows is the percentage of death sentences which actually led to execution. The problem is that the courts, while entering in their records those who were to hang, did not set down in unequivocal terms if the hangings had in fact occurred.[90] Most valuable therefore are the comments on the doing of criminal justice to be found occasionally in official correspondence of the sixteenth century. Thus Wolsey was informed by two justices in March 1525 that of twenty-one persons arraigned for felony at their Durham sessions four had been acquitted, seven delivered by proclamation, and six persons executed out of eight found guilty. A report on the York castle gaol delivery of March 1543 implied that all eight persons convicted of felony had been executed.[91] Particularly interesting are the reports by the council of the north on its joint sessions with the justices of assize and gaol delivery. One such of August 1544 noted that of the seventeen felons convicted sixteen were executed and one dispatched to ecclesiastical gaol. Another report, dated one year later, stated that of the twelve persons just condemned for felony ten had been executed and two reprieved.[92] If these figures reflect the general pattern it would appear that in the later years of Henry VIII's reign about 90 per cent of convicted felons went to the gallows, at least in the north of England.

In the subsequent years of the sixteenth century the proportion of condemned persons who escaped execution, in the north at least, may have slightly diminished. In March 1557 the council of the north reported six prisoners executed and one other to have received benefit of clergy, out of seven felons recently convicted at the York gaol delivery; in August 1564 at York, out of the ten persons condemned for felony, seven were executed and three reprieved, while at sessions at Newcastle on Tyne thirteen were put to death and one reprieved out of the fourteen convicted.[93] At the York gaol delivery sessions of August 1565 fourteen persons were convicted of felony, of whom one was reprieved, two were allowed benefit of clergy and eleven were executed. The March sessions of 1569 saw twelve persons convicted, ten being executed and two reprieved, including a woman who was pregnant. The York sessions of April–May 1577, however, provide a hint that in mid-Elizabethan England fewer of those convicted of felony might have been going to the gallows than hitherto. Of the eighteen persons found guilty ten were executed, two allowed benefit of clergy, four reprieved and two punished for petty larceny only.[94] These post-1550 references to numbers of felons executed, in contrast with the earlier set, show only 76 per cent of those convicted went to the gallows. This was in a region where we would expect benefit of clergy to have been claimed less often than in the south; and possibly, although there is no satisfactory way of determining it, where pardon was obtained less frequently. A factor which may have contributed to the high execution rate and the relatively low percentage of claims for the clerical privilege was the presence of members of the council of the north at the gaol delivery sessions.

We have little proof that the presence of these men hardened the hearts of witnesses, jurors, justices, and officers of the ordinary, yet it would be foolish to suggest there can be no suspicion of this. The various conciliar bodies involved in judicial activities were intended, on the criminal law side, to introduce a note of implacability into such justice and check local pressures which might tend towards more acquittals and fewer executions.[95] The picture we obtain from these northern records of the mid-sixteenth century does not appear to correlate at all closely with that provided by the records of the home circuit of Elizabeth's reign. There the proportion of persons convicted of felony who claimed benefit of clergy must have been almost 50 per cent, while those who obtained a pardon must have amounted to about another 10 per cent, giving a total of around 60 per cent who escaped the gallows. It is quite possible that the council of the north had sufficient political power to block attempts to obtain pardon by any but members of the upper classes. However, the very low rate of successful claims for the clerical privilege in the first part of Elizabeth's reign at the northern gaol deliveries where the council of the north was present contrasts markedly with the high incidence at home circuit sessions. The reason might have been the low standard of literacy among those who lived beyond the Trent, but more likely it was the dominance which the councillors established over the ecclesiastical officers and common law justices attending the sessions and over the justices.

By the fourteenth century the standard punishment for felony was hanging.[96] The customs of various boroughs as enshrined in their charters sometimes stipulated other modes of execution in those places, but probably most had turned to hanging by 1300 even if there was no statute or ordinance which so decreed.[97] We still catch sight of older, sterner, punishments: in 1370 it was noted that the marshal of the prostitutes of the royal household held in serjeanty the office of dismembering adjudged malefactors. Before the 1590s there is no indication in the plea rolls of justices sentencing males to any punishment for strict felony save hanging and they were not even permitted to have them hanged in fetters.[98] To Thomas Smith the sentence for felony, which was to hang by the neck until dead, was a fair and uncruel punishment much different from the brutal execution practices of other nations. The convicted malefactor accepts the penalty in good part, Smith tells us: recognizing the jury 'be his countrie

men, and such as he hath himselfe agreed unto', he 'yeeldes for the most part
unto it and doth not repine'.[99] A felon only suffered an additional punishment if
he assaulted a witness, juror, or officer of the law in court. For such a deed the
hand which struck the victim might be cut off prior to execution. Although the
Tudors were notably inventive in regard to physical punishment for criminals in
general they were not the originators of this particular penalty for there were
fourteenth- and fifteenth-century precedents.[100]

It was the Tudor monarchs, however, who first made a regular practice of
hanging convicted felons in chains or 'in fetters' as it was sometimes put. The
intention was that the body should not be taken down from the gibbet by
relatives or any member of the public but allowed to 'consume' (decompose) as a
warning to others. Hanging in chains seems to have been reserved for notorious
felons, particularly murderers, and the order to do so must have come from the
monarch or his council for Sir John Port argued the practice was 'other than the
law wills' and that a justice who gave such a judgment was in error.[101]
Condemned felons were commonly hanged on the local gallows, that is to say in
or near the town where the gaol delivery sessions had taken place, but this was
not a universal rule. The felon of notoriety was sometimes executed at, or near
the scene of his offence.[102] Thus gibbets might temporarily be found in
Cheapside, St Paul's churchyard, at Mile End, or on the banks of the Thames.
The body of a notorious felon was not necessarily displayed at the place of
execution. George Browne, the murderer in the infamous Sanders case (1573),
was hanged before a huge crowd at Smithfield but his corpse was then suspended
in chains at Shooters Hill, where he had perpetrated the misdeed. Should the
condemned person be a servant of a nobleman he might be executed wearing his
master's livery.[103] The notion behind these practices, quite obviously, was that the
corpse should be a warning to others who were inclined to felony.

We know little about the last hours of condemned felons and their behaviour
in the medieval period for chroniclers, except perhaps where the crime was
treason or heresy, had little interest in the infliction of punishment by the secular
authorities. From the mid-sixteenth century on the other hand there were
produced many short descriptions of gallows scenes, the details of which show the
writers or their informers to have been close bystanders, perhaps the protestant
ministers who prepared the criminals for death during the 'liberty' day usually
allowed condemned felons, and comforted them at the gallows.[104] Here speeches
were expected from those about to die if their crimes had been heinous or their
status was relatively high. A notable example was that of Charles, Lord Stourton,
executed for murder in Salisbury market-place in March 1556. He told his
audience he had come there to die, that he was justly condemned by the law, and
that he wished to be an example to everyone. He asked forgiveness of the
murdered men's relatives and requested those present to join in prayer with
him.[105] At her execution in 1573 Ann Sanders, a wealthy member of the London

merchant class who had commissioned the murder of her husband, when admitting her guilt thanked God for punishing her in this world so as to save her in the next. Her female accomplice, who was hanged at the same time, also admitted her guilt in regard to this crime but took advantage of the occasion to deny other crimes imputed to her.[106] The actual hanging took place when the hangman received a signal from the sheriff or his officer. If the condemned persons were standing with nooses round their necks on a cart it was drawn away; if they were standing on a ladder it was turned over. Occasionally we read of a felon leaping off the ladder before the hangman turned it. Those who were hanged normally died of strangulation, their end being hastened, as a German visitor noted, by their friends, who, with permission, 'pulled them by the legs and struck them on the chest to end their lives the sooner'.[107] Burial was left to relatives or friends.

We have little evidence that the government of the day, whether in the later medieval period or the sixteenth century, believed that too many felons were being hanged. Rather, although direct official comment on this point is lacking, the crown and its advisers appear to have believed that the number of executions, if anything, was insufficient and that law officers and jurors must be admonished to that effect.[108] However, more important to the government than a vast number of felons executed was that example should be made of a good number whose crimes were heinous and criminal records long.[109] Evidence that the crown ever considered removing the death penalty from certain felonies is very slight unless we view the increasing number of successful claims for benefit of clergy or the frequent general pardons as the equivalent. A natural reform in the same direction would have been to turn the non-violent offence of felonious larceny into a non-capital crime, but the nearest the crown came to this concession was to extend the general pardons of 1523 and 1529 to theft of under 20 shillings in value and that of 1576 to theft of under 40 shillings.[110] The earliest direct comment critical of the death penalty seems to have been that of Thomas Starkey in his *Dialogue between Pole and Lupset*. There it is suggested that convicted thieves should be allowed to pay back twice the value of the object stolen to avoid being hanged. Starkey further advocated that felons should be forced to labour on public works. There is, however, no indication these ideas figured in 'official thinking'.[111] Only in the later sixteenth century can we detect any governmental interest in an alternative punishment to the death penalty for some convicted felons: this was the galleys which we have noticed above.

Additionally the statistics on felony themselves imply that there was concern over the heavy use of the death penalty as standard punishment. The large numbers of those arraigned for felony who successfully claimed benefit of clergy in Elizabeth's reign (about 30 per cent in south-east England) or pleaded a pardon (about 5 per cent) amount to over one-third who cheated the gallows through an 'escape hatch'. In contrast the rate of those arraigned in the fourteenth and fifteenth centuries, who successfully claimed the clerical privilege, varied markedly according to period and location but perhaps the average was around 3 per cent. For pardons the rate seems to have been just over 2 per cent. Pardon and benefit of clergy totals combined, therefore, amounted to between 5 and 6 per cent. Since the felony conviction rate over the fourteenth and the first part of the fifteenth century averaged just under 20 per cent of those arraigned it appears that no more than 14 per cent were actually hanged.[112] In the south-east (Essex, Kent, Surrey, Sussex, Hertfordshire, and Middlesex) over the period 1559–99 the conviction rate for felony was about 61 per cent,[113] but, as we have seen, about 35 per cent of those arraigned were excused; therefore only 26 per cent of arraigned felons went to the gallows. Thus the execution rate in the later sixteenth century was almost twice that which prevailed in the later medieval period.

Notes

1 Instructive comments on this part of the trial process only begin to appear in the sixteenth century; see for example R. Holinshed, *Chronicles of England, Scotland, and Ireland* (London, 1808), iv, 4, *State Trials*, i, 1298–1305, W. Roper, *The Lyfe of Sir Thomas Moore* ed. E.V. Hitchcock (Early English Text Society, no. 197), pp. 92–5.

2 Smith, ed. Alston, p. 102. The categories of accused who were eligible for the privilege, the nature of their felony apart, are to be found in Bellamy, *Criminal Law*, pp. 116–17.

3 On those whom the term 'clericus' embraced, and the early methods of determining who possessed this status, see Bellamy, *Criminal Law*, pp. 115–16.

4 Those found guilty by the *ex officio* inquest were handed over to the bishop; those found innocent were set free.

5 Bellamy, *Criminal Law*, p. 119.

6 *Ibid.*, pp. 114, 119.

7 *Ibid.*, pp. 120–1.

8 *Wiltshire Gaol Delivery*, pp. 34–101; Gadbois, p. 11; Tunstall, pp. 65. 72; Ellis, p. 41; Elder, pp. 111, 133, 305–28; PRO JUST 3/210–13. The records of the extreme northern counties of Northumberland, Cumberland, and Westmorland provide only a single instance of benefit of clergy out of 603 persons arraigned, 1439–60: Neville, p. 291.

9 Garay, p. 338.

10 Calculated from PRO JUST 3/145, 191, 210–13.

11 4 Henry VIII c.2, which was not renewed by the next parliament, was the first statute to alter extensively the medieval rules governing the privilege. Perpetrators of petty treason had been denied benefit of clergy by the statute 12 Henry VII c.7.

12 Calculated from Cockburn, *Assize Introduction*, pp. 182–9.

13 *Middlesex County Records*, ii, 245–87.

14 *Letters and Papers, Henry VIII*, viii, no. 457.

15 PRO CHES 21/1 fos. 5–193v.

16 Smith, ed. Alston, pp. 102–3. The church had fought a rearguard action in the fifteenth

century over the issue of who should make the final decision on a prisoner's 'clergy'; but it had counter-attacked strongly over the whole matter of the clerical privilege during Wolsey's supremacy: see Bellamy, *Criminal Law*, pp. 128–41 and also the cases *Year Books*, 34 Henry VI Trin. no. 16, *ibid.*, 7 Edward IV Hil. no. 12, *ibid.*, 9 Edward IV Trin. no. 41, and *ibid.*, 21 Edward IV Pasch. no. 1.

17 For discussion on this see Bellamy, *Criminal Law*, pp. 158–63, J.S. Cockburn, 'Trial by the Book? Fact and Theory in the Criminal Process, 1558–1625', *Legal Records and the Historian*, ed. J.H. Baker (London, 1978) pp. 76–9, and Cockburn, *Assize Introduction*, pp. 119–21.

18 *Letters and Papers, Henry VIII*, Addenda, i (i), no. 1193; R.L. Storey, *The End of the House of Lancaster* (London, 1966), p. 210.

19 Hurnard, *Pardon for Homicide*, pp. 1–4.

20 See for example *Cal. Pat. Rolls, 1334–38*, p. 150; *Cal. Close Rolls, 1409–13*, p. 375; *Cal. Pat. Rolls, 1446–52*, pp. 68, 461; *Cal. State Papers, Domestic, 1598–1601*, p. 30.

21 Or where there had been abuse of authority by an officer of the law. For a pardon granted because the recipient had been compelled to confess out of fear see *Cal. Pat. Rolls, 1381–85*, p. 437; for another where the man pardoned had been convicted because of the labour of enemies see *Letters and Papers, Henry VIII*, iv (i), nos 464/28, 546/11. Justices were, however, only obligated to seek a pardon for a felon if they had personal knowledge that the wrong person had been convicted: *Year Books*, 7 Henry IV Pasch. no. 5.

22 *Rot. Parl.*, i, 444b; 5 Edward II c.28; 2 Edward III c.2; 4 Edward III c.13.

23 4 Edward III c.13; 10 Edward III st. 1; *Rot. Parl.*, ii, 172–3.

24 13 Richard II st. 2 c.1; 5 Henry IV c.2. The Ricardian act amended the rule enunciated in the statutes 27 Edward II st. 1 c.2 and 34 Edward III c.1 that if the 'suggestion' of an interceder was untrue the pardon was void.

25 *Cal. Pat. Rolls, 1555–57*, p. 549 shows that there were two clerks of the crown in chancery in the office there of the clerk for the writing of pardons of treason, murder, and felony (but not homicide in self-defence or general pardons).

26 *Letters and Papers, Henry VIII*, i (i), no. 70; *Cal. Pat. Rolls, 1548–49*, pp. 298–9; *Year Books of the Reign of Edward I, III*, p. 514.

27 The statement is remarkable because it baldly assumes that pardons can be obtained by money alone and not, in part at least, on account of legal reasons. The speaker added that this was 'the safest way', which implies it was more likely to preserve the arraignee from danger than bribing or pressuring the sheriff or the jurors: *Year Books of the Reign of Edward I, III*, p. 504.

28 As the statute 17 Richard II c.10 bluntly put it 'thieves get charters of pardon through long abiding in gaol'; a statement which did not mean they served a specific sentence there.

29 A person accused of felony could only have legal counsel argue his case for him if a point of law was involved. Interestingly the statement referred to in note 27 above was by such an attorney.

30 *Cal. State Papers, Domestic, 1603–10*, p. 602. Some persons close to the king made a practice of seeking his assent to pardons as a means of demonstrating their political influence; for example Jane Shore, the mistress of Edward IV, and Robert Dudley, earl of Leicester: T. More, *The History of King Richard III*, ed. J.R. Lumby (Cambridge, 1883), pp. 54–5; *The Copie of a Leter Wryten by a Master of Arte of Cambridge* (1584), pp. 48–50. Sir William Sandys seeking a pardon for a felon (1519) through Wolsey thought it would help to point out it was the first he had ever asked for: *Letters and Papers, Henry VIII*, iii (i), no. 517.

31   *Letters and Papers, Henry VIII*, ix (ii), nos. 496, 850, 897, 997. On the structure of indictments see chapter one. For an instance where the king was expected to make 4,000 marks out of a pardon see *Letters and Papers, Henry VIII*, vi, no. 204. In Elizabeth's reign Sir John Throckmorton took £1,600 from an accessory to murder towards obtaining one: *Reportes del Cases in Camera Stellata*, p. 137.

32   See Bellamy, *Bastard Feudalism*, pp. 38–9.

33   Those merely indicted of felony had their goods sequestrated into the hands of their neighbours, who were supposed to provide them with food in gaol: *Year Books*, 7 Henry IV Trin. no. 8.

34   Certification into the king's bench seems to have been virtually synonymous in the period under review with being acquitted or pardoned. Sir John Huddleston complained to Thomas Cromwell of a man who had killed his servant being 'removed into the king's bench that he may be saved': *Letters and Papers, Henry VIII*, xiv (ii), no. 406; on royal warrants see *ibid.*, i (i), no. 190/25.

35   We may suspect that the indictment, as it appeared before the court, had deliberate omissions because the clerk who drafted it was in cahoots with the accused or his friends.

36   *Letters and Papers, Henry VIII*, iii (i), no. 278/12; *Cal. Pat. Rolls, 1558–60*, pp. 113, 328, 429; *Cal. State Papers, Domestic, 1595–97*, pp. 11, 457; *ibid., 1598–1601*, pp. 341, 387. Pardons on account of poverty were not peculiar to the sixteenth century: see *Cal. Pat. Rolls, 1334–38*, p. 150.

37   For approvers see chapter one. Thomas More said he had seen many approvers in his career: More, *Works*, p. 976.

38   *Letters and Papers, Henry VIII*, iii, no. 2214/18.

39   *Ibid.*, v, no. 52.

40   *Ibid.*, viii (i), no. 22; *Cal. Pat. Rolls, 1558–60*, pp. 418–19; *Cal. State Papers, Domestic, 1595–97*, p. 457.

41   *Letters and Papers, Henry VIII*, i (i), no. 596; *ibid.*, vi, no. 204.

42   *Ibid.*, xv, no. 398; *ibid.*, xiv (ii), no. 384.

43   *Ibid.*, xvi, no. 954; Bellamy, *Bastard Feudalism*, pp. 135–6.

44   *Cal. State Papers, Domestic, 1547–80, Addenda, 1566–79*, pp. 23, 353.

45   See for example *Cal. Pat. Rolls, 1327–30*, p. 110; *ibid., 1345–48*, p. 518; PRO SP 12/28/63.

46   *Cal. Pat. Rolls, 1381–85*, pp. 206, 399; *ibid., 1389–92*, p. 6; *ibid., 1396–99*, p. 453; *ibid., 1399–1401*, p. 377.

47   *Letters and Papers, Henry VIII*, viii (i), no. 923.

48   *Acts of the Privy Council*, xxiv, 219; *Cal. State Papers, Domestic, 1598–1601*, p. 230. The susceptibility of the crown at this time to the moral improvement argument is suggested in several ways. We even find a prisoner in the Marshalsea in 1597 who asked for a summer of 'liberty' stressing he was sorrowful about his offence and resolved to amend: *Cal. State Papers, Domestic, 1595–97*, p. 445.

49   PRO SP 12/14/60. In 1598 Attorney General Coke devised a new pardon, the principle of which was that should the recipient break the peace thereafter the pardoning of the earlier offence was annulled: H.M.C. Salisbury, viii, 196.

50   See chapter one.

51   The general pardon granted in 1377 to celebrate Edward III's golden jubilee has been called the first (Storey, *End of Lancaster*, pp. 212–13), although the year 1327 also has a claim: see the statute 1 Edward III st.1 c.1. For a general pardon to a particular area only (for all types of offences, committed in this case by the citizens of York) see *Cal. Pat. Rolls, 1381–85*, p. 187.

52   Storey, *End of Lancaster*, p. 216; *Letters and Papers, Henry VIII*, i (i), no. 438 (pp. 203–73).

53   E. Hall, *Chronicle*, ed. H. Ellis (London, 1809), p. 506; *Letters and Papers, Henry VIII*, i (i), nos. 54/5, 54/43, 190/35, 218/6, 313.

54   The general pardon of 1509 was granted by royal fiat alone: *Letters and Papers, Henry VIII*, i (i), no. 11/10; *Tudor Proclamations*, i, 81–2.

55   See the statutes 7 Henry VIII c.11, 14/15 Henry VIII c.17, and 8 Elizabeth c.19.

56   See 4 Henry VIII c.8 and 5 Henry VIII c.8.

57   Those indicted of a statutory felony are few in number in the extant plea rolls of the period.

58   2/3 Edward VI c.59; *Cal. Pat. Rolls, 1554–55*, p. 102; *Tudor Proclamations*, ii, 104–8.

59   The statutes were 27 Elizabeth c.30 and 39 Elizabeth c.28. The general pardon of 1570 was said not to extend to offences triable in ecclesiastical court. In 1593 it was noted that the recent general pardon did not extend to Star Chamber suits: H.M.C. Salisbury, iv, 426.

60   Or their charter of pardon was void: 10 Edward III c.3.

61   *Acts of the Privy Council*, vii, 55. 'Good behaviour' must have meant 'good character' i.e. not bearing a criminal reputation.

62   *Ibid.*, xxiii, 81.

63   Hurnard, *Pardon for Homicide*, pp. 36, 225, 233, 239–40.

64   Plowden writes unequivocally of persons being reprieved from sessions to sessions so they could buy a pardon: E. Plowden, *The Commentaries or Reports of Edmund Plowden* (London, 1816), p. 475.

65   *Wiltshire Gaol Delivery*, p. 16; Hanawalt, *Crime and Conflict*, p. 43; Garay, pp. 338–9; Elder, pp. 305–29; PRO JUST 3/191, 210–13.

66   Elder, pp. 305–29; PRO JUST 3/191, 210–13.

67   These totals are calculated from figures given in Cockburn, *Assize Introduction*, pp. 182–208.

68   Garay, p. 405.

69   Tunstall, p. 77.

70   Hurnard, *Pardon for Homicide*, pp. 245–6; PRO JUST 3/145 mm. 5d, 6, 6d, 8, 8d, 11, 13, 14, 16, 17, 17d, 19, 20d, 21d, 22.

71   Ellis, pp. 121–3, 131–2. Pardons for accidental or self-defence killings were referred to as 'de cursu', i.e. automatic, although technically speaking on the justices' recommendation.

72   The figures are calculated from *Cal. Sussex Indictments and Cal. Essex Indictments*.

73   On the power and the abuse of authority by a gaol keeper in the late sixteenth century (in this case Redhead of York castle gaol) see H.M.C. Salisbury, vii, 515–16.

74   See J.G. Bellamy, *Crime and Public Order in England in the Later Middle Ages* (London, 1973), pp. 162–81 on the general nature of imprisonment in the fourteenth and fifteenth centuries.

75   13 Edward I c.35; 25 Edward I c.10.

76   2 Henry VI c.18; 5 Richard II st.1 c.7.

77   17 Edward IV c.3.

78   See above, chapter one. The two statutes allowing imprisonment at the justices' discretion were 11 Henry VII c.7 and 19 Henry VII c.14.

79   *Letters and Papers, Henry VIII*, x (i), no. 254.

80   3/4 Edward VI c.5; 3/4 Edward VI c.15.

81   1/2 Philip and Mary c.3. This act also imposed a month's imprisonment on those who repeated slanderous news concerning the king and queen.

82   The act against perjurers was 5 Elizabeth c.14. The statute against witchcraft was 5 Elizabeth c.16.

83   18 Elizabeth c.7.

84   PRO SP 12/18/4.

85   *Letters and Papers, Henry VIII*, xvii, no. 1157; *ibid.*, xx (i), no. 812.

86   PRO SP 12/157/38; PRO SP 12/195/74.

87   H.M.C. Salisbury, iv, 258; *ibid.*, xii, 244; *Acts of the Privy Council*, xxxii, 489.

88   *State Trials*, i, 1298–9, 1301–5; R.C. Palmer, 'The Origins of the Legal Profession in England', *Irish Jurist*, New Ser., 11 (1976), 126, 130–1.

89   *State Trials*, i, 1306; *Letters and Papers, Henry VIII*, ix, no. 510; *Acts of the Privy Council*, xxvii, 9.

90   Thus the marginal annotation a capital 'S', or the interlineation 'sus' which we find in many records, is likely to have stood for 'suspendatur' ('let him be hanged') rather than 'suspensus est' ('he has been hanged').

91   *Letters and Papers, Henry VIII*, iv (i), no. 1223; *ibid.*, xviii (i), no. 272. At the Durham sessions the two found guilty who escaped execution were women; they were remanded.

92   *Ibid.*, xix (ii), no. 15; *ibid.*, xx (ii), no. 109.

93   *Cal. State Papers, Domestic, 1601–03, with Addenda 1547–65*, p. 448; *ibid.*, p. 550. At a York gaol delivery in March 1548 of the nine prisoners convicted six were hanged and three, who were women, were reprieved: *ibid.*, p. 376.

94   *Ibid.*, p. 571; *Cal. State Papers, Domestic, Addenda 1566–79*, pp. 74–5; *ibid.*, p. 514.

95   So the correspondence of Rowland Lee, president of the council of the marches, with Thomas Cromwell demonstrates.

96   There were three quasi felonies which begged the rule. The penalty for heresy was burning; beheading was the accepted punishment for 'march' treason. The other exception was where the condemned person was female and had murdered her master, mistress, or husband. This was technically petty treason and she would be burned. In the thirteenth century felons were occasionally beheaded rather than hanged, and *Britton* tells us that burning was the penalty for arson, sodomy, sorcery, and heresy: *Britton*, i, 41–2.

97   See Bellamy, *Crime and Public Order*, pp. 185–6.

98   *Cal. Pat. Rolls, 1370–74*, p. 14. *Glanvill* refers to the abcission of limbs for felony (*Glanvill*, pp. 171, 177) and Bracton talks of the loss of eyes and members (Bracton, ii, 417), i.e. male genitalia, for rape; but there is nothing to indicate such punishments were implemented by the fourteenth century, although a *Year Book* report notes generally that there were occasional abnormal sentences given 'in terrorem': *Year Books of the Reign of Edward I, III*, p. 506.

99   Smith, ed. Alston, pp. 104–6.

100 Stow mentions two Elizabethan felons who had a hand struck off: Stow, *Annales*, pp. 1147, 1564. Heretics who shed blood in a church might be similarly punished: *Acts of the Privy Council*, v, 115. The punishment was not peculiar to felons: see *Select Cases in King's Bench, VI*, pp. 41–2 and J.H. Baker, 'Le Brickbat Que Narrowly Mist', *Law Quarterly Review*, 100 (1984), 545.

101 *The Notebook of Sir John Port*, ed. J.H. Baker (Selden Society, 102, 1986), p. 86; Smith, ed. Alston, p. 104. References to hanging in chains are fairly common in official correspondence in the 1520s. For an early reference to execution in this manner (1366) see *Chronica Johannis de Reading*, pp. 175–6.

102 *Letters and Papers, Henry VIII*, iv (ii), no. 3850; *Acts of the Privy Council*, xxi, 326.

103 *Letters and Papers, Henry VIII*, vii, no. 384; Holinshed, *Chronicles*, iv, 827; *ibid.*, v, 323; A. Munday, *A View of Sundry Examples* in J.P. Collier, *John a Kent and John a Cumber* (London, 1851), p. 92; Stow, *Annales*, pp. 1057, 1163; *A briefe discourse of the murther of Master Geo. Saunders* in R. Simpson, *The School of Shakespeare II* (New York, 1878), p. 218; *Cal. State Papers, Domestic, 1601–03, with Addenda*, p. 301.

104 *A briefe discourse*, p. 211; *Cal. State Papers, Domestic, 1601–03, with Addenda*, p. 301.

105 *Transactions of the Bibliographical Society*, iv (1898), 67.

106 *A briefe discourse*, pp. 231–2, 236.

107 G. von Bulow, 'A Journey made through England and Scotland made by Lupold von Wedel in the years 1584 and 1585', *Trans. Roy. Hist. Soc.*, New Series, ix (1895), 267. On other aspects of executions see Bellamy, *Crime and Public Order*, pp. 187–90.

108 This was the tenor of a great deal of correspondence between justices and officials concerned with the criminal law and Thomas Cromwell. Cromwell, although he obviously believed in the necessity of capital punishment, is not to be considered draconian.

109 See *Letters and Papers, Henry VIII*, xiii (i), no. 152; *ibid.*, xiii (ii), no. 21; *ibid.*, xiv (ii), no. 384.

110 See above p. 145.

111 T. Starkey, *Dialogue between Reginald Pole and Thomas Lupset*, ed. K.M. Burton (London, 1948), pp. 114–15. Opposition to the death penalty figured among Lollard beliefs in the early fifteenth: see *Heresy Trials in the Diocese of Norwich, 1428–31*, ed. N.P. Tanner (Camden Society, 4th ser., 20, 1977), pp. 86, 142, 166.

112 The conviction rate for the fourteenth century and the earlier fifteenth has been calculated from the figures of Hanawalt, Garay, Elder, Ellis, Gadbois, Neville, Tunstall, R. Briggs (*Gaol Delivery on the Eastern Circuit, 1437–1439*, Carleton University M.A. thesis, 1980), and myself.

113 Cockburn, *Assize Introduction*, pp. 175–97 and *Middlesex County Records*, ii, 245–83.

APPENDIX 1

RAPE

To elucidate the history of rape in the period from the late thirteenth to the sixteenth century we must go back a long way. As in the case of homicide, the Anglo-Saxon period was important in giving the crime a character which it never entirely lost, in essence making rape an amalgam of abduction and forcible sexual intercourse. The earliest Saxon laws, those of Ethelbert of Kent, talked of carrying-off of maidens by force clearly enough, but they did not mention assault of females for purposes of copulation,[1] speaking instead of the fines to be paid by those who 'lay with' women of various low social ranks.[2] This may be a reference to mere fornication or adultery, i.e. sexual intercourse with a married or unmarried woman's consent, but there is some slight intimation that it may have covered sexual assault as well. If so, then it implies that the attitude of the woman to such attack, whether docile or hostile, was of no legal consequence at that time. The appearance, therefore, in Alfred's laws of the verb *nidnaeman*, meaning to assault a woman for the purpose of having sexual intercourse, is of considerable significance, the more so because the usual verb for 'to lie with' (*haeman*) became clearly associated with copulation by mutual consent.[3] Although the Anglo-Saxon kings to this time had made special mention in their laws of sexual assault on maidens, and even on girls under age,[4] a more important sign of increasing sophistication in legal notions, and probably of societal pressure as well, was the provision for the punishing of those doing violence with sexual intentions on widows. This was done first in the code of Ethelred, and then with a more precise penalty for the miscreant in the laws of Canute.[5] The rising status of women in the Anglo-Saxon period, or at least society's intention of protecting some sections of the female population from sexual molestation of a less as well as a more serious nature, had been demonstrated by two Alfredian laws which punished the touching of a woman's body in a lustful manner.[6] Quite remarkably, there were no other laws which provided any similar protection in the several centuries from Alfred to the end of the period under review.

In the century subsequent to the Norman conquest, the law of rape seems to have changed only slightly. A novelty, which appears to have altered the scope of the crime, is to be found in chapter twelve of the *Leis Wilhelmi*.[7] By this, married women were added to girls under age, maidens, and widows, in having special sanctions provided against men who sexually assaulted them. The other discernible addition to the law concerned not rapists as such, but would-be rapists. Chapter 18, section one, of the same laws set the compensation to be paid to the lord when a man threw a woman to the ground in order, as it was put, 'to offer violence to her'. If he went further and sexually assaulted her the penalty was a different, draconian, one, namely castration.[8] Lest this punishment be interpreted as one designed especially to suit the crime of rape, we should remind ourselves that William the Conqueror ended the death penalty as such and provided as substitute for the committing of all serious crimes the putting out of eyes, the abscission of feet or hands, and castration, although admittedly he did decree that the penalty inflicted on the malefactor should be in proportion (*secundum quantitatem*) to the crime committed.[9] In later times, as we shall see, castration did become the accepted penalty for rape.

Neither the Anglo-Saxon nor the Norman laws said anything about the proper legal course for a woman to take after she had been raped, but bearing in mind the paucity of information they provide on such procedure in general, we can hardly be surprised. Fortunately a good deal on rape in *Glanvill* is devoted to this very matter, and indeed the course he described became the accepted way of proceeding in later centuries. The woman raped, we are told, must go soon after the deed has been done to the nearest vill and there show to trustworthy men the injury she has received, any effusion of blood and staining of garments by it, and any rending of the latter.[10] Presumably this counted also as raising the hue and cry which custom demanded. She must then similarly inform the reeve of the hundred and later on proclaim the offence publicly in the next county court. Thereafter she might bring an appeal of rape against the miscreant.

Bracton, writing about seventy years later, said very much the same and must have had *Glanvill* before him. There are some slight alterations and additions. The woman raped must inform the 'provost' of the hundred, the sergeant of the king, the coroner and the sheriff. She might by this time make her appeal before the king's justices as an alternative to doing so in the county court, although she would still have to attend there later to have her appeal entered on the coroner's rolls. On receiving notice of the rape, the officials must attach the party accused by two, four, or six persons, the smallest number being used if the rape was not recent and the hue and cry not properly raised. In her appeal the raped woman must say, states Bracton, that the perpetrator came violently and wickedly, lay with her, and took away her virginity.[11] This did not mean that only virgins were protected by the law of rape. The violation of married women, widows, lawful concubines, and even prostitutes was also a serious offence, but the woman raped could not in these cases make the formal charge herself; it must be found in the accusations of a jury of presentment. The reason was, no doubt, that a woman could only make an appeal for the death of her husband or for a hurt to her body. The loss of her pucellage was the corporeal wound which could not be suffered by other classes of women, and thus they had no appeal.

Because we have little other information on the subject, it is unfortunate that Bracton did not exemplify the exact formula of an appeal of rape, being content with generalities. He was much more concerned with the consequences of an appeal. If the man accused denies taking the victim's pucellage she must be examined by four trustworthy women, to find if she is still a virgin or not.[12] If they find she has indeed been deflowered then the man appealed, says Bracton, might perhaps state in his defence that he deflowered her with her consent, and that she now appeals him out of hatred for another woman whom he keeps as a concubine or wife, or because she has been prevailed upon to do so by her relatives.[13] Other responses which may well be successful, if they are accurate, are for the appellee to point out that he was out of the country at the time when the rape was alleged to have occurred, or to take issue with the actual wording of the appeal by showing perhaps that the key word *rapuit* was absent, or there was no mention of maidenhead.[14]

In dealing with the crime of rape Bracton was particularly concerned with the legal aftermath, namely what happened if the man appealed was convicted. Previously, he does not say when, all deflowerers of virgins were hanged,[15] but the penalty now is the loss of those members, the testicles, which had aroused the miscreant's hot lust, because he had deprived the victim of her member, i.e. her maidenhead. Although Bracton does not say so, it seems the woman raped might be required to inflict the punishment herself: at the Kent eyre of 1313–14 it was held that one victim, because the misdeed was done before the promulgation of the Statute of Westminster II, should tear out her attacker's eyes and cut off his testicles (*qe ele eust creue les oyls . . . e cope ses botons*).[16] The penalty of blinding was justified by Bracton on the grounds that it was the assailant's eyes which prompted him to seek possession of the virgin.[17] If the woman raped was not a virgin but a widow or married woman, then the penalty was to be some other severe bodily punishment, but not the loss of life or member. By the end of the thirteenth century all this had changed and hanging was the punishment for rape, as for the other serious crimes.[18] Bracton's especial interest in the penalties for rape may well have arisen through the law on that offence being modified even as he wrote. Two different types of punishment meant there were two classes of victim (virgins and other women) and two types of offence, where there had been but one before. Penalties for the raping of those women who were not virgins were apparently being diminished.[19] Perhaps society now found castration too brutal for all save the most heinous type of rape. Perhaps older women were finding the legal sanctions which protected them from rape more irksome, being likely to drive away potential and attractive abductors. The emphasis current in Bracton's time on the deflowering of virgins, as distinct from the rape of women in general, is shown also by the attention he gives to the legal position of accessories. Those who assisted at the rape of a virgin, he states, perhaps by holding her powerless, were to be proceeded against under the same appeal.[20] If they forcibly copulated with the victim subsequently to the first and principal offender they were to be held as guilty as he, even if they could not take away a pucellage already taken.

As well as in regard to punishment and accessories, Bracton's interest in the aftermath of rape may have extended to the opportunities for reconciling the parties involved, but since this is an *addicio* to the text we cannot be sure; certainly this matter was one which much exercised lawyers at about the time he was writing. Nowadays, states the text, ravishers are sometimes allowed to marry their victims (the latter asking for them as husbands) providing they have the permission of the church and the king although the law does not say as much.[21] This is very similar to what *Glanvill* had to say on the matter, although he had pointed out the parties would, in addition, usually need the consent of their families, and that this concord must be arrived at before the court gave judgment.[22] Although the treatise writers do not mention it, such an agreement had to be made even before the petty jurors gave their verdict; indeed, sometimes the latter announced it to the justices when they returned to the court room. Then the two adversaries were taken into custody and presumably not released until they made a fine. One plea roll demonstrates that the marriage might be solemnized almost immediately.[23] All this suggests that justices played a crucial role in these 'out of court' activities, probably pressing the parties to reach an agreement and informing the jurors when this was achieved.[24] A case heard at the 1313–14 eyre of Kent reminds us that where the rapist was already married there could be no concord, and thus the punishment would always be one of blood.[25] *Glanvill* makes the important point that it was the female appellant's decision in the matter of a concord which was crucial.[26] By agreeing to marriage she was probably saving the miscreant from a cruel fate, but it was essential for society that the decision should be hers, otherwise men of low social station would frequently be raping high born women so as to achieve a profitable marriage. How often these concords were arranged is uncertain. It has been suggested they were relatively frequent, the reason being that many accusations were made with the intention of compelling a marriage, perhaps on the part of discarded mistresses or through the family of a female who had been seduced. They may also have been the product of cases where a woman appealed her lover of rape so as to advertise her 'illicit defloration' and thereby overcome her family's objections to a socially disparaging match. This tendency towards compromise, although we should not doubt its existence, cannot be proven statistically; we do have one or two pieces of quantitative evidence but they are hardly unequivocal. Thus in the crown pleas of the Wiltshire eyre of 1249, appeals of rape occurred in nineteen cases; there was an overt compromise in four instances and the accuser withdrew her appeal or failed to appear in court in eight others. In the Berkshire eyre of 1248 the female appellant failed to appear in court in six out of nine rape cases, but references to concords are entirely lacking.[27]

In the history of rape the most significant occurrences of the later thirteenth century were undoubtedly the promulgation of the Statutes of Westminster of 1275 and 1285.[28] The first of these forbade the ravishing, or taking away by force, of any woman, under age, maiden, wife or other.[29] If any man did so then private suit, possibly in the form of an appeal, might be brought against him within the next forty days. Should there be no such suit the king would start the action. Those found guilty of this category of offence were to be imprisoned for two years and then pay a fine. Failure to meet the king's demands in this respect would result in longer imprisonment as the trespass required. The statute is not easy to interpret. On the face of it a felony had been turned into a trespass, the time in which an appeal might be brought had been slightly lengthened, and the relatively new punishment of imprisonment had been annexed to the crime. Perhaps the law was designed to encourage jury presentments of rape and so to limit the bringing of appeals. Such presentments were very few before the middle of the thirteenth century, although suspected rapists were undoubtedly being put to answer to complaints (*querelae*) made to the justices by means of a bill.[30] The king may have wanted a way of dealing with perpetrators of rape which was more reliable than the personal appeal, with its delays and frequent abandonments. Conviction on a prosecution by the crown by means of indictment would also benefit the king financially, through the fines now instituted. There was also a suspicion of political compromise about the part of the statute dealing with rape. Perhaps it was in order to gain the support of the upper classes for this substantial change in the law, one which Edward must have hoped would produce far more convictions for the crime, that the king agreed to such a mild degree of punishment for charges of rape by indictment. Certainly the distance from the penalties quoted by Bracton was tremendous. Severity of punishment was being exchanged for more certainty of arraignment. The king was also gaining in another manner. Hitherto abduction of females, or of males for that matter, unless they were wards, was no offence at all. Abduction no doubt could have been added to the growing list of presentable trespasses to stand as a new crime in its own right, yet on the face of it it was joined with a felony. For an explanation of this strange association we must take a closer look at the meaning of the words of the statute. Did *ravyse* in the 1275 statute mean 'raped' in the modern sense, or did it in fact mean abducted and thus stand in apposition to *prengne a force*?

The author of a legal treatise of the same reign, *The Mirror of Justices*, seemed well aware of a confusion caused by this statute and by its fellow of 1285 which also touched the subject. 'Rap', he stated, 'est proprement alopement de femme pur desire del mariage.' Assault on a woman for purpose of sexual intercourse, on the other hand, should be called *stuprum* if it feloniously took away a woman's maidenhead, fornication if the woman defiled was unmarried but not a virgin, and adultery if the victim was married. Most significantly the writer suggests that the word 'rape', because of the Edwardian statutes, came to mean something it never had before. Formerly it was a verb which expressed the seizure and taking away of inanimate objects and persons. Now 'by the arbitrary words of the statute . . . the one word rape is used for the forcing of a woman of whatsoever condition she be'.[31] What the drafters of the 1275 act seem to have done was to take the word *ravi*, which in the everyday speech of the thirteenth-century upper class was probably being used in some imprecise phrase like 'he took her' meaning 'he took her virginity', 'he took her away' or both, and use it to cover both rape and abduction.[32] Thereby the latter became a criminal offence, when because of a rise in the number of such cases it was very necessary to make it so. In court records *rapere*, the verb to connote sexual assault, came now to be used for abduction as well. In defence of the act the king, if this was the act he wanted, could say that it did not protect the sexual attacker unduly, since he might still be appealed and thereby suffer a punishment of blood, whereas it was providing a moderate penalty for abduction, hitherto not even a trespass.

Ten years later, so it has been recently argued, the second Statute of Westminster, late in the course of its promulgation, acquired a chapter (no. 34) whose words show evidence of having been concocted in considerable haste, perhaps being taken directly from oral discussion.[33] The chapter decreed that where a man ravished (*ravise*) any woman without her consent he should have judgment of life and member. If he did so but the woman consented to the deed *post facto*, then he was to have the same judgment nevertheless, providing, however, the accusation was by presentment and not by appeal. This amounted to allowing appeals of rape and subsequent concords to continue to be made with the same severe penalties on conviction, if the case reached arraignment and the accused was found guilty, as hitherto, but providing that where conviction followed presentment the punishment should be not imprisonment and fine, as had been the fashion since 1275, but the draconian variety used where the charge was made by appeal. The issue of *post facto* acquiescence by the victim was not entirely new. The statute of 1275 had decreed that the deed, if committed against a maiden within age, was still an offence even if she consented afterwards, and thus the later act was simply making a general application of a rule hitherto reserved for particular victims. Very likely, although we cannot prove it, the pressure for the promulgation of both statutes came from the heads of upper class families who did not wish to see the arrangements for the descent of their lands set at nought, nor women whom they intended to use to achieve alliances with the magnates taking property with them through rape-abduction and subsequent marriage to lesser men. The family of the woman raped no longer had to rely on the victim to charge her assailant with felony. It might under the second Statute of Westminster hope to seek and obtain his indictment instead, and in this way it had some social control over woman, rapist and property.

The remainder of this section of the 1285 statute supports this interpretation of the aim being to protect the property interests of the male head of the family as much as to preserve females from abduction and rape. The taking away of the goods of the husband where the woman carried off was married was made an indictable offence, although no distinction was made between the abductor taking the goods or the woman herself. If a married woman eloped willingly with her 'advouterer' she was to be barred from suing for her dower unless there was a reconciliation and her husband took her back. Abductors of nuns from religious houses, even where the nun went willingly, were to be punished on conviction by three years' imprisonment and a fine, and were to make suitable satisfaction to the religious house the nun had left.[34] All these clauses show how distant the new composite, double-centred crime of rape-abduction was from that of rape, meaning sexual assault, alone. The appearance of this offence in the statute book was to cause considerable confusion among later lawyers, and even historians,[35] for although the meaning of the term in charges could sometimes be ascertained from the method of accusation used, or from the insertion of additional words, on other occasions the exact nature of the offence was concealed.

What effect did the Statute of Westminster II have on the history of rape and abduction in the fourteenth century? An unequivocal answer is impossible. Accusations were made by both appeal and indictment but examples of the latter probably far outnumbered the former.[36] That is not to say that rape-abduction was ever a common offence: in the fourteenth and fifteenth centuries it never amounted to more than 6 per cent of all felonies and commonly provided only 2 per cent, whereas homicide and murder made up as much as 25 per cent at times. If we examine the fourteenth-century plea rolls we notice the crime was reckoned to have been committed feloniously on some occasions yet *vi et armis contra pacem* (or simply minus the word *felonice*) on others, which made it only trespass. Although appeals always made the charge of rape one of felony, it is not true, despite what Maitland said about the thirteenth-century practice, that where the accusation was made by an indictment the offence was only trespass.[37] Rape as a trespass occurred not infrequently in plea roll indictments in the period 1300–80,[38] whereas rape the felony appeared there only from about 1360 onwards.[39] Often modern commentators have argued that the statute of 1285 ended rape as a trespass, and if they have discovered an example which seemed to break this rule they have pointed to it as an exception.[40] In fact there were a fair number of indictments calling the rape trespass, and they were distributed over several widely spread counties.[41] Nor were these indictments essentially charges brought under the section of the chapter allowing the king's suit for any goods (they would have had to have been of minimal value) taken at the time of the offence.

One particularly interesting feature of the history of rape-abduction in the fourteenth century was the wording of the indictments. There were very few instances where a form of the verb *rapere* was lacking,[42] although justices did not as yet, it seems, argue, as their fifteenth-century successors were to, that there could be no charge of rape without it. *Rapuit/rapuerunt* without any other verb was frequent but almost as often we meet *rapuit et asportavit* (or *rapuit et furatus fuit*) signifying that goods had been taken when the victim was raped.[43] In another group of cases *rapuit/rapuerunt* was in tandem with *abduxit/abduxerunt* and referred to the taking away of the woman victim, or of goods, or both.[44] Here the indictments were following that part of the second Statute of Westminster concerning rape which ran *mulieribus abductis cum bonis viri*, a section which by the end of Edward III's reign had become so well known that lawyers talked of 'the statute of *mulier abducta cum bonis viri*'.[45] A third group of rape indictments contained the verb *concubuit, violavit* (sometimes *corporaliter violavit*), *afforciavit contra voluntatem*, or *defloravit*.[46] These were clearly intended to be indicators that the attack on the woman had resulted in forcible sexual intercourse. The words must have been designed to afforce the indictment, making it weightier and thus less likely for the accused man to be acquitted by the petty jury. The use of words based on *abducere*, on the other hand, may have been intended to lighten the indictment, to show this was a less reprehensible kind of rape, possibly in order that there would be no great difficulty in obtaining a pardon. It would perhaps be unsafe to argue dogmatically that the use of *abduxit* alongside *rapuit* always meant the indictors believed the woman victim had been taken for purpose of marriage or cohabitation, for the verb frequently referred to the taking of goods at the time of the assault. On the other hand we must acknowledge that the taking of goods, probably those which were the woman's personal possessions,[47] was a likely concomitant of an abduction which must therefore have occurred. Whether the use of *abducere* should be taken as meaning the indicting jurors had no knowledge that sexual intercourse had been a direct outcome of the attack is an open question, but certainly indictments where *abduxit* was accompanied by *concubuit* or *cognovit carnaliter* were very few. We can, however, say that the insertion of words like *concubuit* or *carnaliter cognovit* alongside *rapuit* show that in these instances the jurors were sure copulation had occurred and that they were willing to support such a charge despite the statute of 1285, or indeed the one of 1275, making no mention of such terms. Whether it was the justices, the justices' clerks, the bringers of bills of indictment, or the jurors of presentment who originated the practice is unknown, but that there was pressure within society for better definition of rape than was to be found in the Edwardian statutes cannot be doubted. Finally there is the important question of whether the insertion alongside *rapuit* of words like *carnaliter cognovit* or *violavit* was intended, and able to make the offence a felony. In Henry IV's reign the judges appear to have agreed that that indeed was the effect.[48] In this they seem to have been reporting accurately practice in the courts, for although there appear to be exceptions to this rule in the plea rolls of the fourteenth century they disappear by the fifteenth.

There was only one piece of legislation with an important effect on procedure in cases of rape in the fourteenth century, namely the statute 6 Richard II st.1 c.6. There had been, it is true, a short-lived act (2 Richard II st.1, c.5) passed four years earlier, which mentioned the ravishing of women and lying in wait to maim and murder persons so as to have their wives and goods. The remedy which was provided was the arrest of suspects without waiting for their indictment, but the statute's importance to the history of rape was limited to its demonstration that in certain parts of the realm the prevalence of rape-abduction was a major cause of disorder. The act passed in the parliament which met in October 1382 spoke of rape-abduction of noble and other ladies and ordained that where such women when so attacked gave their consent to the misdeed, which a parliamentary commons' petition shows they had frequently been doing to the encouragement of male fortune-seekers,[49] then the rapist as well as the raped should be barred from challenging for any inheritance, dower or joint feoffment. More important from the procedural viewpoint was a provision that the husband, or lacking him the father or next male by blood to the victim, might sue the offender and have him convicted to the loss of life and member, even if the woman attacked had, after the event, given her consent to the misdeed.[50] These stipulations meant the second Statute of Westminster was amended so that the rapist as well as the victim was denied the right to inherit both from his own family and that of the woman assaulted; furthermore the husband, father, or nearest male kin could now bring suit apparently by means of appeal against the miscreant, which was a very necessary arrangement in cases where the woman by definition had consented to the crime and therefore given up any intention of accusing the assaulter on her own account. The statute, whose continuance in force the parliamentary commons had to ask for in 1384, was no dead letter. This was shown by a *Year Book* case in Henry IV's reign in which one judge was quoted as saying that an appeal of the rape of a woman should be brought by her *baron*, i.e. husband.[51] In another relevant case, one heard at Michaelmas term 1409, it was specifically stated that the appeal of rape in the matter under consideration was brought against the miscreant by the husband of the assaulted, yet consenting, woman under the Ricardian act, and in the case of Athern versus Bigg in 1 Henry VI James Strangways, defending counsel, made the point that only this statute gave the husband appeal of rape where his wife was victim: 'nulle appelle de rape fuit done al baron solement mez par lestatut suisdit' (i.e. 6 Richard II st.1 c.6). John Hals J.C.P. solved one perplexing point for historians when he argued in the same case that the statute gave no appeal by express words, only implicitly by its stating the husband should have power to have the assailant convicted of life and member.[52]

There was a third statute of Richard II's reign which directly affected rape. This was the 'pardon' act of 1390.[53] As long before as 1347 the parliamentary commons had complained of the frequency of, among other crimes, rape-abduction and also of the pardons granted to the perpetrators.[54] On that occasion no remedy was forthcoming save for a promise on the king's part that there would be no such pardon 'otherwise than conformably to the honour and profit of himself and his people'. In the statute of 1390, as we have seen, the king announced that no pardons would be allowed by the justices for treason, murder (slaying by ambush, assault or by deliberate plan), or rape if the type of offence was not specified in the pardon. Quite likely one of the fairly recent outrages against public order which prompted this statute was the rape-abduction at Fulborn manor house, just outside Cambridge (where the second parliament of 1388 met) of Margaret, widow of Sir Thomas Shardelow, and some goods by Sir John Pelham.[55] Later Pelham married her, thereby gaining her estates. He was pardoned through the intervention of the earl of Derby in November 1389. The issuing of individual pardons for felony which excepted offences of treason, murder, and rape had occurred fairly frequently from 1378 and was to remain the fashion throughout the fifteenth century.[56] General pardons offered by the crown on special occasions, like those of 1387, 1399, and 1404, usually contained the same qualification.[57] Clearly rape-abduction was considered a most dangerous offence; not, of course, because of the injury or affront to the woman but because it might lead to quarrelling or feuding, and serve as an excuse for the raising of armed forces by the upper classes.

Before we examine the legislation against rapists and abductors in the fifteenth century we must consider why women continued to bring appeals of rape in the later middle ages when they might instead offer a bill of indictment to the justices and avoid the procedural obligations of the older method of accusation. One reason must have been an awareness that in an age rife with maintenance, embracery, and political pressure in the courts, there was no certainty their accusation would ever be found '*billa vera*' and the accused ever arraigned. Another factor may well have been a belief based on actual observation that bringing an appeal of rape, as with bringing one of homicide or robbery, meant there was a greater chance of the accused being convicted by the petty jury. Since appeal was in many ways a private suit the victim-appellant might have to employ counsel, which could be costly, but she would have the satisfaction of knowing that the accused might be kept awaiting his fate for a considerable length of time, which he might find a wearing experience. More importantly she might expect, because of the private nature of the suit, that the accused might approach her discreetly and offer her some reward if she defaulted in her suit. The concern that a potential female appellant might cause in the mind of a possible appellee is demonstrated in the correspondence of the Paston family and is very relevant to appeals of rape, even if the case in question was one of homicide.[58]

Harassment by means of appeal had been common since the thirteenth century at least. Often the appeals were prompted by the enemies of the man accused, who sought to use women, even females under age, as a means of troubling a disagreeable neighbour or a rival. Such is the implication of a celebrated appeal which was brought in the London eyre of 1321.[59] Joan, the daughter of Eustace le Seler, a girl of eleven, appealed Raymond of Limoges, a merchant, of taking her from outside her father's house to his lodgings and raping her there. Joan defaulted in her suit but then the crown indicted and arraigned Raymond, but he was acquitted; the jury said further he had suffered £40 damages and that Joan's father and four other men had abetted the appeal. No doubt encouraged by this, Raymond sued the five for £100 damages. Somehow, despite Raymond's acquittal, Joan appealed him a second time, on this occasion before the London coroners, and the case came before the justices in eyre. There Raymond was able to show record of his acquittal of the charge before the king's bench. Because she was under age Joan was, however, excused the penalties of an unsuccessful appeal. The vindictive nature of this appeal is suggested by the jury's verdict concerning damages and abetment, and also quite possibly by the wording of the appeal itself, the precise detail being probably designed to prevent exceptions on the part of the accused. Maybe it was the appeal's detailed description of the actual committing of the rape which gained such notoriety amongst the lawyers and secured it a place in the *Novae Narrationes*.[60] Remarkably, as yet no other examples of the actual words of an appeal of rape have been noted with which we can compare it, and therefore we cannot be sure that the details were exceptional. Suffice it to say the form was similar to that of an appeal of homicide, telling where the deed was done (the assailant's chamber), how the victim was physically seized (laid on the floor and derobed), what type and size of weapon was used (the penis, of certain dimensions), and what injury was received (bruised her watershed, 'laid her open so that she was bleeding', and ravished her maidenhead). Only in this legal form are we to find actual detail of sexual assault because medieval men, for all their lurid accounts of death and suffering, were extremely reticent when it came to describing sexual offences.[61]

The Seler case, if for a moment we accept the veracity of the appeal, was one of rape in the modern sense. True the miscreant first took the girl to his lodgings, but the essence of the crime was assault for the purpose of sexual intercourse, not abduction with or without the intention of marrying. In the fifteenth century the gentry and nobility, keen to enjoy the property of upper class widows and heiresses, found ways of avoiding appeals and indictments of rape by using pressures more subtle than assault, physical and sexual, to force ladies, abducted against their will, into marriage. There was no copulation with the woman taken until she had married. This way they could not be accused of rape, for all they had committed was abduction, which was not yet a felony. After the woman had been taken by force or dissimulation she was then held captive until she had entered into an obligation carrying financial penalties for its non-observance. By threat of levying these, the abductors would later coerce the woman into marrying a man she did not wish to.[62] This oppressive behaviour could not be found an offence under the common law because the statutes on rape-abduction demanded a sexual assault or forced matrimony, which was lacking here. The remedy the king approved was that the abducted woman should have a writ which would bring her harasser before the chancellor, his assignee, or the justices of assize in the county where the offence was committed, and if the oppressor failed to appear or if, on examining the parties they found that she had been pressured into such an obligation, it should be void.[63]

There is in addition other evidence that in the mid-fifteenth century some elements in society were much concerned with the ineffectiveness of the courts to deal with rape-abduction; it is to be found in the rolls of parliament. In 1436, in response to a bill which said that William Pulle had 'horribly ravysshed' and led Isabel, the widow of Sir John Boteler, into the wilds of Wales, the assailant was ordered to attend before the justices in Cheshire or stand convicted of high treason.[64] In 1439 Margaret, the widow of Sir Thomas Malefaut, claiming she had been abducted and forced to marry Lewis Leyshon of Glamorgan, asked in her bill that if he failed to answer in one of the next eleven county courts to charges of felony and rape he should stand automatically convicted of high treason with its severe penalties and expensive pardons.[65] The problem these petitioners faced was probably an inability to bring their abductors into court because of the political influence such men had in their own counties. The other crime which caused petitions to parliament and the approval of novel procedure with very severe punishments for the putative offenders if they failed to appear in court, was the notorious murder, which demonstrates how rape also could be a *cause célèbre* at this time.[66]

Whether it was Isabel Boteler and Margaret Malefaut themselves who petitioned in parliament for the punishment of their abductors we cannot tell, but from what we know of the contemporary social scene it was more likely their families who were seeking remedy for the loss of property the eventual marriage would cause. We are lucky to have, in the Paston family's letters of the same period, a good example of how relatives and friends might react to the abduction of a propertied woman, as well as a graphic description of the tribulation caused.[67] The woman was Jane Boys and after abduction she apparently said it had occurred with her consent. John Paston did not believe this, and compiled a list of points to prove to his correspondent that she had been taken against her will, despite her subsequent denial. 'Whan she was set upon her hors', wrote Paston, 'she revylid Lancasterother', i.e. the abductor, 'and callid hym knave and wept and kryid owte upon hym pitowsly . . . and fel doune of her hors unto that she was bound . . .'; 'Item whan she was bounde she callid upon her modyre, wheche folwyd her as far as she myght on her feet'. When she saw her mother could go no further Jane cried to her 'and seid that what so ever fel of her she shuld never be weddyd to that knave, to deye for it'. As she was carried along, wherever she saw anyone 'she kryid owte upon hym and lete people wete whos dowtyre she was and how she was raveshid a-yens her wyll, desyeryng the people to folwe her and reskew her'. Whether in fact Jane's friends got any legal satisfaction we do not know, but the chances were against it once she had consented.

Lancasterother's priest 'wheche shroff her' said Jane had told him in confession that she would never wed her abductor but would rather die; he added that he would not marry the pair even if he was offered £1,000 to do it. This moral revulsion felt by a third party is interesting to meet, for we have little information about the way contemporaries who were not actually involved in the crime as principals or accessories, viewed it. Upper class women were inclined to seek the punishment of those having illicit sexual intercourse whether force had been used or not, particularly if they discovered it amongst their social inferiors. Edmund Paston wrote that his mother had secured the dismissal of his servant Gregory because he had been seen 'to swhyve a quene'.[68] John Paston II, writing to his brother John in August 1478, adopted a non-moralistic tone in telling him, rather in the manner of one 'man of the world' to another, that the youthful William Brandon had been arrested because he had 'by force ravysshyd and swyvyd an olde jentylwoman and yitt was nott therwyth easyd but swyvyd hyr oldest dowtre and then wolde have swyvyd the othere sustre bothe'.[69] However, the writer allowed that for these deeds 'men sey fowle off hym, that he wolde ete the henne and alle her chekynnys'. There was even talk of a trial in which the king would participate.

The accession of Henry VII to the throne was soon followed by the establishing of a very sensible remedy for the problem of wealthy women who had been manoeuvred into marriage by kidnapping and the taking of bonds. The statute 3 Henry VII c.3 stipulated quite simply that those who took maidens, widows and wives having lands and tenements (the possession of which was the object of the crime) against their will, unlawfully, were committing felony; so were their procurers, abettors and receivers. Seemingly it made a felonious offence out of abduction *per se* and although in the preamble it referred to victims being forced to consent to marriage or be deflowered (*deflorez*) it did not do so subsequently. Only in Mary's reign, apparently, do we find a statement that rape or forced marriage were necessary elements in the felony of abduction. Introducing judgment of death for mere kidnapping was a striking afforcement of the late medieval criminal law, one comparable in novelty to the enactment by the same parliament which stated indicted murderers should be arraigned within a year of the offence without awaiting any appeal.[70] The cause of the abduction statute, so it has been argued, was not a recent glut of such cases but one notorious example. Yet the fact that another investigator has suggested a different celebrated case should remind us that there existed a more general problem.[71] In addition to its vagueness regarding the nature of the offence the Henrician statute was also unclear about victims. The introduction or preamble referred to the problem of abduction of maidens, widows and wives 'having substance', but the actual remedy which was enacted omitted those two words. Did this mean therefore that the abduction of any woman was now felony? The drafters of the Elizabethan statute 39 Elizabeth c.9, the one which deprived those found guilty (or the technical equivalent) under 3 Henry VII c.2 of having their clergy, referred to the latter act as making it felony to take away 'heiresses', an entirely novel word which seems to suggest that since 1487 it had been the practice to limit the act's application to cases involving the abduction of wealthier women.[72] Yet in the *Newe Book of Justices of the Peas* of 1538 Anthony Fitzherbert, or whoever the author was, quoted the Henrician act as it was set down in the statute rolls in 1487 and minus the preamble, that is to say without any reference to the abducted woman's wealth. However, between this time and the publication of the treatise *L'Office et Aucthoritie de Justices de Peace* in 1584 the element of wealth had become accepted as an integral part of the rubric, for in Crompton's improvement of Fitzherbert the statute is given as stating 'if anyone takes a damsel, married woman, or widow, against her will who has lands, goods or chattels or who is heir apparent to her ancestor . . .'.[73] If the statute 3 Henry VII c.3 was usually interpreted by the crown and the judges as being only relevant to richer women this may account for the paucity of indictments based on it during the sixteenth century, yet clearly it was never forgotten by the upper classes, as the passing of the amending act of 1596 demonstrates.[74]

What form did indictments of rape generally take, then, in the sixteenth century? Those who compiled legal treatises or justices' manuals in the Tudor period directed their readers' attention, when the offence was rape, mainly to the second Statute of Westminster.[75] The 'charges' given by justices to indicting jurors, where they have survived, take a similar approach.[76] The act of 1487 was seemingly ignored, which shows that in the courts where these men would officiate 'rape' was now rape in the modern sense. What might be termed the release of the verb *rapere* to mean solely forcible sexual intercourse did not, surprisingly, do away with supplementary phrases which would confirm the rape had been such an attack and not abduction. The phrase *carnaliter cognovit* and its synonyms,[77] which as we have seen began to appear in the fourteenth century, continued to be used in conjunction with *rapuit*, presumably in order to afforce the charge,[78] that is to say as a way of hinting to the petty jury that the accusation was well substantiated. There is no evidence of any official move in the early Tudor period to abolish *rapere* from indictments entirely and use words like *carnaliter cognovit* or *corporaliter violavit* instead, although in the reign of Edward IV it seems indicting juries might on occasion have done just that.[79]

By the middle of the sixteenth century the law of rape and abduction had become much clearer, and the only problem causing serious concern and debate was where girls rather than women were involved. The statute 4/5 Philip and Mary c.8 was intended as a remedy for the inveigling into marriage of youthful heiresses against what was taken as the better judgment of their elders. Such 'maidens, women, and children' of 'great substance in goods and chattels', as it was put, were being talked and bribed (by trinkets) by intermediaries ('light persons') into disparaging marriages. Therefore anyone conveying away a girl under sixteen against the wishes of her father or guardian was, on conviction, to suffer two years' imprisonment and a fine. Anyone who abducted such a girl, or promoted her abduction, and then deflowered her, or contracted matrimony with her against her father's or guardian's wishes, was to be punished with five years' imprisonment without bail, or pay a fine assessed by the council. Neither of the offences was rated a felony. The statute was dealing with situations which occurred when the female was a willing party, and this touched only abduction, not rape. The concern was not with the physical and emotional well-being of the girl but, as in the related statutes of the later middle ages, with her position as a property heiress. Thus the statute stipulated that in the event of such an illicit marriage any lands which she might inherit subsequently were to go for her lifetime to her next of kin.

Yet we should be wrong to assume there was no concern in the sixteenth century over the sexual abuse of young girls. In the statute 18 Elizabeth c.7, which had as its prime purpose the forbidding of benefit of clergy to those who were convicted of felonious 'rape, ravishment or burglary', section four stated that for the 'playne declaracion of lawe' it was now enacted that 'carnally knowing and abusing' of 'women children' under the age of ten was to be felony. This was the first use in legislation of the phrase 'carnally knowing'. Edward Coke in his *Third Institute* argued that this statute sprang from a particular case heard in the king's bench in 1571 and which was reported by Dyer. The accused was one W.D., a Scot, who was indicted of the rape of a girl aged seven.[80] By 'good evidence of divers women, matrons' he was found guilty, but, the report adds, 'the court doubted of rape in so tender a child. But if she was nine years or more it would have been otherwise'. How the court's doubts affected the judgment given we do not know, but it does sound as though there might have been some mitigation of the normal severities. It is worth noting that in the early fourteenth century appeals of rape were brought by girls who were not yet ten. The 'good evidence of divers women' in the 'W.D.' case was less likely to be their testimony as to the dwelling place of the accused, or the prior movements or subsequent distress of the girl, than a report of the physical inspection of the girl's abused parts. In the earlier seventeenth century such women might be assisted by a surgeon, and a report made on whether there had been, as Coke put it, '*res in re*'.[81]

What we should like to know in regard to sixteenth-century trials of rape is whether the female sexually assaulted was allowed to give evidence in court on oath, as was the practice in the following century. Hale was of the opinion that if the victim was too young to be sworn because she would not understand the obligations of the oath, she should be heard without such preliminaries since her information was usually the most useful. Her mother, in whom the girl had probably confided, was, however, to be heard on oath; she was not reckoned to be as great a help in ascertaining the truth as was the daughter. Hale was the first to set down what lawyers for many centuries must have felt about the trial of rape. It is, he said, 'an accusation easily to be made and hard to be proved, and harder to be defended by the party accused tho never so innocent'. It was for these reasons he advocated the checking, in modern detective style, of the testimony against the 'circumstances of fact', that is to say whether the victim-witness was of good fame, whether she announced the rape immediately, whether she made pursuit and showed the circumstances and signs of the injury, and where the deed had occurred (in well-travelled areas or remote byways); all these would show the greater or less probability of her story.[82] All this seems very sensible when put in such a manner, yet it is surely very akin to the behaviour expected by Bracton and the lawyers of his day if the woman who brought the appeal of rape was to have any chance of success. This should warn us against viewing procedure in cases of rape as a customary charade of little practical value.

Although rape was considered a grave offence and was certain to achieve prominence and notoriety in the area where it had been committed, its incidence amongst the whole range of felonies perpetrated in any one period was relatively low. It could of course be committed only against one half of the population, but even if we allow for this and procedural factors like its exclusive attachment until the late thirteenth century to appeal by the woman assaulted, the total of rape cases is still small. For example, the pleas of the crown in Gloucestershire for the year 1221 provide only 13 accusations of rape as against 255 of homicide. In the Wiltshire eyre of 1249, whereas there were 110 accusations of homicide, by appeal, presentment or indictment, there were only 18 charges of rape, and all by female appellants.[83] Two Northamptonshire rolls of sessions of the peace of the period 1314–20 give only a single rape amongst 31 felonies which included 10 homicides (3.26 per cent). The rolls of the Kent keepers of the peace of roughly the same period (1316–17) contain 289 cases involving felony, of which only 5 concerned rape (1.73 per cent).[84] An Essex 'peace' roll of 1351 has only one rape among 88 felony indictments (1.14 per cent), while another of the same county which covers the years 1377–9 has 3 among 51 accusations amounting to felony (5.88 per cent). Using gaol delivery rolls, Hanawalt found for the period 1300–48 rapes amounting to only 0.7 per cent of all felonies in Yorkshire, a miniscule 0.2 per cent in Norfolk, and 0.1 per cent in Northamptonshire.[85] Since Pugh found only two charges of rape in the one thousand which were heard before the justices delivering Newgate gaol in 1281–90 we must suspect that this extremely low incidence in this class of record was caused in part by a procedural factor, such as the trial of rapists being usually held before other types of justices (i.e. as a trespass before keepers/justices of the peace).[86]

Rather than decline, the incidence of accusations of rape if anything slightly increased in the later fourteenth century and early fifteenth. In Lincolnshire peace sessions rolls of the period 1360–75 the percentage of rapes in the total of felonies of all sorts was 2.49; in similar records of the same county for 1381–96 it was 3.85. The surviving Warwickshire and Coventry peace rolls for the period 1377–97 give a figure of 5.88 per cent, those of Nottinghamshire for 1393–6 give 5.55 per cent, those of Staffordshire for 1409–14 give 5.70 per cent, although in neighbouring Salop for very similar years (1400–14) the percentage was a much smaller 2.25.[87] These figures seem to suggest that the complaints in the parliament of 1378 about rape being a major cause of disorder were accurate, as was the one in the parliament of October 1382 about the prevalence of that offence and abduction. Unfortunately we cannot ascertain if this relative increase in accusations of rape continued into the mid and late fifteenth century, because few specimens of this class of record are extant. The Norfolk quarter sessions files of the regnal year 24 Henry VIII suggest that by the time of the Henrician reformation accusations of rape were in relative decline, for they comprised only 2.53 per cent of the total of all felonies.[88] The assize indictments of Elizabethan Sussex support this thesis and provide some indication that the diminution continued throughout the sixteenth century. In that county there were in the years 1558–1603 only twelve indictments of rape, amounting to a percentage of 1.13 of the total of all charges of felony.[89] This accords very well with the incidence of rape in Essex in the same reign, as shown by the indictments in the records of the coroners, the quarter sessions, the assizes (i.e. gaol delivery sessions), and the queen's bench: the figure there was 1.12 per cent.[90] The Cheshire assize records of the period 1569–98 show an even smaller proportion, a mere 0.45 per cent.[91]

Those who were formally charged with rape probably knew there was only a small chance of their being convicted. The pleas heard in 1221 before the abbot of Reading and his fellow justices itinerant in Gloucestershire contained thirteen cases (all brought by appeal), but none of the accused was found guilty. In six cases the appellor failed to prosecute her appeal, in three she died before her day in court, in one the accused was found not guilty, in another the appellor was non-suited but the appellee fined; in one other case the accused was outlawed.[92] In the Wiltshire eyre of 1249 there was not one suspect among the twenty accused actually convicted of the offence in court, although only six were stated to have been found not guilty. In four instances the appellor failed to appear or withdrew her appeal; in another case she had died before the day of the trial. In three further cases the verdict was technically the equivalent of 'guilty' since the accused was outlawed; however, the likelihood of any of these offenders being executed was remote. In the Berkshire eyre of 1248, where there were nine cases of rape, the only two men accused as principals who were found guilty in court were those already claimed by the ordinary and therefore known by the inquest to be safe from lay punishment. In the five cases of rape in the surviving rolls of the Kent keepers of the peace for 1316–17 involving fifteen assailants, only a single accused is known to have been found guilty.[93] The rolls of the justices of the peace for the parts of Lindsey in Lincolnshire for the period 1381–96 contain seven cases of rape. The principals in five of these were reported as being in exigend in the king's bench, and those accused in the other two cases appear to have been acquitted. No evidence has been discovered that any of the accused was ever punished by life or limb. In twelve indictments of rape in the surviving peace sessions rolls of Warwickshire and Coventry for the years 1377–97, the four for which we have information about the outcome were all acquittals.[94] A study of the gaol delivery rolls of a large number of counties between 1388 and 1409 has failed to discover a single conviction in 493 cases where rape was the sole crime charged. Only in the sixteenth century was there a substantial number of rape convictions. The Sussex assize indictments for the reign of Elizabeth show a percentage of 41.7 found guilty, and those of Essex for the same period one of 24.0.[95] In contrast with the figures for convictions for murder and manslaughter, or grand larceny, verdicts of 'guilty' never seem at this time to have outnumbered acquittals.

The factors which may have contributed to the rise in convictions for rape in the sixteenth century we have met for the most part when considering murder and manslaughter. The fact that many indictments must have derived from the bills of individuals, and that the veracity of the charge was by this time attested by witnesses, must have played a part, as must the general climate of a rising conviction rate for other felonies. Another consideration is the passing of the act 3 Henry VII c.2, which made some types of abduction into felony. This may well have made jurors from that time incline to finding verdicts of guilty more frequently when the crime was rape in the modern sense. Essex indictors of the later sixteenth century seem to have made a practice of supplying the age of youthful female victims of rape even when they were over ten. Because this suggests that society found the crime particularly heinous we might perhaps expect to find a higher proportion of convictions in such cases; in fact we do not. Nor do we where the girl raped was said to be under ten, the crime having been made a felony in 1576.[96] Indeed the only category of rape in which the acquittal rate was clearly higher was where masters were charged with sexually assaulting their own servants or those of others.

The majority of rape indictments in the plea rolls of the fourteenth and fifteenth centuries as well as mentioning the attack itself give the additional information that goods were taken. Although we cannot prove it, there is every likelihood that this property was in the personal possession of the victim and that she was being abducted for the purpose of marriage, or at least cohabitation, rather than being sexually assaulted *in situ*. These indictments usually state that the miscreant had broken into the house of X, raped his wife, and taken his goods, but since the charge was very likely based on the husband's bill of indictment or his information to the indicting jury, the breaking-in may in fact have been a letting-in and the goods, in practice, the wife's.[97] Rape indictments of the reign of Elizabeth, in contrast, rarely mention the taking of goods and thus the evidence that in the sixteenth century the verb *rapere* referred usually to sexual assault alone seems confirmed. When in the later middle ages only one assailant was indicted of rape and goods were said to have been taken we may suspect the crime was abduction and that there was a lack of resistance to it on the woman's part. The naming of several assailants, a feature not infrequent in fourteenth- and fifteenth-century indictments may, in contrast, be taken as showing that while the intention was abduction the woman was expected to resist or have servants who would do so. Rather surprisingly, all of the five rape cases in the rolls of the Kent keepers of the peace for 1316–17 involved more than one assailant, although none mentioned more than four. On the other hand only one case out of the twelve in the peace sessions' rolls of Warwickshire and Coventry for 1377–97 was reckoned to have been perpetrated by more than a single man; similarly there was only one such case out of seven in the same type of records for Lindsey, Lincolnshire, for 1381–96.[98] We may suspect that often abduction was not much different from elopement. If there were more than one or two occasions when a group of men were each accused of 'raping' a woman in the sense of abducting her, there seem to have been very few cases of rape where more than a single attacker had sexual intercourse with the victim, at least they do not appear in fourteenth-, fifteenth-, and sixteenth-century indictments. Where the intent included abduction the plurality of assailants was to effect the kidnapping more efficiently; the man of substance who ordered his servants or asked his friends to help in accomplishing the deed was clearly not expecting them to take liberties with his intended spouse. Nonetheless, there must have been occasions when, with no thought of abduction or marriage, a member of the upper classes told his servants to hold the woman while he copulated with her. It was common talk in 1542 that Thomas Culpeper, the lover of Katherine Howard, had once got three or four of his attendants to hold down a park keeper's wife for him in a thicket.[99]

The Elizabethan indictments do not suggest that at that time upper class rapists ever came to trial, and indeed when we examine the charges of rape in medieval times we find the squirarchy and above absent at that time also. The rapes charged in the Elizabethan Essex and Sussex records were said to have been committed by labourers (24.3 per cent) and artisans/tradesmen (24.3 per cent) for the most part. Yeomen were accused in 21.6 per cent of the cases, husbandmen in 10.8 per cent and miners in 8.11 per cent. The rolls of the fourteenth- and fifteenth-century sessions of the peace contain a fair number of accusations of rape against chaplains and tradesmen,[100] and even one or two against servants, but seemingly few against labourers. The Elizabethan Essex and Sussex assize records contain only two men who were accused of more than a single rape. One, an Essex baker, was held to have raped one female twice and two others once. The other, a Sussex miner, was charged with the rape of two of his women servants. Both were acquitted on all counts. As to the victims in these Elizabethan records, 13.5 per cent were servant girls, 40.5 per cent were called 'spinsters', and 21.6 per cent were between five and twelve years old.[101] Women in the first category would probably be without immediate adult male protection, and the same would likely be true of the young girls if they had many brothers or sisters. A noticeable difference between these Tudor rape indictments and those of the fourteenth and fifteenth centuries was the large number of victims in the latter who were called the wife of X or the daughter of Y, X and Y being the owners of the houses entered. Sometimes every rape victim in a roll of the peace sessions was listed as one or the other, wives predominating in a roughly two to one ratio, but no information about age or social status given. The high proportion of wives as victims in late medieval rape was probably because the offences were really abductions or elopements rather than because Tudor rapists sought out as their victims women who had no husband or home (i.e. of lesser social standing), but to prove this is not possible.

The English law of rape for a great part of the period under review, we may say in conclusion, reflected particularly the attitudes of the male heads of upper class families. It must have been their political influence which decided two parliaments of the later thirteenth century should propel abduction into the sphere of rape and then turn the amalgam into felony. It must have been the same paterfamilial section of society which promoted directly or indirectly the disinheriting of abductor-rapists in the later fourteenth century and provision for prosecution in cases where the woman was known to have subsequently assented to the misdeed and was therefore of little use as an instrument of accusation. In 1487 Henry VII, utilizing what was to become a fairly common device for maintaining public order, made simple abduction (i.e. without any suggestion of sexual assault) into a felony. Thereby those who sought to bring the miscreant to court must have been relieved of the necessity of having to show forcible coition, which must have been a difficult thing to prove when so many rapes were really elopements. The *rapuit* cases of the later sixteenth century therefore were probably about rapes in the modern sense, that is assaults for sexual purposes, which may account for the big rise in the incidence of convictions. By the later sixteenth century also there were indications that society was considerably more concerned with the sexual violation of females than hitherto. This is suggested not only by the increasing incidence of rape convictions but also by the promulgation of statutes in 1558 and 1575 which in the one case protected girls from those who sought to persuade them to run away from their families and in the other attempted to guard girls under ten from sexual assault. This concern may have derived once more from paterfamilial interest, but there is also the possibility that at last the younger male generation and even the female part of the population were beginning to make their voices heard.

Notes

1 They do, however, mention compensation for 'injury' to a maiden: *Laws of the Earliest English Kings*, pp. 7, 9.

2 The Anglo-Saxon verb here was *geligeth*.

3 *Laws of the Earliest English Kings*, pp. 71, 75, 77 (Alfred cc.10, 25, 29).

4 The compensation to be paid by those who raped girls under age was to be the same as when the victim was an adult woman of the same rank.

5 *Laws from Edmund to Henry I*, pp. 103, 203.

6 *Laws of the Earliest English Kings*, pp. 71, 73 (Alfred cc.11 and 18).

7 *Laws from Edmund to Henry I*, p. 259.

8 *Ibid.*, p. 263.

9 *Ibid.*, p. 251.

10 *Glanvill*, pp. 175–6.

11 *Bracton*, ii, 415–16.

12 *Ibid.*, ii, 416.

13 The *Mirror of Justices*, which dates from the end of the thirteenth century, suggests a good defence is to say the woman has borne a child by the man she appeals: *Mirror of Justices*, p. 103. The argument is based on the contemporary belief that a woman could not conceive as a result of a sexual assault, but only if she consented to copulation: see *Britton*, i, 114. In a case heard in the eyre of Kent of 1313–14 a woman who said she had been raped appeared with a child in her arms, which she claimed was the offspring of the union. The reporter tells us men said this was a wondrous thing because 'un enfaunt ne pout estre engendre saunz volunte des ii': *Eyre of Kent*, p. 111.

14 Bracton states that trial in appeal of rape, because the appellor was female, was always to be by jury, not battle or, as in Glanvill's time, by ordeal: *Bracton*, ii, 416.

15 *Bracton*, ii, 415: 'since such persons were not clear of the crime of homicide'. Presumably this was because a virgin life had ended.

16 *Eyre of Kent*, p. 134.

17 *Bracton*, ii, 414–15. This, of course, was the theory of punishment. How frequently such penalties were actually inflicted we do not know; probably not very often. There is, however, some suggestion that blinding, perhaps for rape, perhaps not, was still practised in Edward I's reign: *Cal. Pat. Rolls, 1281–92*, p. 192.

18 *Mirror of Justices*, p. 141.

19 It has been pointed out that there are no emasculations (or exoculations) mentioned in the extant rolls of the 1230s or 1240s: *Crown Pleas of the Wiltshire Eyre*, p. 79.

20 *Bracton*, ii, 418.

21 *Ibid.*

22 *Glanvill*, p. 176.

23 *Crown Pleas of the Wiltshire Eyre*, no. 461.

24 The announcement of the concord by the jurors was probably *pro forma* for the record. The formula used in a Cornish plea roll of 1201 was 'by leave of the justices they made concord on the terms of his espousing her': *Select Pleas of the Crown, 1200–1225*, ed. F.W. Maitland (Selden Society, 1, 1888), no. 7.

25 *Eyre of Kent*, i, p. 134.

26 *Glanvill*, p. 176.

27 See J.B. Post, 'Ravishment of Women and the Statutes of Westminster', *Legal Records and the Historian*, ed. J.H. Baker (London, 1978), pp. 152–3; *Crown Pleas of the Wiltshire Eyre, passim*; *Berkshire Eyre, passim*.

28 3 Edward I st.1 c.13 and 13 Edward I st.1 c.34.

29 The French was 'qe nul ne ravys ne prengne a force . . .'.

30 See for example *Select Pleas of the Crown, 1200–1225*, no. 96; *Procedure without Writ*, no. 131.

31 *Mirror of Justices*, p. 28.

32 One of the causes of the difficulty was that hitherto all legal records had been in Latin but the statute rolls were for the most part in French.

33 See Post, 'Ravishment of Women', p. 156; T.F.T. Plucknett, *The Legislation of Edward I* (Oxford, 1949), pp. 121–2.

34 Abduction of nuns had last appeared in English laws in the code of Canute. Perhaps this earlier use decided the drafters of the statute to use the word 'abductor' rather than 'those who rape'.

35 See footnote 37. In the earlier thirteenth century abduction seems to have had little connection with rape in legal terminology; a case in *Rolls of Justices in Eyre for Lincolnshire, 1218–1219, and Worcestershire, 1221* ed. D.M. Stenton, (Selden Society, 53, 1934), p. 579 shows abduction and rape as quite separate notions and charges.

36 It has been pointed out that an incidental result of the new law on rape seems to have been the rise of a trespass action for ravishment of wife, often with chattels: Post, 'Ravishment of Women', p. 159.

37 *History of English Law*, ii, 491–2n.

38 Thus in *Kent Keepers of the Peace*, although there were six rapes reported, not one of the indictments contained the word *felonice*.

39 As shown by the rape cases in *Proceedings*, ed. Putnam, *passim*.

40 As for example in B.H. Putnam, *The Place in Legal History of Sir William Shareshull* (Cambridge, 1950), p. 274.

41 See *Northamptonshire Sessions, passim*; *Proceedings*, ed. Putnam, *passim*, and *Kent Keepers of the Peace, passim*.

42 One example is *Proceedings*, ed. Putnam, p. 190 (no. 68).

43 For example see *Proceedings*, ed. Putnam, pp. 112 (no. 63), 132 (no. 17), 135 (no. 31), 302 (no. 33), *Records of some Sessions of the Peace in the city of Lincoln, 1351–4, and the borough of Stamford, 1351*, ed. E.G. Kimball (Lincoln Record Society, 65, 1971), no. 1, *Warwickshire Sessions of the Peace*, pp. 47 (no. 176), 135 (no. 101), 146 (no. 114), 170 (no. 58), *Records of some Sessions of the Peace in Lincolnshire, 1381–1396, ii*, ed. E.G. Kimball (Lincoln Record Society, lvi, 1962), no. 142.

44   For example, *Proceedings*, ed. Putnam, pp. 185 (no. 33), 406 (no. 18), 442 (no. 57), *Sessions of the Peace in Lincolnshire, 1381–96, ii*, nos. 32, 163, *Sessions of Lincoln and Stamford*, no. 10, *Warwickshire Sessions of the Peace*, pp. 101 (no. 28), 133 (no. 62), 151 (no. 133), *Essex Sessions of the Peace*, nos. A42, B279, and *Northamptonshire Sessions*, p. 101.

45   *Year Books, Liber Assisarum*, 42 Edward III no. 16.

46   See *Proceedings*, ed. Putnam, pp. 99 (no. 30), 100 (no. 34), 119 (no. 157), 184 (no. 26), 188 (no. 49), *Sessions of the Peace in Lincolnshire, 1381–96, ii*, no. 736.

47   Although belonging technically to the husband.

48   Fitzherbert, *La Graunde Abridgement*, f. 249.

49   The immediate cause of this act was apparently the rape-abduction of Eleanor, daughter of Sir Thomas West, by Nicholas Clifton: see J.B. Post, 'Sir Thomas West and the Statute of Rapes, 1382', *Bull. Inst. Hist. Res.*, 53 (1980), 26–7.

50   To persuade superior lords not to abet the rapists they were awarded his escheats on conviction. Another point worthy of notice was that no one accused under the statute could opt for trial by battle.

51   *Year Books*, 8 Henry IV Pasch. pl. 2.

52   *Year Books*, 1 Henry IV Mich. no. 20; *Year Books of Henry VI, 1 Henry VI, 1422*, ed. C.H. Williams (Selden Society, 50, 1933), p. 1. Athern made the appeal by bill (p. 7); Strangways on behalf of Bigg made the exception that the writ sued was one of trespass, since it did not contain the words 'feloniously raped' (p. 2).

53   13 Richard II st.2 c.1.

54   *Rot. Parl.*, ii, 172a.

55   See R.L. Storey, 'Liveries and Commissions of the Peace, 1388–90', in *The Reign of Richard II. Essays in honour of May McKisack*, ed. F.R.H. Du Boulay and Caroline M. Barron (London, 1971), p. 134. The abduction was in late September 1387.

56   See chapter four.

57   Normally these pardons covered those accused by appeal as well as indictment.

58   Late in 1469 the duke of Norfolk persuaded the widows of two men killed by the Paston faction in the siege of Caister castle to appeal John Paston and others of their husbands' deaths. He paid their expenses to travel to the court in London and even persuaded one of the women to enter into an obligation not to marry for two years so the appeal would not automatically abate. The appeal was still proceeding at Hilary term 1472: *Paston Letters and Papers of the Fifteenth Century, i*, ed. N. Davis (Oxford, 1971), pp. 363, 550, 560, 561.

59   *Year Books of Edward II. The Eyre of London 14 Edward II. A.D. 1321, i*, ed. H.M. Cam (Selden Society, 85, 1968), pp. 87–93.

60   *Novae Narrationes*, ed. E. Shanks and S.F.C. Milsom (Selden Society, 80, 1963), pp. 341–2.

61   It is worth noticing that the appeal also contained phrases used in the later fourteenth century to afforce indictments, for example 'in ambush and assault prepense'.

62   It was symptomatic of the times that the abductor was not necessarily abducting the woman in order to marry her himself; he might have been doing it to oblige a client.

63   The statute was 31 Henry VI c.9.

64   *Rot. Parl.*, iv, 497a.

65 *Ibid.*, v, 14b, 15.

66 See *ibid.*, iv, 447b, v, 111.

67 *Paston Letters and Papers*, ed. Davis, no. 45. The year may have been 1452.

68 *Ibid.*, no. 395.

69 *Ibid.*, no. 312.

70 English Reports, Dalison 22 and see also note 74; 3 Henry VII c.2.

71 Compare A. Cameron, 'Complaint and Reform in Henry VII's Reign: the Origins of the Statute of 3 Henry VII c.2', *Bull. Inst.Hist. Res.*, 51 (1978), 82–6, and E.W. Ives, ' "Agaynst taking awaye of Women": the Inception and Operation of the Abduction Act of 1487' in *Wealth and Power in Tudor England*, ed. E.W. Ives, R.J. Knecht and J.J. Scarisbrick (London, 1978), pp. 21–44.

72 D'Ewes states that the part of 39 Elizabeth c.9 touching receivers had to be redrafted by the attorney general, but does not mention heiresses: *The Journals of all the Parliaments during the reign of Queen Elizabeth* (London, 1682), 528.

73 Fitzherbert, *Newe Boke*, f. xix; A. Fitzherbert and R. Crompton, *L'Office et Aucthoritie de Justices de Peace* (London, 1584), p. 37.

74 Coke says that at a judges' conference in 3/4 Philip and Mary it was decided there was no offence under the 1487 act unless the woman was (a) possessed of property, (b) taken against her will, (c) eventually married to the ravisher or was carnally known by him. If Coke was right on the third point, and he claimed he had the information from a manuscript of Dyer, then the original intent of the act may well have been changed in 1556: E. Coke, *The Third Part of the Institutes of the Laws of England* (London, 1797), p. 61.

75 *Boke of Justyces of Peas*, A.vi; Fitzherbert, *Newe Boke*, f. xx; Fitzherbert and Crompton, *L'Office et Aucthoritie de Justices*, p. 37; W. Lambard, *Eirenarcha* (London, 1588), p. 324. Marowe does not mention rape apart from incidentally. As well as drawing their readers' attention to the second Statute of Westminster it was common form for the authors of legal treatises to add that a pardon for rape must specifically mention it was granted for that offence.

76 B.M. Additional MS 48047 f.64v; Middleton MS (in Nottingham University Library) Mi.02/1 f.11. Compare *Proceedings*, ed. Putnam, p. 11 (a justices' charge of 1403–4) which states enquiry shall be 'de toutes maniers de rapes dez femmez cibien des dames, comme des aultres femmes quelsconques'.

77 *Concubuit* seems to have been much less popular, and *copulavit* made appearances.

78 For example Norfolk Record Office, Norfolk Quarter Sessions Files, 24 Henry VIII, nos. 5a, 56; 34 Henry VIII no. 158; 3 Edward VI, no. 127.

79 But the judges were against it. See *Year Books* 9 Edward IV Trin. pl. 35.

80 Coke, *Third Institute*, p. 60; English Reports, 3 Dyer 304a. The case was primarily concerned with a Scotsman's claim to trial *per medietatem linguae*.

81 'Res in re' was how Coke decorously defined penetration. However, in commenting on a case in 5 James I he said there must be both penetration and 'emissio seminis' for the assault to be rape: *English Reports*, 12 Coke 36.

82 Hale, *Pleas of the Crown*, i, 628, 634–5.

83 *Pleas of the Crown for the county of Gloucester*, ed. F.W. Maitland (London, 1884), *passim*; *Crown Pleas of the Wiltshire Eyre*, *passim*.

84 *Northamptonshire Sessions, passim; Kent Keepers of the Peace, passim.*

85 *Essex Sessions of the Peace, passim;* B.H. Westman, *A Study of Crime in Norfolk, Yorkshire and Northamptonshire, 1300–1348* (Ph.D. dissertation, University of Michigan, 1970), p. 136.

86 Pugh, *Proc. British Academy*, 86.

87 The Lincolnshire total of felonies was 281 for 1360–75 and 416 for 1381–96. The Warwickshire and Coventry total was 204, that for Nottinghamshire 54, that for Staffordshire 158, and that for Salop 178. There seems to have been an abnormally large number of clerics accused of rape.

88 Norfolk Record Office, Norfolk Quarter Sessions Files, 24 Henry VIII, *passim.* It should be mentioned here that historians are not sure to what extent in the earlier sixteenth century felonies were ceasing to be tried before justices of the peace.

89 *Cal. Sussex Indictments, passim.*

90 See Samaha, p. 20. The quinquennium 1579–83 accounted for 0.53 per cent of this.

91 PRO CHES 21/1 fos. 43–199.

92 *Pleas of the Crown for Gloucester, passim.*

93 *Crown Pleas of the Wiltshire Eyre, passim; Kent Keepers of the Peace, passim.*

94 *Sessions of the Peace in Lincolnshire, 1381–96, ii, passim; Rolls of Warwickshire, passim;* Garay, p. 345.

95 *Cal. Sussex Indictments, passim;* PRO ASSI 35/1 to 35/44. The comparable Chester indictments of 1569–97 provide a conviction rate of 100 per cent but this is probably a freak arising from the very small number of offences.

96 Taking those cases in the Elizabethan assize indictments for Essex where the age of the young woman is stated, we find the proportion of acquittals to convictions was seven to two. If we consider only cases where the female was under 10 we find a total of three acquittals and no convictions.

97 By claiming the theft of goods worth more than one shilling the husband could make the offence a double felony.

98 *Kent Keepers of the Peace, passim; Warwickshire Sessions of the Peace,* p. 133; *Sessions of the Peace in Lincolnshire, 1381–96, ii,* no. 32.

99 *Original Letters relative to the English Reformation,* ed. H. Robinson (Parker Society, 1846–7), i, 2237.

100 Cases where a chaplain was named as a principal malefactor accounted for 25 per cent of all rape indictments in the rolls of Warwickshire and Coventry peace sessions, 1377–97, and 28.6 per cent in those for the parts of Lindsey, 1381–96.

101 *Cal. Sussex Indictments, passim;* PRO ASSI 35/1 to 35/44.

APPENDIX 2

LESS FREQUENT FELONIES

In addition to the major felonies already studied above, which provide the vast majority of capital cases in the plea rolls, there were in medieval times a fair number of other, less frequently perpetrated offences, falling within the same category. Most of these felonies, in their basic form, predated the arrival of parliamentary statutes.

Bracton stated clearly that to make fire with felonious intent was to be punished by a capital sentence. The inclusion of this crime of arson within the category of felony was confirmed for later lawyers by a passing but decisive mention in Edward I's first Statute of Westminster (c.15).[1] This stipulated that the structure burned or to be burned (where presumably the fire had been extinguished quickly) must be a house, although burning a barn if attached to a house was rated as arson by the end of the fifteenth century.[2] One curiosity connected with the definition of the offence was the making of extortion of money from the occupant of any house by threat of arson into treason, which was done in the parliament of 1429–30.[3] The aim was probably to prevent the extortionists from obtaining benefit of clergy. In the extant gaol delivery records of the fourteenth and fifteenth centuries arson rarely seems to have been the cause of any more than one per cent of any set of arraignments.[4]

The author of *Glanvill* in an unspecific manner mentions another of these felonies, the crime of falsifying: it belonged to the king's courts and was to be punished either capitally or by loss of members. *Britton* more expansively tells us that in his time the crime of forgery included counterfeiting the king's coin, putting in more alloy than was the usage at the royal mint, and coining money whether good or bad without the king's leave. These offences, the writer makes clear, are felonies.[5] This is surprising for as is well known the great treason statute of 1352 declared counterfeiting (i.e. making a false imitation of) the king's money to be treason.[6] Responsibility for the change cannot be attributed entirely to Edward III and his judges and their attempts to extend the scope of treason in the later 1340s since there is evidence from the previous reign of the same classification. An entry in the records of the king's bench for Michaelmas term 1320 refers to a man indicted of forging the king's money in Norfolk, an offence which, so the roll states, 'is a special form of treason'.[7] We may take it, therefore, that although there is no administrative order to that effect now extant the crown between approximately 1280 and 1320 managed to increase the heinousness of money forgery. By two statutes of the early fifteenth century (3 Henry V c.1 and 2 Henry VI c.9) a new money felony was created: the introduction into the realm of certain continental coins for use in payment of purchases or debts. On the statistical side we should notice that gaol delivery records of the late thirteenth century suggest that at that time forgery of the king's coin accounted for the arraignment of a mere 0.04 per cent of accused persons.[8]

The law concerning persons who broke out of gaol, as it stood for the major part of the thirteenth century, was notable for its severity. Bracton implied that whatever the offence for which the prisoner was incarcerated, his escape amounted to felony. *Britton*, written in Edward I's reign, even states that the mere intent to break prison (i.e. where no overt act to that purpose had been perpetrated) is felony.[9] Thus in one respect the author placed escape in the same category as so heinous a crime as treason. A radical change in the law was, however, at hand. From the parliament of 1295 came a statute which stipulated no one should suffer capital punishment for breaking out of gaol unless the crime for which he was imprisoned carried such a penalty (i.e. was felony or treason).[10] Escape from prison as an offence seems to have comprised less than one per cent of indictments in the thirteenth and fourteenth centuries. The incidence may have been a little greater in the earlier fifteenth century but there can be little doubt that the number of such offences in any gaol delivery calendar was minimal.[11]

An offence with a considerable history as a felony was purveyance, the requisitioning by the crown of provisions for the king and his entourage at a set price, done illegally. The nature of the crime hardly seems to us to justify a capital sentence but the statutes which defined it demonstrate strong popular hostility. By the *Articuli super Cartas* (28 Edward I c.11) purveyors taking goods without a royal warrant were to be treated as felons, and an act of 1332 (5 Edward III c.2) stipulated the same penalty should the 'prise' not be made by constables and the men of the vill. By the act 20 Edward III st.2 c.15 purveyors were commanded not to take sheep before shearing on pain of being treated as thieves and robbers. In 1362 there were several legislative provisions (36 Edward III cc.2, 4, 5, 6) concerning purveyance: it should be at the current market price, in areas only where there was no dearth, and the amount was to be no more than necessary.[12] Offenders in this respect and royal purveyors who took more than they delivered to the king, if convicted, were to suffer as felons. Illegally performed purveyance became thus one of the most statutorily defined of all felonies, but it is no surprise to discover that royal servants who perpetrated the offence rarely suffered the proper punishment. The very few cases of the crime to be found in the plea rolls show the accused indicted for trespass rather than for felony.[13]

If medieval legislation against illegal purveyance was the result of popular outcry there were some other types of misbehaviour, also declared felony by statute, which must have been promoted by particular groups which had at that moment the ability to obtain parliamentary approval and royal assent. The statute 34 Edward III c.22 made it felony to steal or abduct a hawk: it stated that the miscreant was to be treated as a thief who had stolen a horse. The reign of Henry VI produced several examples of these new felonies. Thus the act 3 Henry VI c.1 made it a felony to cause masons to meet for the purpose of trying to destroy the effect of the Statute of Labourers; the act 18 Henry VI c.15 made a felon of anyone convicted of taking wool anywhere abroad other than to the Calais staple; those who procured the removal of law records so that judgment in a case was reversed could be convicted of felony (under the statute 8 Henry VI c.12) as could anyone who simply embezzled a court record by 2 Richard III c.10; an act of 1454 (33 Henry VI c.1) established procedure to secure the appearance before the chancellor of servants suspected of embezzling their masters' goods: failure to appear in response to writs of proclamation was to result in their being held as felons. Somewhat more likely than the above to produce indictments and therefore suspects in court was the statute 18 Henry VI c.19, which was concerned with the problem of soldiers in the French war who, after receiving their wages, deserted their captain.[14] It was not desertion as such which drew punishment; rather it declared they would on conviction be held as felons should they not return the wages.

A notable weakness of English medieval criminal law in the fourteenth century was its failure to provide adequate remedy for serious assault. The victim could seek the indictment of his assailant for trespass, which on conviction would normally result in a modest fine or, occasionally, imprisonment, but nothing more. Bracton tells us that in the earlier thirteenth century the victim might, if his wounds were severe enough to render him incapable of success in trial by battle, bring an appeal of mayhem. This he was entitled to call a felony if he so desired. In the reign of Edward I the author of *Britton* was able to state that mayhem was a felony which did not carry the death penalty if the charge was made by indictment rather than appeal, which may have heralded a decline in its perceived heinousness. In the early fourteenth-century plea rolls appeals of mayhem are not apparent, although the verb 'to maim' appears sometimes in indictments of battery and wounding and thus only as trespass.[15] The only vestige of the felony of mayhem is perhaps to be noticed in the statute 5 Henry IV c.5, which declared that henceforth the cutting out of tongues or putting out of eyes, brutalities designed to ensure that the victim would not give evidence, should carry the penalty for felony.

There were also two offences, newly rated as felony in the fourteenth century, in which the king, or at least his judges, must have had a particular interest. A statute of 1390 (13 Richard II st.2 c.3) made felons of those convicted of bringing or sending into the realm summons, sentences, or excommunications connected with the implementation of the Statute of Provisors. The second offence was referred to as 'discovering the king's counsel' and is rather mysterious for there exists no statute containing a reference to it. Furthermore on the few occasions it appears in extant indictments it is more often a trespass than a felony. Even to provide a definition is not easy. It seems to have amounted to the illegal revelation by jurors of indictment to persons other than the justices of suspects they had just indicted, or the giving of warning to the latter. The offence secures mention in a list of articles for inquest in the king's bench where the 'discovery of the king's counsel' is very definitely linked to the giving of warning to those who have been indicted. There were also, however, instances in which the charge was used where the sense is that the jurors have revealed advice given them by the king's justices, the 'advice' presumably being suggestions as to whom they should indict.[16]

There were considerably more types of offence turned into felony by act of parliament in the Tudor period than between about 1280 and 1485. The notion that the face of the common law could be drastically altered by statute began to take strong root. The new felonies fell into a number of clearly defined categories: to do with religious doctrine and observance; to do with hunting and parks; practices which were seditious but not quite treason; assembling for illegal purposes and refusing to disperse; deserting and demobilized soldiers; dangerous prophecy; forcible abduction; sexual offences; sorcery/witchcraft; wandering persons; embezzlement; and a number which were one of a kind.

In the first group was 31 Henry VIII c.14, which made felons of those who denied five articles of religion, and 35 Elizabeth c.1, which did the same to those who refused to go to divine service and instead went to unlawful conventicles. In the second was 31 Henry VIII c.12 (entering parks in disguise at night, retaining possession of the king's hawks, stealing falcons' eggs on royal manors), 32 Henry VIII c.11 (killing deer in enclosed parks by night or when the miscreant wore a disguise), and 3/4 Edward VI c.5, which was concerned with those (more than twelve) who attempted to break down park enclosures and would not disperse on warning. By a very odd statute of 1486 (1 Henry VII c.7) those who hunted in disguise and on arrest refused to admit their crime were, if subsequently found guilty, to be treated as felons. The act 3/4 Edward VI c.5 might also be placed in the 'illegal assembly' category with 1 Mary st.2 c.12, which rated as felony the gathering together of twelve or more persons in order to alter the laws, the price of food, or to destroy enclosures or houses, and who refused to disperse on warning. Dealing with disobedient soldiers were the acts 2/3 Edward VI c.2 and its revivor 4/5 Philip and Mary c.3, which stipulated that soldiers departing from the army with booty without permission were, on conviction, to be held felons. 5 Elizabeth I c.5 extended this rule to mariners and gunners and 39 Elizabeth I c.17 made felons of idle and wandering soldiers and mariners who did not possess a testimonial from a justice of the peace.

Dangerous prophecy was the subject of three sixteenth-century statutes. 33 Henry VIII c.14 rated as felony the making of false and 'fantastical' prophecies while 35 Henry VIII c.14 made felonious the declaring of prophecies based on the interpretation of nobles' badges and armorial bearings. Making a more direct connection of prophecy with sedition was 23 Elizabeth c.2, which declared as felony the writing or printing of seditious books and repeating slanderous tales about the queen, and also making prophecy as to how long the queen should live. The forcible abduction of women who possessed property or were heiresses, as we have seen, was made felony by 3 Henry VII c.2, while the act 43 Elizabeth I c.13 did similar in regard to the taking for ransom of inhabitants of the three most northerly counties and the bishopric of Durham. Two kinds of sexual offence were made felony: buggery 'with mankind or beast' by the statute 25 Henry VIII c.6 (annulled in 1547 but restored by 2/3 Edward VI c.29); raping a girl under ten years of age by 18 Elizabeth I c.7. The provoking of 'unlawful love' as well as destroying people's bodies or goods, or discovering lost articles by means of pictures or images, was made felony by 33 Henry VIII c.8.

This statute is commonly regarded as the original secular law on the crime of sorcery/witchcraft. In the later middle ages, in England at least, sorcery, the ancestor of witchcraft, was considered the business of the church. A sorcerer was defined as one who co-operated with devils to do wicked things. Since such co-operation necessarily involved agreement sorcery was viewed as denying the Christian faith and thus heretical. This was the attitude of the church from the mid-thirteenth century onwards yet the usual punishment it imposed was only excommunication, which probably reflected the equivocal comments on magical arts by contemporary ecclesiastical writers. However, in the late thirteenth century, if we believe *Britton*, both heresy and sorcery were regarded as being the concern of the state also. Thus, whereas no earlier treatise writer or legal code (since Edmund) had mentioned sorcery, that offence, together with heresy, was included by the author of *Britton* among the articles of the sheriff's tourn. The punishment, for those presented by the jurors of the hundred and convicted, was to be death by burning. A little later the compiler of *Fleta* affirmed this and added, rather obscurely, that proof should be by reputation and hurtful deeds, which may be a hint that he thought hard evidence of injury by sorcery difficult to discover.[17]

In the extant common law court records of the late thirteenth century, and the fourteenth and fifteenth centuries, sorcery is noticeably absent. On the other hand the king's council appears to have handled a small number of instances. In one case (1331) it made use of the king's bench and a local jury to enquire if death (which had not in fact occurred) was intended, and it imprisoned the accused when a positive verdict was returned.[18] The case suggests that sorcery had no certain place in the field of secular law. Although the relevant records are almost entirely lost to us it seems that sorcery at the end of the middle ages was normally tried in court ecclesiastical and that cases usually ended with the suspects purging themselves with the assistance of neighbours. There is no sign of homicide being attributed to sorcery at this time: the offence, in the church courts, was merely intent to harm or kill. The mental jump from this charge to an accusation that a person had actually been killed by magical means (called 'witchcraft' by that time) cannot at the moment be shown to have occurred before the reign of Elizabeth I. The statute 33 Henry VIII c.8, as we have seen, made it felony to use images of various sorts to destroy a person in body or goods, but what 'destroy', not a word in the common law lexicon, meant is not clear. Thus when it figured in a fifteenth-century Irish statute the meaning was 'to oppress' or 'to impose a heavy burden'.[19] It is possible that 'to destroy' in the Henrican act incorporated 'to kill' but no record evidence has been found which proves this, and it is just as likely that 'to destroy' meant not 'to kill' but rather 'to make diseased' or 'to drive a person distraught'. The word-form of the subsequent sorcery/witchcraft statute, 5 Elizabeth I c.16, points in the same direction for although in one section it made it felony to invoke spirits so a person should be 'killed or destroyed' (terms apparently here synonymous), elsewhere it referred to witchcraft as the misdemeanour which 'hurt' or 'destroyed' a person in his body but did not cause death. The latter type of destruction seems to have amounted to the loss of a limb or acquiring a debilitating disease, the witchcraft offence in the statute 33 Henry VIII c.8.

Another category of Tudor statutes on criminal law concerned wandering persons. Those convicted a second time of being rogues or vagabonds were deemed felons by the act 14 Elizabeth I c.5, a severer version of 27 Henry VIII c.25 which stipulated the punishment only for the third offence; by 39 Elizabeth I c.4 dangerous rogues who had been banished from the kingdom, should they return illegally, were to be held to have committed felony. Similarly Egyptians (gypsies) who had entered the country were to be deemed felons should they not leave it again within a month under 1/2 Philip and Mary c.4, while 5 Elizabeth c.3 did the same for any person who lived among them for a month or disguised himself as one. There were two relevant statutes concerned with what was called 'embezzlement'. By 21 Henry VIII c.7 servants to whom goods had been entrusted and who had then 'withdrawn' themselves intending to steal were to be felons if convicted; the act 31 Elizabeth I c.4 was concerned with those who deliberately conveyed away military equipment or supplies of the crown worth more than 20 shillings, and made such offences into felony.

Among statutes creating new felonies in the sixteenth century which lacked a close relationship with any other was 5 Elizabeth I c.14. This made felons of persons who forged charters, evidences, or deeds for the purpose of obtaining freehold property if they were convicted of the offence a second time. Also without connection was 8 Elizabeth I c.3, which made felons of those convicted a second time of shipping sheep out of the kingdom, and the statute 23 Henry VIII c.11, which stipulated that it was felony for a clerk convict to break out of ecclesiastical gaol, the laws against escape from prison, apparently, hitherto not extending to those who had successfully claimed benefit of clergy.

The felonies declared by statute of the Tudor period produced only a few indictments if we judge by the assize records of the home circuit for the reign of Elizabeth I. The offences which accounted for the greatest number of persons arraigned in the Sussex records between 1559 and the end of the century were counterfeit coining (1.5 per cent), arson and buggery (each 0.4 per cent), and desertion from the forces (0.2 per cent). The number of those arraigned for Tudor statutory felonies overall in this county was only a very modest 3.3 per cent of all prisoners put to answer. The Kent assize records for the same period show a slightly more substantial total of 4.5 per cent of those arraigned were indicted of such felonies. The three crimes which produced most of these charges were counterfeit coining, breaking out of gaol, and witchcraft at just over one per cent each, while buggery provided about 0.6 per cent of cases. Analysis of those arraigned in Essex in this period shows desertion was the offence in about 1.4 per cent of indictments, breaking gaol in about 1.2 per cent, while being an Egyptian or consorting with the same made up about 0.9 per cent; counterfeit coining amounted to just under 0.8 per cent, buggery 0.36 per cent and arson 0.3 per cent. Witchcraft, however, provided a very substantial 9 per cent out of the overall 'statutory felonies' total of 14.7 per cent of indictments. Were it not for the incidence of witchcraft cases in Essex we might say that the arraignments which did not involve the basic felonies of culpable homicide, robbery, burglary or larceny were negligible in number.[20]

Notes

1 *Bracton*, ii, 414; *Stat. Realm*, i, 30.

2 *Year Books*, 11 Henry VII Mich. pl.1.

3 The commons of parliament petitioned for this; the reason was the activities of a gang operating in Cambridgeshire and Essex which practised extortion. Its members were indicted for traitorous and felonious arson and conspiracy. The leader, John Muston, was convicted and hanged: *Rot. Parl.*, iv, 349b; PRO JUST 3/8/14/29.

4 As calculated from the plea rolls mentioned in chapter one.

5 *Glanvill*, pp. 176–7; *Britton*, i, 25.

6 *Stat. Realm*, i, 319 (25 Edward III st.5 c.2).

7 *Select Cases in King's Bench, IV*, p. 102.

8 Calculated from *Wiltshire Gaol Delivery*.

9 *Bracton*, ii, 350; *Britton*, i, 43.

10 *Rot. Parl.*, i, 138.

11 These are my calculations from *Wiltshire Gaol Delivery, Sessions of the Peace in Lincs., 1360–75*, and *Sessions of the Peace in Lincolnshire 1381–96*. The statistics of Elder (pp. 305–29) show a rate of 4.5 per cent for the south-western circuit, 1416–30. The Yorkshire gaol delivery records for 1439–60 give an incidence of 1.6 per cent: PRO JUST 3/211 and 213.

12 *Stat. Realm*, i, 137, 266, 322, 371. There was also the statute 20 Edward III st.5 c.15, which commanded that sheep should not be taken by purveyors before shearing on pain of their being treated as thieves and robbers.

13   See *Proceedings*, ed. Putnam, pp. 362, 365.

14   18 Henry VI c.19 is an example of a statute dependent for its implementation on the putting in of bills of indictment since no English jury of presentment would have had knowledge of such offences.

15   *Bracton*, ii, 408, 411; *Shropshire Eyre*, p. 275; *Britton*, i, 98.

16   *Year Books, Liber Assisarum*, 27 Edward III pl. 44; *Proceedings*, ed. Putnam, pp. cliii, 54, 65, 192.

17   *Britton*, i, 42, 179; *Fleta*, II, p. 10.

18   *Select Cases in King's Bench, V*, pp. 53–7.

19   *The Statutes of Ireland newly perused and examined*, ed. R. Bolton (Dublin, 1621), p. 9.

20   *Calendar of Assize Records, Indictments, Eliozabeth I*, for Sussex and Kent; PRO ASSI 35/1–41.

GLOSSARY

Appeal of felony	A formal accusation of felony, usually made by a victim against the perpetrator. It obviated the need for an indictment brought by a jury.
Approver	One (male) who confessed to felony and accused his confederates in order to delay his own execution.
Arraignment	Putting a person to answer (i.e. make a plea of 'guilty' or 'not guilty') in court.
Bailee	Person to whom an owner entrusts his goods without intending to transfer ownership.
Captus	In the legal sense a person arrested on suspicion but without a formal charge laid against him.
Compurgation	Attempt to prove the innocence of the accused by the oaths of others as to his good character.
Eyre	An eyre was a judge's circuit, but the 'general eyre' was a judicial visitation by judges of central courts. 'Articles of the eyre' were instructions for enquiry by presenting jurors in the county visited.
Frankpledge	Compulsory association of men into groups of ten with each acting as surety for the behaviour of the others.
Gaol delivery	Trial, by visiting justices, of prisoners being held there.
Grand Jury	Title sometimes given to juries which provided indictments. Occasionally used to indicate jurors drawn from the whole county rather than a single hundred.
Hundred	An administrative and judicial section of a county.
Indictment	Accusation of crime affirmed by jurors of presentment/indictment. A bill of indictment was an accusation in writing intended to gain the approval of the jurors and thus become an indictment.
Inquest	Inquest or inquisition was an enquiry made by a jury before an officer of the crown or franchisal lord.
Judgment	Sentence on a person convicted.
Mainour	Loot which a thief or robber took from his victim; also called pelf.
Manucaption	Giving of surety for the appearance of a person in court or for his good behaviour in the future.
Ordinary	Bishop's officer who, when an accused in secular court claimed benefit of clergy in regard to his felony, decided if he should be allowed the privilege.
Outlawry	Failure to appear in court to answer a charge of felony could lead to this equivalent of conviction after about five months.
Oyer and Terminer	Commission to justices to enquire of and try particular offences or persons.

Peine forte et dure	Refusal at trial to plead 'guilty' or 'not guilty' to an indictment would lead to imprisonment on a starvation diet (or, in the sixteenth century, to being weighed down with heavy objects) in order to extract a plea.
Petty jury	Trial jury.
Privata	Secret report to the justices by jurors of presentment about those they suspected.
Querela	Informal complaint to justices.
Reeve	Head peasant in a village.
Sheriff's tourn	Session of a hundred court before the sheriff for enquiring into offences.
Trespass/Misdemeanour	Offence against person or property which did not carry the death penalty.
Unamendable crime	One for which the perpetrator could not escape legal consequences by payment to the victim or his kin.
Veredictum	Charge laid by jury of presentment (thirteenth century).
Vill	Village, township.
Wer	Value, according to rank, set on a man's life and thus payable by his slayer.

NOTES ON COMMENTATORS

Bracton	Bracton's *De Legibus et Consuetudinibus Angliae*, written *c.* 1250, is the classic medieval treatise on English law. It is a systematic work by a judge and shows Roman and canonical influence. The section on criminal law is about a fifth of the whole work; it emphasizes prosecution by appeal and outlawry.
Britton	Treatise written purportedly on royal authority, *c.* 1290. It is well organized, practical, and emphasizes procedure. Although it draws a lot from Bracton it contains several important pieces of information on the criminal law which the latter lacks. Comment on the criminal law comprises nearly half the work.
Dialogue of the Exchequer	Written (*c.* 1180) essentially on the workings of the exchequer but it also contains an explanation of presentment of Englishry and passing comments on a variety of offences.
Fleta	A commentary on the law (*c.* 1290) drawing much from Bracton and emphasizing the judicial supremacy of the crown.
Fortescue	*De Laudibus Legum Angliae* is a tract written by an ex-chief justice of the king's bench, John Fortescue, when in exile in France in the 1460s. Disturbed by continental criminal law procedure he sought to demonstrate the superiority and innate fairness of the English system. This he did in an almost journalistic manner without making reference to the legal treatises of earlier centuries. He viewed the jury system as being of the greatest benefit.
Glanvill	Treatise written in about 1190. Authorship uncertain. Demonstrates the employment of the inquest and Henry II's legal reforms in general. Criminal law occupies only a small part of the work but the court system and the older forms of trial are clearly delineated.
Graunde Abridgement	By Anthony Fitzherbert (printed 1516). Modelled on earlier abridgements it is a collection of reports from *Year Books* arranged by subject matter. It has, therefore, been a source particularly well used by historians and lawyers. The criminal law is to be found under the title 'Corone et plees del corone'.
Lambard	William Lambard, a very committed and learned Elizabethan justice of the peace, who wrote on several historical topics. His most famous work was probably his *Eirenarcha* (1581), an exhaustive commentary on the powers of justices of the peace.
Law Reports	The English law reports, which begin in the sixteenth century, were notes made by judges on cases which had come before them. On the criminal law

side they record details of offences and professional opinions about them. Particularly valuable are those by Spelman, Plowden, and Dyer.

Laws of the Pre-conquest and Norman kings
In rudimentary form the elements and scope of what were the later medieval felonies are to be found in the laws of the Anglo-Saxon and Norman kings, notably of Ine, Alfred, Athelstan, and Canute, and in the *Leis Wilhelmi* and *Leges Henrici Primi*.

Marowe
Thomas Marowe's reading on the peace in 1503 at the Inner Temple (in theory on chapter one of the Statute of Westminster I (1275)) carefully analysed the powers of the justices of the peace.

Mirror of Justices
Possibly written late in Edward I's reign, probably by Andrew Horn, chamberlain of London. The accuracy of some sections of this legal treatise is doubted by historians although a desire to emphasize certain London legal and judicial idiosyncracies may account for some of its distinctive flavour.

More
Most of Thomas More's revealing comments on the English common law criminal justice system are to be found in his *Debellacion of Salem and Byzance* (1533) in which he was retorting to Christopher St German's criticisms of the ex officio procedure used by ecclesiastical courts, particularly in regard to the trial of heretics.

Smith
Thomas Smith's *De Republica Anglorum* (written *c.* 1565, published 1583) provides the clearest account of the period of the criminal law system and the trial process. It remains essential reading for all students of the topic. In praising the merits of the English criminal trial Smith was probably prompted, like Fortescue, by his experience of the continental torture-based systems.

Staunford
William Staunford's *Les Plees del Corone* (1557) has claims to be regarded as the first large-scale treatment of English criminal law since the thirteenth century. It owes much to Fitzherbert's *Graunde Abridgement*. Conservative in tone, its aim seems to be the listing of royal rights. The author shows much interest in benefit of clergy and accusation by appeal.

Year Books
A very important source even if the space devoted to criminal law is extremely small compared with the coverage of private law. The comments on cases by judges were recorded by apprentices of the law sitting in the courtroom, or so it is believed. Unfortunately the recorders frequently fail to provide the precise context in which the remarks were made. The *Year Books* extend from 1283–1536. The section richest on criminal law is the so-called *Liber Assisarum*, which covers the reign of Edward III.

NOTES ON SOURCES

The English criminal trial of the later medieval period, even of the time of the earlier Tudor monarchs, is a subject which has received relatively slight attention from historians and lawyers. Maitland, in his *History of English Law* (Cambridge, 1898), devoted some pages to its form in the twelfth and thirteenth centuries but through the major part of the twentieth century a direct approach to its study was not undertaken. Over the last three decades the new-found popularity of the history of crime has created a fair amount of interest in certain aspects of the criminal law, notably the trial jury, but progress has been on a relatively narrow front.

The major reason for this is clear enough. The criminal trial of the period from Edward I to the end of the fifteenth century is not a topic for which there is a substantial amount of contemporary material for the historian to draw on – rather the reverse. Legal and administrative records must be trawled for small pieces of relevant evidence hitherto lying unnoticed. Subsequent to Edward's reign there was only a single commentator on the subject before the sixteenth century. The chroniclers of the period, even if they were competent to deal with the topic, which in the main they were not, were uninterested. Those notable records of government the statutes (*Statutes of the Realm* [Record Commission, 1810–28] and the rolls of parliament, *Rotuli Parliamentorum* [1272–1503], ed. J. Strachey et al. [1767]) provide only opaque glimpses of the trial process and ambiguous definitions of the felonies. More useful are the rolls of chancery, the best being the patent rolls (PRO C 66; *Calendar of Patent Rolls, 1216–1509* and *1547–* [London, 1891–]). The indexes of the calendars for the medieval period are particularly deficient on subject matter and the text must be read *in extenso*.

Invaluable, despite their laconic nature, are the rolls and files of the courts which handled criminal business, especially those of the gaol delivery/assize sessions (PRO JUST 3), of coroners (PRO JUST 2), and of justices of the peace's sessions. On the last see particularly *Proceedings before the Justices of the Peace in the Fourteenth and Fifteenth Centuries, Edward III to Richard III*, ed. B.H. Putnam, Ames Foundation (London, 1938), and other similar proceedings edited by Putnam and her followers for English local record societies. The Ames Foundation volume contains a revealing analysis of the indictments by T.F.T. Plucknett, who pioneered the notion of exploring the vocabulary they contained. Also to be included in this category is the class of records known as 'Ancient Indictments' (PRO KB 9), often the records of lower courts being moved into the king's bench, and the rolls of the king's bench itself (PRO KB 27). Part legal record and part commentary are the important reports on cases to be found in the *Year Books*. Some of the latter were printed in the Rolls Series, some by the Selden Society, some by the Ames Foundation; the remainder are best approached through the so-called 'Maynard's edition' of 1678–80.

The search to establish the nature and scope of particular felonies takes us back to the early middle ages. The laws of the Anglo-Saxon and Norman kings (see *The Laws of the Earliest English Kings*, ed. F.L. Attenborough (Cambridge, 1922), *The Laws of the Kings of England from Edmund to Henry I*, ed. A.J. Robertson (Cambridge, 1925), and *Leges Henrici Primi*, ed. L.J. Downer (Oxford, 1972) are invaluable here. It has also been necessary in the aforegoing text to study earlier Tudor records for the same purpose, but more so in order to flesh out the mechanics of accusation and trial as they were at the end of the medieval period. Here we are fortunate since the first two Tudor reigns provide much useful information. In addition to important cases in the *Year Books* there are relevant, if chance, references in the records of the king's council (*Select Cases in the Council of Henry VII*, ed. C.G. Bayne and completed by W.H. Dunham (Selden Society, 75, 1958), PRO STAC 1 and 2, and Star Chamber records printed by local record societies). The law reports of John Spelman, edited with a lengthy introduction by J.H. Baker (Selden Society, 93–4, 1977–8), and the opinions of Thomas Marowe and Thomas More (especially in his *Debellacion of Salem and Byzance*) are similarly informative. Providing much insight from another angle is the correspondence of Thomas Cromwell (*Letters and Papers, Foreign and Domestic, of the reign of Henry VIII*, ed. J.S. Brewer, J. Gairdner, R.H. Brodie [1862–1932], vols. v–xv and Addenda); this source throws light on pressures put on jurors and justices, on relations between justices and administrators, as well as on sentencing and pardoning policy.

Gaol delivery records, with a few exceptions, do not survive from about 1440–1550 and peace commission records are similarly lacking. Since it is difficult to gauge what may be called the efficiency of the later medieval criminal law system without a comparable set of records of a different period, the home circuit assize (i.e. gaol delivery) indictments for the reign of Elizabeth I (PRO ASSI 35 1–67, *Calendar of Assize Records, Indictments, Elizabeth I*, ed. J.S. Cockburn [London, 1975–82]) have been utilized together with similar records of Middlesex and Cheshire. For the same purpose and for information on post-trial practice not available elsewhere, use has been made of privy council records (*Acts of the Privy Council of England*, ed. J.R. Dasent et al. [London, 1890–1964] and the State Papers, Domestic (PRO SP 10, 11, 12 and the printed calendars for the period 1547–1603). It is only from the mid-sixteenth century onwards that we encounter detailed descriptions of particular criminal trials. Unfortunately nearly all are concerned with treason or witchcraft.

INDEX

abduction, 117, 148, 150, 162, 164, 166–82
abscission (of bodily parts), 70, 72, 154, 163, 167, 187, 189
accessories, 39, 60, 110, 134, 142, 164
accidental killing, 68, 148
acquittal, 30, 118, 120, 122
adultery, 143, 162, 166
afforcement of indictments, *see* indictments
Alfred, King, 162
apparel, excessive, 26
'appeachers', 142–3
appeals, 8, 9, 15, 21, 29, 31–2, 36–9, 40, 46–7, 71, 72, 82, 97, 99–100, 103, 109, 110, 144, 148, 149, 150, 163, 164–8, 170–2, 177–8
approvers, 36, 39–42, 47, 80, 108, 139
arrest (*see also captus*), 12, 19, 60, 67, 106, 115, 170
arson, 40, 145, 187, 193
articles, justices (*see also* eyre), 19, 23, 30
artisans, 180
Ashton, Nicholas, 34–5
asportation, 21, 32, 35, 119, 169
assault, 11, 20, 39, 73
   in court, 154
   indecent, 162
   serious, 82, 189
Athelstan, King, 69–70
Athern, William, 170

bail, 39
bailees, 31–2, 72, 78
bailiffs, 26, 43, 44, 45, 47, 102, 119
bakers, 181
Bamborough, 59
banishment, 151, 192
barns, 145, 187
bastard feudalism, 11, 12, 15, 37, 48, 107, 115, 116, 118, 120, 122, 123, 149
battery, 189
battle, trial by, 31, 36–7, 41, 57
beasts, 78

benefit of clergy, 29, 65, 75, 84–5, 118, 125, 134–7, 150, 152–3, 155, 156, 178, 187, 192
Berkshire, 165, 179
Bigg, John, 170
blinding, 163, 164, 189
Boke of Iustyces of Peas, 64, 83
books, making seditious, 145, 191
boroughs, 153
Boteler, Isabel, 173
Boteler, John, 173
Boys, Jane, 173, 174
Bracton, Henry, 8, 19, 20, 58, 59, 71–3, 163–4, 177, 187–9
Brampton, John, 43
branding, 137, 150
Brandon, William, 174
breaking bulk, 79
bribery, 10
Britton, 8, 20, 30, 59, 71–2, 74, 187–9, 191
Brooke, Robert, 65, 66
Browne, George, 154
buggery, 191, 193
Buildwas, 59
burglary, 13, 15, 36–7, 39, 40, 44, 72–6, 78, 81–6, 93–5, 97, 125, 136, 142, 145, 148, 151
burning, execution by, 191
Bury St Edmunds, 101

Cambridgeshire, 73, 114
Cantilupe, William, 60
Canute, King, 69, 72, 162
captus cases, 42–6, 104, 105
Carles, William, 59
castration, 163, 164
Cecil, William, Lord Burghley, 10
certiorari, writ of, 141
challenge of trial jurors, 100–1
chance medley, killing in, 61–6
chancellor, 139, 141, 144, 173, 189
chancery, 139, 141, 145
   records of, 8, 59, 76

chaplains, 181
Chapuys, Eustace, 143
charges, justices, *see* justices charges
charters, 79
Cheapside, 154
Cheddar, Richard, 33
Chester, palatinate of, 24, 68–9, 136–7, 138, 142, 173, 178
Choke, Richard, 79
chronicles, 9, 41
Clarendon, assize of, 19, 57
clericus, 117, 134, 135
clerk of court, 28–9, 30, 48, 109, 115, 134, 139
Clifford, John, 60
closes, breaking, 75–6
Coke, Edward, 99, 176
   The Third Part of the Institutes of the Laws of England, 176
collectors, subsidy, 115
common fame (*see also* notoriety), 23, 29, 30, 35, 43–4, 75, 102, 144
common law, 8, 36, 106
compositions, 32, 38, 62, 69, 70, 149
compurgation (ecclesiastical), 135, 137, 191
concealment by juries, 33
concording, 165
concubines and mistresses, 163–5
confessions, 39, 101, 108, 142
confrontations in court, 109–10
conscience, 14, 97, 115, 122, 151
conspiracy, actions of, 29, 34–5, 47, 102, 106
constables, 24, 26, 27, 44, 45, 67, 188
conviction rates, 9, 14, 33, 37, 40, 63, 69, 75, 82, 86, 93, 95–8, 111, 117–18, 123–4, 137, 152, 179, 181
coroners, 25, 31, 40, 60, 66, 101, 115, 163, 172, 178
correspondence, 8, 24, 25, 47
council, King's, 11, 13, 33, 34, 42, 43, 101, 108, 120–3, 139, 145, 146, 151, 152, 154, 176, 191
counsel, legal, 80, 100, 113, 140, 151, 171
counterfeiting, 43, 187–8, 193
county court, 20, 70, 163
Coupland, John, 60
Coventry, 81, 178, 179, 180
Crompton, Richard, 175
Cromwell, Thomas, 97, 101, 119–22, 140, 143, 149, 151

Culpeper, Thomas, 180
Cumberland, 95
cut-purses, 136

Dacre of the South, Thomas Fiennes, Lord, 65, 143
Dalton, Michael, 85
damages, 21, 31, 33, 72, 148
Daulton, Mr, 109
death penalty, 70, 72, 77–8, 80, 107, 116, 125, 138, 148, 155, 167, 187, 188
debt, 21
deeds, 21
deer, king's, 101, 148
defloration, 164–5, 174, 176
depositions, 105, 108–9, 119
Derby, Henry Bolingbroke, earl of, 171
Derbyshire, 73
desertion from army or navy, 189, 190, 193
'destroying' a person, 191, 192
detective techniques, 26
Devonshire, 12, 46, 101
Dialogue of the Exchequer, 70
'discovering the king's counsel', 189
Diss hundred (Norfolk), 101
Diversite de Courtz et lour jurisdictions, 31
dower, 168, 170
Dublin, 22
duration of trials, 110, 113–15
Durham, palatinate of, 138, 152
Dyer, James, 65, 176

ecclesiastical courts, 191
Edmund II, King, 138, 191
Edward I, King, 19, 21, 22, 40, 42–3, 72, 81, 82, 86, 93, 96, 189
Edward II, King, 27, 34, 100
Edward III, King, 15, 44, 47, 75, 80, 104, 124, 187
Edward IV, King, 24, 25, 97, 119
Edward VI, King, 65, 141
Egyptians (gypsies), 192, 192
ejectment, 21
Elizabeth I, Queen, 38, 42, 67–9, 86, 95, 97, 107–9, 114, 122, 123, 136–7, 143, 144, 146, 147, 150, 193
Ellis, Dr, 66
Elliot, Richard, 64
eloining, 71

elopement, 168, 180
embracery, 12, 121, 122, 171
Englishry, presentment of, 58
Essex, 44, 68, 69, 81, 86, 93, 95, 96, 123,
    136, 147, 148, 156, 177, 178, 179,
    180, 181, 193
Ethelbert of Kent, King, 69, 162
Ethelred II, King, 162
evidence, 25–6, 32–3, 35, 39, 48, 97,
    102–3, 205, 106, 107–8, 113, 115,
    119, 121, 176, 189, 191
  hearsay, 47, 109
  King's, *see* 'appeachers'
ex officio inquests, 134
examination, 15, 26–7, 47, 101, 105–9,
    111, 119, 120, 121, 173
exchequer chamber, 13, 75
excommunication, 189, 191
execution, 70, 120, 138, 143, 152–6
eyre, general, 19, 21, 22, 23, 24, 25, 30,
    74, 77, 78, 104, 164, 165, 171–2, 177

fama, inquests *de gestu et*, 46, 103, 105
Fastolf, John, 25
fines, 102, 139, 146, 148, 149, 162, 166
Fitzherbert, Anthony, 29, 38, 83, 175
Fleet gaol, 33, 145
Fleta, 71, 72, 191
Fletham, Robert, 59
forcible entry, 11, 12, 15, 120, 121, 122, 149
forfeiture, 8, 31, 62, 79, 81, 85, 141, 142, 145
forging charters or deeds, 150, 192
Fortescue, John, 8, 99, 102
frankpledge, 71
Fulbourn, 171

galleys, 151, 155
gallows, 16, 154, 155
  speeches at, 154, 155
gaol delivery, circuits of, 36, 38, 40, 45, 68,
    82, 85, 86, 94, 95, 96, 97, 112, 114,
    124, 125, 135, 136, 147
  commissions of, 11, 23, 64, 98, 103,
    104, 113
  sessions and records of, 8, 9, 24, 26, 31,
    38, 40, 43, 45, 48, 68, 73, 74, 81, 85,
    86, 95, 97, 100, 101, 105, 108, 109,
    112, 114, 120, 135, 136, 146, 148,
    152, 178, 187
Garay, K., 94, 147

girls, young, 162, 175, 176, 179, 181
Glamorgan, 173
Glanvill, 57, 58, 70, 163, 165, 187
Gloucestershire, 177, 178
goods and chattels, 8, 71, 180
Gower, John, 64
great seal, lord, 146
Green, T.A., 61, 63

Hale, Matthew, 177
Hales, John, 115
Hals, John, 170
Hampshire, 24, 27, 76
hamsocn (*see also* burglary), 72, 73
hanaper, 139, 143
Hanawalt, B.A., 68, 81, 82, 93, 116, 146,
    177
hanging, 152–5, 164
  in chains, 154
heiresses, 175, 176
Henry I, King, 70
Henry II, King, 19, 134
Henry III, King, 25
Henry IV, King, 63, 68, 77, 94, 116, 124,
    147, 169, 170
Henry V, King, 9, 94, 147
Henry VI, King, 9, 45, 81, 94, 108, 125,
    144, 147, 189
Henry VII, King, 32, 101, 122, 125, 144,
    149, 174, 181
Henry VIII, King, 25, 42, 64, 65, 83, 117,
    119, 136, 140, 141, 142, 143, 144,
    145, 149, 152, 178
Herbert, George, 65, 66
Herefordshire, 81
heresy, 26, 154, 191
Hertfordshire, 44, 93, 124, 156
Holforde, Robert, 142
homicide, 12, 25, 32, 35, 36, 38, 39, 40, 58,
    59, 93–5, 97, 101, 108, 115, 145, 168
horses, stealing of, 136, 145
household, court of the steward and
    marshal of the royal, 102
houses, 72–5, 84–5, 187
Howard, Katharine, 180
Hudson, William, 122
hue and cry, 35, 58, 163
hundreds, 19, 24, 27, 31, 33, 57, 74, 98,
    99, 100, 101, 163
Huntingdonshire, 22, 81

Hurnard, N.D., 58, 146, 147
husbandmen, 180
Hussey, John, 140, 141

Ilchester, 41
imprisonment, 13, 16, 21, 30, 31, 39, 41,
    46, 47, 70, 112, 135, 137, 141,
    148–51, 166, 176
  charges for, 141, 148
  escape from, 145, 148, 188, 193
indictments, 11, 14, 20–2, 28, 37–8, 48,
    80, 96–7, 99, 103, 109, 115, 116,
    168, 177, 179, 180, 189
  afforcement of, 29, 30, 44, 63, 75, 76, 85
  bills of, 15, 20, 22–6, 32, 33, 34, 35,
    47–8, 103, 105, 118, 119, 171, 179
  insufficiency of, 141, 151
  multiple charges in, 124
  sessions for, 12, 103, 120
Ine of Wessex, King, 69
infangthief, 70
informing, 15, 24, 25, 34, 35, 46, 102,
    106, 118, 121, 179
inheritance, 170
Inns of Court, readings at, 8, 13, 83, 100
insanity, 138, 139
Institutes of Justinian, 71
Ireland, 22, 146, 192

James I, King, 85, 114, 140
jointures, 170
judgement, 134, 138, 151
judges, *see* justices, professional
juries, grand, 24, 27, 46
  indictment, 15, 20, 24–8, 33–4, 46, 48,
    102, 103, 111, 118, 122, 190
  presentment, 19, 20–4, 28, 32, 33, 47, 48,
    57, 75, 106, 118, 119, 163, 167, 191
  trial, 14, 15, 19, 27, 28, 29, 32, 63, 75,
    95, 97–126, 151, 154, 165
  special, 99–100
jury, foreman of, 27, 115, 116
  retirement of, 113–15
justices' charges, 63, 74, 77, 83, 175
justices' clerks, 25, 45, 74, 140
justices of assize, *see* justices of gaol delivery
justices of gaol delivery, 9, 10, 12, 26, 33,
    44, 46, 47–8, 103, 107, 110–12, 116,
    121, 137, 141, 143, 146, 151, 152, 190
  behaviour at trials of, 110–11, 151

justices of oyer and terminer, 8, 10, 47,
    103, 111
justices of the peace, 9–12, 23, 24, 25, 26,
    27, 33, 34, 44, 47, 48, 60, 75, 101,
    103, 104, 105–7, 109, 111, 115, 119,
    123, 177, 190
justices, professional, 9–11, 12, 39, 65, 75,
    78, 79, 80, 98, 106, 107, 126, 135, 187

Kaye, J.M., 58–9, 61, 65–6
Kent, 27, 33, 43, 69, 73, 74, 78, 86, 93,
    95, 108, 123, 136, 147, 156, 164,
    165, 177, 179, 180, 193
kin, 35
king, 8, 9, 121
  attorney of, 65, 108, 121
  solicitor of, 33, 65
king's bench, 8, 9, 10, 13, 38, 43, 73, 78, 101,
    116, 141, 172, 178, 179, 187, 190, 191

labour laws, 11, 15, 106, 149
labourers, 106, 181
Lambard, William, 22, 99
land wars, 11, 62
larceny, 13, 19
  felonious, 12, 15, 36, 37, 38, 40, 59, 61,
    69–86, 93, 94, 95, 97, 125, 136, 145,
    148, 150
  petty, 13, 70, 72, 78, 116, 153
Lavenham, Hugh, 41
law reports, 8
lawyers, *see* counsel, legal
Lee, Rowland, bishop of Coventry and
    Lichfield, 143, 152
Leges Henrici Primi, 57, 70
Leis Wilhelmi, 57, 162
Leyshon, Lewis, 173
Limoges, Raymond, 172
Lincolnshire, 73, 81, 178
Lindsey, 179, 180
Lisle, Arthur Plantagenet, Lord, 140–1
literacy, 84, 135, 137
  test of, 135, 137
Littleton, Richard, 31, 100
L'Office et Aucthoritie de Justices de Peace, 175
London, 42, 93, 101, 150, 172

maidens, 162, 166, 174
mainour (loot, pelf), 29, 31, 32, 37, 42, 43–4,
    69, 70, 71, 80, 81, 104, 105, 117, 144

mainpernors, *see* sureties
maintenance, 11, 12, 15, 121, 171
Maitland, F.W., 8, 57, 70, 168
Malefaut, Margaret, 173
Malefaut, Thomas, 173
malfeasance of officials, 19, 25
manifest offences, 70, 71
manslaughter, 15, 61–9, 116, 136, 145, 148, 150
Manwood, Roger, 10
Marowe, Thomas, 22, 76, 82
Marshalsea gaol, 142, 145
Mary, Queen, 15, 65, 105, 107, 174
mayhem, 61, 170, 189
mayors, 119
Meekings, C.A.F., 20
Middlesex, 93, 95, 123, 136, 137, 150, 156
Middleton manuscripts, 84
Mile End, 154
Milsom, S.F.C., 80
miners, 180, 181
Mirror of Justices, 71, 72, 73, 166
misdemeanours (criminal trespasses), 8, 11, 15, 19, 20, 38, 94, 117, 120, 138, 148, 166, 188–9, 192
Moile, Walter, 35
Montgomery, 59
moral improvement, 144
More, Thomas, 8, 25–6, 31, 32, 98, 105, 107, 109, 119
murder, 15, 19, 33, 39, 57–69, 85, 97, 101, 136, 139, 143, 144, 145, 148, 170, 171, 173
murdrum fine, 57, 58, 62
mutilation, punishment by, 70, 72

Newcastle on Tyne, 152
Newe Boke of Justices of the Peas, 83, 175
Newgate gaol, 69, 93, 124, 144, 150, 177
Norfolk, 40, 43, 81, 96, 101, 121, 177, 178, 187
Norfolk, Thomas Howard, fourth duke of, 108
north, council of the, 120, 121, 152, 153
Norris, John, 140
Northampton, assize of, 57
Northamptonshire, 43, 177
Northumberland, 59, 95
notoriety, criminal, 29, 30, 35, 42, 154
Nottinghamshire, 73, 178

Novae Narrationes, 172
nuns, 148, 168

oaths, 25, 34, 46, 72, 102, 105, 106, 108, 109, 177
officials, killing of, 67, 144
ordeal, 14, 57
orders, ecclesiastical, 135
ordinary, 135, 137, 150, 178
outlawry, 20, 178
Oxford, 101
oyer and terminer, commissions of, 8, 10, 14, 59, 120

palatinates, 95, 138
pardons, 29, 41, 59, 60–3, 64, 137–48, 153, 155, 156, 170, 171
    conditional, 60, 143, 144
    costs of, 62, 138, 140, 141, 144
    crimes excepted from, 145, 146
    general, 65, 75, 144–7
    interceders for, 138, 139
    persons excepted from, 144, 145
    reasons given for, 138
parishes, 99
parliament, 8, 9, 11, 12, 28, 60, 85, 138, 139, 144, 145, 178, 181
    petitions in, 9, 12, 42, 60, 170
    rolls of, 59, 173
Parvyng, Robert, 28
Paston, John I, 173
Paston, John II, 174
patronage and clientage, *see* bastard feudalism
peace commissions, 111
    records of, 8, 9, 20, 73, 74, 76, 81, 177, 179, 180
    sessions of, 13, 23, 120, 178
        quorum at, 12
Peasants' Revolt, 60
peine forte et dure 12, 35
Pelham, John, 171
perjury, 101, 121, 150
Pike, L.O., 93
pillory, 72
piracy, 143, 144, 145
Placita Corone, 38
plague, bubonic, 93, 97
plea, entering, 134, 135
Plucknett, T.F.T., 74, 80

Port, John, 154
Porter, Ralph le, 59
Prene, William, 22
presentments, 19, 23–4, 28, 29, 166, 177
prices, 125
Prideaux, John, 65
prisoners of war, 151
privata, 19, 20
privy seal, keeper of the, 139
proclamations, 34–5, 45, 46, 64, 102–3, 104, 120, 152, 189
prophesies, 149, 150, 190, 191
prosecutors for the crown, 26, 108–9, 110
prostitutes of the royal household, 153
protestantism, 123, 144
pucellage, 163, 164, 166, 172
Pugh, R.B., 93, 177
Pulle, William, 173
punishment, 9, 62, 148, 149, 166
purgation in court ecclesiastical, 29, 135, 137, 191
pursuit of felons, 30, 31, 177
purveyance, 188
Putnam, B.H., 23, 27, 74

quarter sessions, *see* peace commissions
querelae, 21, 31, 42, 166

rape, 12, 13, 15, 32, 35, 36, 39, 63, 85, 117, 139, 144, 145, 150, 151, 162–82
rapere, 164, 167, 169, 175, 180
ravi, 166, 167
Reading, abbot of, 178
receiving, of felons, 19, 34, 40, 60, 79–81, 148, 174
    of stolen goods, 79–81
record, process by, 15
reeves, 24, 46, 104, 105, 163
reform (of the criminal law), 126
regulation, commercial, 12, 15
remanding to gaol, 135, 140, 148
reporters, court, 13
reprieving, 12, 120, 121, 140, 146, 148, 151, 152, 153
restitution of stolen property, 13, 21, 31, 32, 37, 38, 39, 82, 117, 119, 142, 143
retainers and retaining, 10, 11, 12, 15, 118, 121, 122
revenge, 30, 33, 36, 37, 115, 117

Richard II, King, 29, 60, 69, 77, 94, 124, 147
riot, 11, 12, 15, 26, 120, 121, 122, 190
robbery, 15, 19, 36, 37, 39, 40, 41, 44, 62, 69, 72, 76–7, 81, 82, 84, 85, 86, 93, 94, 95, 97, 106, 108, 125, 136, 145, 148
Rochester, Salomon of, 21, 22
rogues, 192

St German, Christopher, 32
St Paul's cathedral, 154
sakbere, 30–1
Salisbury, 154
Salisbury, John Vane, 66
Salisbury, Richard, 66
Sanders, Ann, 154, 155
Sanders, George, 154
Sandes, William, 27
Saunders, John, 67
Savoy, liberty of the, 102
Scochere, Robert, 22
seditious words, 108
Seler, Eustace le, 172
    Joan, daughter of, 172
self defence, killing in, 58, 63, 117, 138, 139, 148
sequestration of possessions, 71, 141
serjeants at law, 11
    king's, 11, 106, 108
Serjeants' Inn, 13, 65
servants, 35, 154, 179, 180, 181, 189, 192
settlements between victim and accused, 37, 39, 48, 118, 165
Shardelow, Margaret, 171
Shardelow, Thomas, 171
Shareshull, William, 76, 80
sheriffs, 24, 43, 46, 57, 70, 99, 103, 105, 112, 118, 134, 140, 148, 155, 163
Shooters Hill, 154
Shropshire, 81, 178
Skell, Adrian, 140
Smith, Thomas, 8, 13, 22, 25, 99, 100, 105, 110, 114, 115, 119, 121, 134, 137, 153
Smithfield, 154
Somerset, 33
Song on the Venality of the Judges, 10
sorcery (*see also* witchcraft), 145, 191
Southwark, 151

Spelman, John, 38, 84
Staffordshire, 178
Star Chamber, court of, 101, 121, 122
Starkey, Thomas, 155
statutes concerning felony, 8, 26, 36, 109,
    145, 151, 188
  of Westminster I, 74, 78, 148, 165, 187
  of Gloucester, 38
  of Westminster II, 43, 148, 164, 165,
    167–8, 169, 170, 175
  of Winchester, 43, 74, 76
  28 Edward I c. 11, 188
  9 Edward II st. 1 c. 6, 75
  2 Edward III c. 1, 77
  2 Edward III c. 7, 77
  5 Edward III c. 2, 188
  5 Edward III c. 14, 44, 75, 77
  10 Edward III st. 1, 75, 77
  20 Edward III st. 2 c. 15, 188
  of Labourers, 106, 189
  25 Edward III st. 5 c. 3, 28
  27 Edward III st. 2 c. 13, 77
  28 Edward III c. 9, 46
  28 Edward III c. 11, 75, 77
  34 Edward III c. 1, 44, 77, 106
  34 Edward III c. 22, 188
  36 Edward III c. 2, 188
  36 Edward III c. 4, 188
  36 Edward III c. 5, 188
  2 Richard II st. 1 c. 5, 60, 170
  6 Richard II st. 1 c. 6, 170
  13 Richard II st. 2 c. 1, 63, 64, 139, 170
  13 Richard II st. 2 c. 3, 189
  1 Henry IV c. 18, 75
  5 Henry IV c. 2, 139
  5 Henry IV c. 5, 189
  2 Henry V st. 1 c. 4, 106
  2 Henry V st. 1 c. 9, 75
  3 Henry V c. 1, 187
  2 Henry VI c. 9, 187
  3 Henry VI c. 1, 121, 189
  8 Henry VI c. 12, 189
  18 Henry VI c. 15, 189
  18 Henry VI c. 19, 189
  33 Henry VI c. 1, 189
  2 Richard III c. 10, 189
  1 Henry VII c. 7, 190
  3 Henry VII c. 1, 33
  3 Henry VII c. 2, 38, 149, 175, 179,
    191

  3 Henry VII c. 3, 174, 175
  11 Henry VII c. 25, 121
  19 Henry VII c. 4, 101
  4 Henry VIII c. 2, 65, 84, 136
  7 Henry VIII c. 11, 145
  14/15 Henry VIII c. 17, 145
  21 Henry VIII c. 1, 145
  21 Henry VIII c. 7, 79
  21 Henry VIII c. 11, 32, 111, 119, 123
  22 Henry VIII c. 14, 64
  23 Henry VIII c. 1, 84, 136
  23 Henry VIII c. 11, 192
  24 Henry VIII c. 5, 64, 85
  25 Henry VIII c. 3, 85
  25 Henry VIII c. 6, 191
  26 Henry VIII c. 4, 114
  27 Henry VIII c. 25, 192
  31 Henry VIII c. 12, 190
  31 Henry VIII c. 14, 190
  32 Henry VIII c. 11, 190
  33 Henry VIII c. 8, 191, 192
  33 Henry VIII c. 14, 190
  35 Henry VIII c. 14, 190
  1 Edward VI c. 12, 136
  2/3 Edward VI c. 2, 190
  2/3 Edward VI c. 29, 191
  3/4 Edward VI c. 5, 190
  5/6 Edward VI, c. 9, 85
  1 Mary st. 2 c. 12, 190
  1/2 Philip and Mary c. 4, 192
  1/2 Philip and Mary c. 13, 119
  2/3 Philip and Mary c. 10, 119
  4/5 Philip and Mary c. 3, 190
  4/5 Philip and Mary c. 8, 176
  5 Elizabeth I c. 3, 192
  5 Elizabeth I c. 5, 190
  5 Elizabeth I c. 14, 192
  5 Elizabeth I c. 16, 192
  8 Elizabeth I c. 3, 192
  8 Elizabeth I c. 4, 136
  14 Elizabeth I c. 5, 192
  18 Elizabeth I c. 7, 85, 137, 176, 191
  18 Elizabeth I c. 24, 145
  23 Elizabeth I c. 2, 109, 191
  31 Elizabeth I c. 4, 192
  35 Elizabeth I c. 1, 190
  39 Elizabeth I c. 4, 192
  39 Elizabeth I c. 9, 175
  39 Elizabeth I c. 17, 190
  43 Elizabeth I c. 13, 191

Staunford, William, 38, 42, 65, 66, 76, 83, 84
stewards of liberties, 47
Stourton, Charles Lord, 154
Stow, John, 42
Strangways, James, 170
stuprum, 166
submission by the accused, 116
Suffolk, 21, 23, 115
suicide, 68
summary or truncated process, 12, 31, 32
sureties, 11, 47, 104, 139, 145
surgeons, 176
Surrey, 93, 109, 123, 136, 147, 156
suspicion, discovery by, 106
Sussex, 68, 86, 95, 136, 147, 148, 156, 178, 179, 180, 181, 193

talesmen, 98
'testifying', 104
Thimbleby, Dionysius, 107–8
Thorpe, William, 76, 78
Throckmorton, Nicholas, 107
tonsure, 135
tourns, sheriffs', 20, 24, 44, 46, 47, 74, 103, 191
Tower of London, 145
tradesmen, 181
trailbaston commissions, 23, 42, 59
treason, 8, 9, 14, 63, 101, 108, 112, 139, 142, 154, 171, 173, 187, 188
  petty, 110
trees, felling of, 78
Tresilian, Robert, 29
trespass, 8, 166, 168, 189
  action of, 21, 31, 71
  criminal, *see* misdemeanours

Udall, John, 108, 109, 113, 151
unamendable crimes, 57, 62, 138
vagabonds, 150, 190, 192

verdicts, 15, 16, 28, 63, 113, 114
  'partial', 117, 125
veredicta, 19, 20, 21
victims, 16, 24, 25, 27, 30, 31, 32, 35, 48, 102, 103, 107, 109, 111, 113, 115, 117, 119
vills, 20, 21, 24, 46, 57, 58, 99, 104, 105, 112, 163, 188
virgins, 163, 164

wage rate, 125, 149
Wales, marches of, 114
  council of the, 120, 121, 143, 144
Warwickshire, 81, 178, 179, 180
Welsh counties, 95
wer, 57, 70
Westmorland, 95
widows, 162, 164, 174, 175
William I, King, 163
Willoughby, Richard, 25, 27, 28, 96
Wiltshire, 40, 42, 81, 82, 96, 135, 146, 165, 177, 178
witchcraft (*see also* sorcery), 27, 145, 150, 192, 193
witnesses, 25, 27, 28, 31, 32, 33, 34, 39, 48, 101, 104, 105, 106, 107, 109, 111, 113, 115, 117, 120, 121, 123, 151, 154, 179
  for the accused, 107–8
wives, 162, 164, 166, 170, 174, 175, 181
Wolsey, Thomas, 120, 152
women, accused, 124

Year Books, 13, 25, 34, 38, 42, 47, 73, 75, 80, 83, 99, 100, 102, 106, 119, 170
Yelverton tract, 76, 83
yeomen, 180
York, 152
Yorkshire, 36, 38, 40, 43, 68, 69, 73, 81, 82, 95, 96, 101, 116, 124, 125, 135, 136, 147, 177